D1630405

CAPE HORN

is not a

GIFT!

The First Circumnavigation of South America

FREYA

HOFFMEISTER

FOR MY BELOVED SON HELGE

Index

Panama

Colombia

Ecuador

Venezuela

Trinidad

Guyana

Suriname

Fr.-Guiana

Peru

Brazil

Chile

Uruguay

Argentina

Cape Horn

Prologue
ONE MUST HAVE STORIES TO TELL

"Why are you so determined to paddle around South America?" This is the question I was often asked before I set off. Well, similarly, one might as well ask why climb mountains? Because they are there, and mountaineers can. For us sea kayakers, the greatest challenge is not "Mount Everest" or "K2", but "Around Iceland" or "Circumnavigating New Zealand". For me, this is comparable. I love sporty challenges - the bigger, the better. After going around Iceland, New Zealand and Australia, the islands of the world were not big enough.

Besides Australia, no continent has been circumnavigated by kayak. Down under, I was only the second person, but the first woman, to circumnavigate Australia by kayak, and I was much faster than Paul Caffyn who did the same trip twenty-seven years prior. After Paul and before me, many attempts have failed.

Done Australia, and now what?

Even in the last weeks of my Australian adventure, my thoughts strayed to my potential next journeys. I contemplated what would tickle my fancy: Around Africa? Impossible, too dangerous. Asia? No, too exotic. Europe, no, too close and too familiar. North America? Not yet... South America? That seemed doable!

New Year 2011, I was ready to make my plans public: "Think Bigger – South America" I proclaimed on my website. I announced confidently, that I would be the first person to circumnavigate South America in a sea kayak. The press leapt on it at once. My new trip was announced on the front page of thirteen daily papers. Now, there was no way back - not that I wanted there to be one.

I am the first person to even contemplate a complete circumnavigation of

South America by kayak. Prior to my embarking on this journey, only partial sections had been done. In comparison to Australia, South America would be my first "real" continent. Australia could still pass as an island, as it is a single country. South America is enormous, and has many different faces: It stretches south to the fifty-sixth latitude and northwards to the fifteenth - I would be crossing the equator twice! During my circumnavigation, I would enter thirteen different countries. Eight of them use Spanish or Portuguese as their main language, which I barely had knowledge of when I started. Along the journey, I learnt to communicate with hands, feet and "Spanglish".

I originally had planned my historical circumnavigation of more than 16,000 miles with two three-month breaks. As I would be the first person to do this feat, I could set my own standards, and did not have to prove to anyone I could do it faster. My Danish partner Peter was not particularly delighted when I presented him with a fait accompli just before New Year. "Can't you plan some smaller adventures?" he asked me quite appalled, and inadvertently gave me the idea for the motto for this journey - "THINK BIGGER!"

Peter and I became partners after my Australian trip in summer 2010, having first met in 2002 on a sea kayak tour around the Danish island of Samsö. He ran the tour, and I was a raw beginner. In the following years we continued to meet at varying events, but not until he organized a lecture for me in Copenhagen did the magic happen. On our first tour as a twosome through the Kattegat, the old teacher could test his ex-student for progress, but it was the old teacher who lost his paddle in high waves as he did not tie it to the boat.

After a few weeks, Peter had digested my South American plans, and was fully behind me with support. Especially, his IT knowledge was an incredibly vital aid to my endeavor.

Werner, the well caring father of my then fifteen-year old son, declared he would support me again; both live close by. People were asking me how I could leave my beloved son alone for so long. Prior to the split from his father, Helge and I were extremely close, but during our peaceful divorce, we decided Helge would spend more time at his father's house. It was hard for me to be so close, yet so far and not to always see him. I preferred to start a complete new life, but the relationship between my son and I continues to be special and indestructible.

Many potential adventurers fail due to the available time off. The dilemma: "Much time, but no money - Much money, but no time", prevents many adventure-hungry fellows to follow up their ambitious plans. The separation from my son and family was a high price to pay for my free time. As for my current financial independence, I had laid a foundation with seriously arduous work during the first years of my working life.

These days, I can concentrate on my "third job", and the income from lectures and the support of sponsors help me cover the higher expenses in my shops, as I need more and better qualified staff. I would not like to have to live on the income from my adventuring. Due to my fantastic long-term managers Ilona Sierks and Andrea Höhn and all the staff that are caring for my Janny's ice-cream cafés and Christmas shop in Husum, I can be gone for such extended periods.

My elderly mother had to fight against a lump in her throat at the thought of my new endeavors, and proclaimed she would not be able to breathe freely until my successful finish. Thankfully, she was not able to follow the blog posts in English, as some of the dangerous situations would have worried her too much. My late father, a marine biologist and Cape Horn veteran, would have been proud of me!

After 850 days travelling, of which I had been paddling for 606 days, 16,000 miles and thirteen countries, I do now have a few stories to tell...

Chapter 1
DEPARTURE

Argentina, Part 1: Buenos Aires to Península Valdés

August 30th - October 8th, 2011

I will soon be off! My two kayaks have arrived in Buenos Aires via air freight. It is the end of August, and I have been here for two weeks already, preparing for a tour that will take me around the whole South American continent. From Buenos Aires in Argentina, through thirteen countries in a clockwise manner, I expect this circumnavigation is to cover more than 16,000 miles. I will paddle around Cape Horn, through the Panama Canal and back down again.

I got the permit for my solo tour along the Argentine coast down to Tierra del Fuego only a day prior to my intended start date. Alejandro, my Argentine host and helper, a vet by trade and sea kayaker by heart, had sent me a few emails promising me his help. He was the one to hustle for my paperwork.

In this respect, South America is a strange kayaking territory. Everywhere else in the world, you just get your kayak into the water and off you go. But here, I need to get an official written permit from the coast guard. It needs a multi-page, multi copy application, with exact description of the planned route and all overnight stops. A muscle powered kayak is of course very dependent on the impact of the wind, weather and waves. It is impossible, not even in the morning of a day's start, to predict where one will make landfall at night. How then am I supposed to devise a plan for the whole coast line? I prepare a lovely document with fitting words and pretty pictures, hoping they will accept my imaginative document as a base for the formal permit.

Alejandro and I are on the way to pick up my kayaks from the airport. We have mixed feelings as we approached the customs office. Argentina has infamously high import taxes - the import tax costs about the same amount as the price of the airfreight. I am hoping, the kayaks will be classed as oversized luggage, otherwise, how else am I to bring sporting equipment too big for regular luggage size?

The officer thankfully sees reason, and does not charge import tax. On the way home, I am getting worried about my kayaks, they seem in greater danger in the maniac traffic than in the air or on the water. Alejandro's manner of driving, and everyone else's here, is quite hair raising compared to European standards. My kayaks will only be safe with me paddling, even if I am likely to have a few hard landings.

Today, August 30th, I will be on the water! I was researching the general wind direction around the continent, and it seems to make most sense to go clock wise, instead of anti-clockwise as I have originally intended. And this way, I can tackle the more difficult section of the south first.

Alejandro has organized a small press conference and goodbye party in the fancy Puerto Madero Yacht Club. Representatives of the German embassy, the town council of Buenos Aires, the Argentine Coast Guard and local paddlers are in attendance. I give a short slide presentation about my upcoming journey, stick the flag of my first host country on both sides of the kayak, and answer the many curious questions of the press, the officials and my paddling friends.

But now, it is time to peel myself out of my presentation gear, and to don paddling trousers and jacket. I swap high heels for sandals, tie up my hair and pull down my sun visor. On this first stage, I am paddling an "Epic 18x Sport" kayak, five and a half meters long, fifty-six centimeters wide and twenty-two kilograms empty. I pack my luggage: Food, water, camping gear, clothes and many items of technical gear like phones, cameras, laptop and GPS.

I wave good bye with a smile to the many cameras, but I am actually just happy to be on the way to escape the crowd. At half past two, I paddle slowly and proudly out of the harbor, a light breeze behind me, accompanied by several boats of the Prefectura Naval Argentina. Alejandro and his friend Juan Pablo act as kayak escorts either side of me. Good bye Buenos Aires! We will meet again, in two and a half years, on my 50th birthday!

The planning stage is over, the reality is upon me. What would be happening along the way, both the horrible and amazing ones, I am not able to imagine at this point.

The long goodbye ceremony has already created a delay in my daily schedule, my target for the day is not far. I only like to do a manageable twelve miles to the next Yacht Club along the broad mouth of the Rio de la Plata. My daily average is close to thirty miles, in about ten hours of paddling time. The water is brown and opaque like a chocolate lake, but my mind is clear and cheerful. The sun is shining, I am back on the water!

The first night in my tent, I am ailing a little. A cough and headache plague me, caused by too little sleep, too much partying and the constant smog hanging over Buenos Aires. Harsh treatment for my lungs. Does "Buenos Aires" mean "Good Air"? A good night's sleep and the fresh sea breeze will put me back together. My body quickly remembers the earlier strains, and adapts quickly to the even efforts of a steady paddling pace. The next two days, I cover more than 35 miles each.

The tidal range is a noticeable six and a half feet. If the current comes towards me, I paddle close along the coast, and can avoid the sharp steep waves, inspect potential camp sites, and watch the many animals along the shore. Occasionally, the water becomes so shallow I get stuck, and I must get out to drag my kayak into deeper water. A herd of wild horses is grazing peacefully by the banks, they feel disturbed by my approach, and run right in front of my kayak into the river. The water is so shallow, the distressed creatures can run in a wide berth around my kayak, and come to a stomping and snorting halt behind me.

Snow white egrets and many stork-like wading birds in the low shrub do not see me as a threat. I often spot a jumping fish. I wonder, if they want to show me how happy they are in this brown broth? Or would they like to escape it for a moment? Fishing boats and many nets show, the fish from this mud bath are quite edible - or the digestive systems of the locals have been toughed up.

A lot of huge beached buoys are washed up high and dry. This large river can carry much more water than in this dry spring month at the start of the southern summer. I spot a car - its occupants are wearing the well-known sand colored uniforms of the Argentine Coast Guard. Are they watching me?

Only three days in, and everything seems to go wrong. My plan is modest: I only like to cover twenty miles to the start of the seventy-five-mile-wide Bahia Somborombon. Should I get started in this strong wind? The sea looks calm, and the wind is following. I start too late to push my kayak easily off my high grassy knoll. The tide has been running out for a few hours. I need to pull the empty kayak six hundred feet across an exposed sandbank, and make more trips with my three heavy gear bags. In the meantime, the water continues to run out, I must move everything another sixty feet to become afloat. It is arduous work to drag a fully laden 220 pounds boat across wet sand!

There is only one way to do it: Stand facing backwards with both legs spread across the bow, and then jerk the kayak forward gripping the front cockpit. Sometimes, the sand is so gooey, not even this method works. The only remedy would be unloading gear. After seven miles of paddling, I am already fed up. The shallow water seems to suck my boat to the bottom, and does not allow it to glide smoothly. Further out is nothing but breaking surf. I check on a landing spot. Punta Indio looks like an old harbor town, and I am hoping to find deep water to not get stuck in the mud on low tide. Wrong! 900 feet to go, and the water is too shallow to paddle.

I can pull my laden boat another hundred feet, and can walk on a firm sandy surface. With two heavy bags on my shoulders, I set off. With worry, I notice that the firm sand is getting covered with mud. It comes up to my ankles, and soon it is knee-deep. I barely make it to the shore, coated in mud from head to toe, and need to return to fetch my third bag.

As I arrive, I discover the first catastrophe. The rear hatch cover was not properly tied to the kayak, and has blown away. I cannot see it anywhere on this flat sandbank. No way to continue without hatch cover. I am thinking about options on how to get a replacement. A young man digging for worms I can ask for help with my kayak, gesticulating with hands and feet. While he is pulling my empty boat, I am on the return trip of my second luggage run. Suddenly, he triumphantly holds up the missing hatch cover. He found it! Thank God for that.

I have been paddling on the Rio de La Plata since Buenos Aires. The mighty river merges after 100 miles in the Atlantic. The current drops all sediments south into the Bahia de Somborombon. It is very shallow, and looks like viscous chocolate. The sweet river water has already blistered my hands, and now, the concentration of sediments in the water is continuing the bad job. Entering the bay, I keep my distance to a few barely visible submerged rocks, only occasional splashes show their position. The coast consists of low grassland, with few suitable landing places.

I like to make it to Rio Salado today, and cover the last miles an hour before sunset. I must have miscalculated the tidal flow. When I arrive at the river mouth, the water is already receding! There are sixty feet of thick, sticky deep mud between my barely afloat kayak and the shore. I turn around quickly, and paddle to the spot where I thought I had seen a landing with firm grass. Dusk is closing in. In the last light, my GPS does not show progress, although I am paddling hard - but am just shoveling mud. I am stuck! I begrudge spending my energy on fighting yet another mud bath. About a mile off the grassy coast line, I need to prepare for a cold damp night on the water in my kayak.

It is important to stay warm, but I am only wearing my Gore-Tex paddling jacket, a fleece jumper and my damp Sealskin pants. I have been yearning for my dry suit already at other wet starts and landings. My warm camp clothes are inaccessible in the front hatch, which I cannot open without sinking deep into the mud. Within reach, inside my cockpit bags, there is only a thin foil rescue blanket. I loosely wrap it around myself, like wrapping a bunch of flowers. This needs to do. I doze off occasionally, despite shivering.

By 1am, I hear gurgling water noises. Is the tide already coming in? I am hoping my deeply stuck kayak will be lifted by the incoming water. It is spooky to be trapped in this pitch-black night in this bog, like a Viking corpse of old. But with creaks and groans, my mud-wreck comes afloat with the rising tide. I paddle back to Rio Salado for 3.5 miles, and hope I can land now. At 3am, I see nothing inviting, only a wet meadow covered in cow shit and bird dung. I better continue paddling into the night!

Sunday morning, the first rays of sunshine are promising. But shortly after, a heavy storm with thunder, lightning and hefty wind whistles around my ears. I am a mile and a half away from shore, can still touch the ground with my paddle, and will not have a chance to escape the lightning any better on the flat wet land. A nasty situation! By 2pm, I can approach the coast, and find a nice bit of grassland with a higher ledge where I can easily land. All grass is soaking wet, only a pile of reeds is halfway dry to set up my tent. It is high time for a good rest!

By 4pm, I think I am hallucinating: I see the head of another paddler! Really, it is Alejandro! He started paddling at high tide to look me up from a bit further down south. He finds me from the GPS position I posted on my blog yesterday, and is bringing me the dry suit I was longing for. Many thanks!

The next morning, I still feel my maltreated body and the lack of sleep. I decide to put in a complete day of rest. I cannot see any water anyway, and only heaven knows on these complicated diurnal tides, when it will be rising again. At 4pm, I surface from my day dreams in my sleeping bag, and see the muddy-brown soup swapping right in front of my tent. Spontaneously, I decide to leave: "Now, or never!"

Forty minutes later, I have packed, slip into my dry suit and I am ready to set off. The forecast is promising a quiet night. I have a bad conscience, as my permit prohibits paddling after dark. This is my second night out!

A thousand stars are sparkling in the cloudless sky at night, with the sickle of the moon shining over a calm sea. The outgoing tide and a light breeze push me along at about two miles per hour, even when I am having a break. Throughout the night, I am taking it easy. I am in no rush, and hope to land at dawn on a sandy beach. I am singing to stay awake, old folk songs with silly made up words. A large fish jumps on my spray deck. Does he want to be my dinner?

During the second half of the night, bioluminescence develops, and it becomes idyllic. I am so happy to have escaped the muddy hell! With the wide Bahia Somborombon and its chocolate-colored water behind me, I will see the clear sea by daybreak.

On the morning of day eight, a gorgeous yellow sandy beach is glowing in the sun. I feel I have entered a different world! It is no more of the muddy coast line, but not yet the freedom and solitude in untouched wild nature I am looking for. For miles on end, I am passing seaside towns with cute cottages, but also ugly high-rising apartment blocks, which look either half finished, or half broken down. Or both together. Endless docks stretch into the water. Holiday season is over, hence most of the cottage windows are shuttered, and there is a hint of a ghost town about all the communities. Only a few young people on quad bikes are racing over the dunes.

I am under intense surveillance - a large boat of the coastguard has picked me as a training target. Six men cannot stop looking at me and my tent all day. I am almost flattered to receive such VIP treatment, but must hide behind a bush to shower and change.

My blisters, due to spending the last days in muddy river water, are painful as hell, and not healed yet. The first stages of a tour are physically demanding, no matter how well one has prepared. I urgently need a paddle-free day, and decide to take my first pit stop after twelve days in Mar del Plata.

But first, I must fight my way through the unclean sewage of the city - quite an unwelcome confrontation with the civilization. Over an hour, I am floating through a thick soup of human effluence, garnished with everything that goes down the toilet. I pull my scarf up over my nose, try to breathe as shallowly as possible, and try not to get splashes onto the deck and my hands. As the water gets halfway clear again, I try cleaning the kayak and paddle. A shower would be delightful, but that will have to wait another few hours.

With regards to using toilet, of course, I do have human needs. I mostly cannot take care of them on land, while paddling for over ten hours per day. The small business can be done without too much of a problem, even when wearing a dry suit. While sitting in my kayak, I open the horizontal zip designed for men, fit a funnel style attachment to my private parts, and let it run into a plastic bag. This is a simple and mostly dry affair, unless a cheeky wave pops over the cockpit rim right into the open zipper while in action. Or, I might forget to close the zip again, and have a cold shower of the nether regions while landing in waist deep water. Most men also use a bag or bottle, despite telling that they hang the hose straight overboard.

The first day without paddling is pure stress. I clean, overhaul and repair all gear and my body, and go food shopping plus packing it into my dry bags. I write up the blog, research the next stage, answer emails and visit the coast guard, plus having nice meals and chats with my hosts. They take me to an ice-cream café late afternoon, and I feel quite at home.

It is well past midnight, and I can somehow settle down. A paddle-free day in town may be a physical rest, but my mind runs on full power. It is the reverse on the water. Only weather days on beaches without being online are really relaxing for both body and soul. I could stay here longer, but when the calm weather calls, I feel I must get going again. It is part of my adventuring nature to follow this inner need, and it does help to keep the journey on pace. I stay longest three days in a town, or I become sluggish and lose my motivation.

Next morning, I set off again to enjoy a perfect day on the water. As dirty as the water was north of Mar del Plata, as clean and clear it is south of the city. I am a fortnight on the trip. Small penguins, fat seals and many sea birds are all around me, and the first whales show up with their steaming spouts. I love whales! Big and majestic, they surface out of the water when least expected, sometimes right next to the kayak, sometimes right in front. One more paddle stroke, and I once would have slid straight down the rising back of one, kayak and all.

A heavy storm pushes me on. It is absolutely bucketing down. Despite the rain, I feel fine in my dry suit with a layer of warming fleece underwear. Only my hands and feet are continuously cold. My hands stick in neoprene open palm mitts, but they keep away only the worst of the chilly wind. Even a second layer of gloves offers limited protection, and I stick one or the other finger into my mouth for defrosting. I cannot paddle properly with closed or thicker gloves. Pogies, closed gloves attached to the paddle, might be warm, but they are just too cumbersome for me. My feet are wrapped in thick, fluffy woolen socks inside the Gore-Tex-booties of the dry suit, inside thin neoprene socks, inside thin foldable booties, inside sandals. This layering system protects the suit membrane from getting rubbed by encroaching sand. As I am not moving much while paddling seated, my feet are having a tough time getting and staying warm. The best would be to do some heavy cardio work out before setting off, but I rarely take time for that. Occasionally, I boil up some sea water, and pour it into my high booties to get my feet warm, but still dry.

My friend Alejandro from Buenos Aires has planned to pop in and paddle for a day with me tomorrow, but he will not make it. A text message informs me that a car repair has tied him up in town, but he will be driving the 400 miles all through the night to get here.

Alejandro and his wife arrive at 3.30am, but they let me sleep. He wrote a message into the wet sand: "Ale was here!", but I do not see it in the thick fog when I get up at 6am. I have no other message from him, and cannot see a car, and my assumption is he did not make it. I climb up my "office hill" to get mobile phone reception to answer a few texts when out of nowhere, Alejandro stands behind me. He scares me to death, but I am glad he has done this arduous journey.

We are checking if the chart chip he brought works in my GPS. I stupidly lost my chip at sea when I changed batteries, and despite being equipped with a second GPS, I have only one chart chip. The card holder inside my GPS is insufficient, a piece of sticky tape will fix that problem in future. Alejandro finally leaves me his GPS with the chip only cooperating in his machine. He is really a sweetheart, and I am incredibly grateful. I am feeling naked without a GPS system, I am so much used to electronic navigation. It would feel strange to just have a compass, or even a sextant or such other ancient gear. On my GPS, I can follow up my speed and recognize when wind, current and waves slow me down, that I might not reach my intended destination in time. With currents and wind from aside, I can check my drift off the bearing and re-adjust easy. I can see my position on the chart, and the calculated estimated time of arrival (ETA) anytime, in case I need to re-adjust to a new landing place. Additionally, I have the tides, currents and sun and moon times included for any spot in the area. It leaves a track on the chart I upload later to my trip map. Despite it swallows close to two AA batteries per day, it is a real magic machine for my needs! "Keep South America to my right" would only be quite a marginal navigation approach!

Unfortunately, Alejandro does not have enough time to paddle with me. He does not know what he will be missing! At 9am, he is pushing me in. Thick fog stays persist over the water, and it is a bit spooky to float about in this thick soup without being able to see the coastline. I am so thankful for the functioning GPS!

The first whales show up soon. Today, most of the time they show up as a twosome, and I can watch their flirting. A whale lifts out of the water quite close to me, and noisily spouts out of his breathing hole. Suddenly, it is raining despite the sunshine! My first whale encounter was at night in Newfoundland 2006, and I found it very spooky. Before you can even see the huge animals, their breath-fountain is first audible, and then visible from quite a distance.

A second whale, a smaller female, joins my mighty neighbor. They roll over and around each other like an energetic couple on a waterbed. My kayak is at the center of their activities. Is this a show just for me? I can look directly into the eyes of the female just a yard away, and can see under the long black eyelashes her faithful, unsuspecting expression. I am convinced, both know exactly where I am, and all of us know we will not hurt each other. I am their playmate, confident that no unintended whack with a fin or fluke will sweep me off my spectator spot. But just in case, I wedge my legs under the edge of the cockpit, ready to roll any moment.

This romantic interlude is also fascinating some spectators on the shore. Are they waiting for a new "Moby Dick" show, or the headline in tomorrow's news: "Kayaker swallowed by whale!"? These two whales should belong to only me! I feel disturbed by the gatecrashers standing on the roof of their cars with binoculars watching this love play. For over an hour, I get to enjoy our frisky threesome.

Just before landing this evening, I get to see another two of these massive marine mammals rolling around each other. This time, it looks more like rough showing off than gentle love plays. Their thirty-six feet long bodies weigh tons, yet jump entirely into the air. Their fins slap the water so hard it sounds like cannons firing. I better keep my distance. As opposed to the lovers, these young guns might not know what they are doing.

After this stirring day of whale performances, it is now my turn to delight the beach visitors with a stunt. On approaching the coast for landing, an unexpected large breaker throws me, and I capsize to do my first roll of this journey. Many more will follow, some will not work, and I will have to bail out and to go swimming. From offshore, the surf is always looking lower than it is. And even with the best judgement and sharpened rolling techniques, an ambitious paddling professional will take the occasional swim on launching or landing. The dry suit is useful, but does not enclose my head. Wet, cold and salty long hair is not pleasant at either end of the day. A baldy has it easier there.

I nearly lose my helmet stowed in the net behind me. I swear to myself to always wear it in future on a surfy launch and landing. The same goes for my personal floatation device (PFD), which would protect me from collecting some knocks, should I get washed out of my kayak in the surf. Attached with only one cross bungee on the back deck right behind me, my PFD would hang on a capsize in the surf like an unpleasant anchor on the side, and hamper a required roll. I will not wear it on a normal calm long-distance paddle day, particularly not over my buoyant dry suit. It would be too warm, and only rub the Gore-Tex suit or my skin, but I would put it on in rough seas. This is my own personal decision for safety. Offshore, I am always attached to my kayak with my bow line, in case of an unlikely open water capsize.

Forty-eight hours later, it is the 22nd day of my tour, and I am trying to land that evening in a small river mouth. I like to save myself a trek of a third of a mile to dry land, but I fail pitifully. I can surf into the mouth over some rough cross waves, but when I want to paddle upriver, I either get stuck in the mostly shallow water, or fight against the current where the water is over knee deep. No high and dry river bank is in sight, where I would be able to exit in comfort. I work myself upriver, always watched by some fishermen, wondering what this strange person is trying to achieve. Finally, I have enough, but the same tortuous stop-start is waiting downriver. How much easier this would have been at high tide! Half a mile south, after the little holiday resort of Balneario Oriente, I finally land right on the open coast.

A beach buggy is passing, and I quickly do my best to look like a weak and feeble woman, barely able to pull the kayak up the beach on her own. The good heart of the driver allows me to tie my bow line to his tow bar. We pile the heaviest bits of luggage and myself onto the loading platform, and off we go in style! We drive a third of a mile up the beach to a large bush offering shelter for my camp behind the high tide mark. Just what I needed this evening, after that superfluous, exhausting odyssey up the river mouth. I pitch my tent first, that it can dry in the wind. I had to pack it this morning dripping wet and coated in sand. The floor inside is wet, I get down on my knees and mop it up with a towel. Just done, the wet contents of my boots spills onto my dry housing floor. Cursing roundly, I start over again.

Unfortunately, I find even more reason to curse. My normally bone-dry front hatch is taking in water. It must be getting in through a leak of the bulkhead. How can that seam split, it has held up in a comparable boat all those thousands of miles around Australia! I made a repair on this bulkhead after the rough air freight to Buenos Aires, and now, it seems the other side has come loose. The damage must have occurred two days ago on launching. I have crashed twice six feet down a steep wave with the heavily laden boat. Normally, this is not something out of the ordinary, but having been weakened previously, the seam did not hold such beating.

I am only forty miles off my planned rest day in Monte Hermoso. No paddling tomorrow, I have boat repair to do instead. An interesting task on this flat and windy beach, with the sand whipped along. I move my tent a second time to improve the shelter in the lee of the big bush, and start the repair of the bulkhead. After extensive cleaning and sanding, I drench a sheet of fiberglass in a mix of epoxy resin and hardener. Wearing one-way gloves, I carefully smooth it over the gap and hope I got the mix ratio just right. Not enough hardener, and it stays sticky; too much hardener and it will be brittle and break like glass at the smallest amount of stress. Now, all I can do is wait and see tomorrow, if my repair was successful. All my gear is in small, individual, waterproof bags stowed in the boat, but still, there should not be water in the boat. You never know when the dry bags also start to leak!

In the evening, I have further shocking news: My laptop will not start! I keep seven batteries, none can start the magic box. A local takes me to the nearest village, and I hope to revive it with mains power, but it does not come alive again. I am writing a daily entry on my blog with my position and events. My family and the coastguard can see I am well, and my faithful fans can enjoy my journey in near real time. My blog entry updates my Facebook pages, marks my position on my trip map, and updates an easy readable trip table. I send my text via satellite- or cell-phone connection directly to my website. Thanks to my partner Peter, a professional software developer, who has arranged it all. In a town with good Wi-Fi, all what is left is to upload my pictures and GPS tracks, to document my journey in the most efficient way. Without the laptop, I am only able to send a brief SMS from the satellite phone, or shorter texts via my smart phone. Peter can help me from where he is in Denmark, and after a horrible long time, the magic little machine is starting again. But to be on the safe side, he recommends me to send it in for a proper repair.

The locals worry about me. With great concern, they watch the crazy gringa, who wants to camp another day next to the bush on the flat beach with worst weather forecast. The tide this evening is meant to come another 500 yards closer. I gratefully accept the offer to move into a holiday house in the village. The bags go into the scoop of a digger, the kayak onto the flatbed trailer, and off we go on a bumpy ride through the dunes.

Next morning, September 23rd and day twenty-five of my tour, the mayor himself comes along to take me to the beach and to inspect the waves. The sea is high from last night, but the launching looks doable, albeit a bit tricky. The wind is a north easterly, I must use that to my advantage, so I give it a thumb up. I am good to go! A tractor takes my gear and myself to the beach. Many villagers have gathered, and with an audience of this size, I am getting nervous. I put on my helmet and PFD, and with the help of a young man who quickly strips down to his underpants, I aim my kayak to the breakers and paddle across the first line. For the next, my timing is poor, and my position unfavorable. I get the full force of the breaker and capsize. I roll up, come around straight to the waves again, and wait for another chance. Smack! Again, wrong timing, I go over and greet the fish. After the second roll, I surface sideways to the breaker line. The next one catches me side on, and washes me back onto the beach. Directly to the feet of the spectators. Embarrassing. I finally listen to the advice of the fishermen, and agree to try again later. In two hours' time, the tide will be more favorable, the surf lower, and not showing so many lines. I leave my loaded kayak on the beach, and return to the village with my tail between my legs.

On my second attempt at about 11am, the narrow area in front of the breaker field is calmer and wider. I can wait out ten to fifteen breakers in the surf, until I spot a gap and can sprint out with full power. "Now... Now... Now..." I cheer myself on, adrenaline pumps into my veins, and I barely leap out over the last higher wave. The spectators must do without a further rolling show!

Finally, I am on the open water! I take a deep breath, remove my helmet and check, if my integrated rudder blade has self-deployed out of my moving stern section. On the beach, I have threaded a long string through a loop on the skeg from one side of the cockpit and back. I would be able to loosen the blade if little bits of sand and gravel get stuck in the housing. I can make some good distance for seven hours now, and am just regretting not having taken off last night, as this strong northern wind might have carried me right across Bahia Blanca.

There are three days to go before the crossing of the "White Bay". To avoid being blown out to sea by the twenty knots wind, my bow is constantly facing towards the coast. After three miles, my progress comes to a halt. I need to land. It is torturous to load and unload the kayak with horizontally driven sand creeping into all nooks and crannies. Before I can close the hatch, I must scrape the sand out of the seal. A sand storm nearly buries my tent, and invades through every opening. Everything is looking sugar coated, and sand even crunches between my teeth.

I receive my freshly repaired laptop, a delivery service straight to the beach from a friendly local. I am hoping the computer can cope with this flying sand, fresh off the operating table. One of my cameras and the busted e-reader use this nice and easy beach service for a trip back to Alejandro in Buenos Aires.

The tide range will be giving me grief over the coming days and weeks. Landing on low tide in the afternoon turns into a right slog. The next day is such one with unpleasant tides. Offshore, the waves are getting continuously steeper. It is time to surf in, and to try paddle closer to land. It is a bit early to camp; the wind is giving me still a strong push. There is a shallow water zone with lower breakers I mostly can brace into, but again, and again, I am getting fully washed up the beach and must start over. These starts and stops are quite tiring, and somehow surreal. To my left is the trashy surf belt, to my right nothing but sand, but I can paddle somehow, that is if I am not deciding to better drag my kayak along.

At lowest tide, nothing goes, not even dragging my kayak. Four miles before a river mouth might come to my rescue, all I get to my right is 800 yards of ankle to calf deep mud. Twice, I must traverse this mud with my heavy gear bags, and I contemplate tying the kayak securely to a tree trunk that was washed ashore. But what is "secure" in the sea? I would not be able to sleep. For the third time, I stomp through the mud, the light empty kayak sticking to the ground, and the bowline tearing new blisters on my palms. I need to have a rest day.

By the early morning high tide, I feel guilty for not trying to get out. Could I walk the loaded kayak over the flooded sandy plain, or even paddle? But I cannot motivate myself. Tomorrow is another day. I feel more like getting engrossed painting my toe nails, do a thorough shave here and there, plus other pampering of my body. I do not like to be the unkempt "expedition zombie", never mind how far into the wilderness and seclusion I travel, or what strains and danger I experience. Who knows who you might bump into, even in desolated wasteland. Some light flashes on my tent. Is someone approaching already? And again, again...it is only sheet lightning, soon followed by hefty thunder. The storm is lasting until an hour after sunrise, and is holding me off my beauty sleep.

It takes me two hours to get into deep enough water to be able to paddle. Good heavens, why is the sandy plain not flooded this morning like yesterday? The difference of the tides is only a few inches. I notice a small, but dry sandy strip between the water and this wide muddy area. Could I have camped there, and saved myself the triple battle with the mud?

My GPS chart is not precise enough to securely navigate the labyrinth of islets and mud humps in a direct line to Bahia Union. I am mentally prepared for a night in the kayak, having run somewhere dry. I paddle where there is water, and manage to find the one and only bush for miles on the elevated west side of Isla Culebra, where I can pitch my tent without trekking for miles. How refreshing! I dispose of all superfluous clothing and play Robinson, dipping boldly my precious body in the cold sea.

Another morning, I see a boat of the coast guard bobbing up and down far out on the white capped sea. I am paddling relaxed and swiftly, only two yards off the steep cliff in a strong, but calm following current, and chuckle. I lose the laughter landing this evening. A massive wave lifts my stern, I lean back as far as I can, to avoid pitch poling vertically. The shower descending onto my exposed body is at least a ton of water, and creates a merry foam. I can neither submerge with the buoyant clothing on my upper body, nor does it give grip for my paddle to enable me to roll.

"What the heck! I am so near the sandy flat beach, I will just get out!" I think defiantly, and wade ashore in the strong side current. My abandoned kayak washes up a further hundred yards down the beach, with a cockpit full of sandy water. It weighs a ton, I turn it over to empty it out, and notice with horror, the carbon skeg blade of the integrated rudder has sheared off. Only a sad stump remains, not enough to stay on course with a strong side wind. Around Australia, I have never broken my rudder fin! I only have one reserve blade, and I stupidly left it in Buenos Aires. Thankfully, Alejandro can send it to my next host at Balneario El Condor via bus express.

Tonight, my tent is secured with added lines and thin short pegs buried under piles of stones. I cannot drive the long broad sand pegs into the rock-hard ground. Next morning, my originally white kayak looks like a corpse, buried under sticky black sand. My red tent also is wearing a black skin, its repellent protective silicone coating is sandblasted off. A little brush does sterling work, and soon all original colors are restored.

I spend a stormy day on this lonely beach, with an abandoned nearby farmstead as my neighbor. A rusty, wind powered waterwheel is squeaky pitifully, trying to pump brackish water from the well. I would use this water only in an emergency. Stray dogs are howling a duet with the wind, and it is a bit spooky here.

The distance to Balneario El Condor is forty miles. I fly along with a good current and following wind at about six miles per hour - my regular speed is three. I notice the missing skeg in the last five miles, as I turn right and get the wind from the side. For two hours, I only use the right paddle blade with wide sweep strokes to stay on course.

Exhausted, I am desperate to escape the breakers in the river mouth, and am getting washed ashore with an elegant roll a mile beyond my intended take out point. A lift in my host's pick-up truck directly from the beach counts as a reward for my efforts today. They let me use a fully equipped holiday house with a hot shower, and help me change the rudder fin. I really appreciate the hospitality and helpfulness of the locals! I try to return favors by adding the host to my blog entries with pictures, and by telling tales from first-hand experience. I also present a signature card attached to a bottle of wine or the like. It is a bit tricky to buy those unnoticed while I am food shopping, as I am mostly accompanied by my hosts!

The offer of the shops in the tiny sea side resorts or fishing villages cannot be compared to European standards, but it keeps me fed. I am not even thinking of posting sponsored packs of special athlete's food to the right place, at the right time, and in the right amount. It would be a hopeless exercise, especially in South America. Instead, I can buy oats and powdered milk for breakfast, plus pasta and rice, garnished with tuna or salami and various sauces for dinner. As snacks during the day serve anything, that will withstand the current temperatures. Right now, cheese, chocolate and butter are possible, but later in the tropics, they will melt away. I buy crackers, sweet and salty nuts, bars of all healthy and unhealthy kind, fresh fruit and veggies...whatever may be available in places with a limited choice.

Apples and carrots last well, everything else is a luxury. I have neither the time nor ability to fish or hunt, and dragging a line behind the kayak would only attract sharks. I shop food for two to three weeks, and stow everything in daily portions into zip lock bags. Water bags get brim full, six bags with four liters each fit with some effort into the fully laden boat, and last for about a week. A minimal fresh water shower in the evening is included. Altogether, my fully stocked floating home weighs 220 pounds, and about a quarter each is water, food, gear, and the boat itself. Add to that, yours truly at 165 pounds, and it is a veritable battleship, which I am moving along with only muscle power.

Chapter 2
DELIGHTS OF THE NATURAL WORLD

Argentina, Part 2: Peninsula Valdés to Puerto San Julian
October 9th - November 18th, 2011

I am not a friend of detours on a circumnavigation like this. If there is a bay, I will be crossing. It is more entertaining to see land, but being near the coastline is not a promise of safety. Paddling into each bay would also add several hundred miles to my endeavor. When circumnavigating Australia, I went across the 400-mile-wide Gulf of Carpentaria, and slept seven nights in my kayak. There was no other vessel around, only water, water, water everywhere! South America has only a few large bays to offer, but to reach the striking Peninsula Valdés, could I not just cross over the Golfo San Matías?

Yes, I can! No long thinking, I am off. After only one rest day, I am back in my kayak. I put the northernmost point of the Peninsula Valdés into my GPS, and follow the arrow for hundred miles. Wind, tides and waves are pleasant, and in a good mood, I am "chatting" to the massive brown Albatrosses, which are majestically gliding above, or nosediving right next to me. "Get away, you vultures, I am not a prey for you!" I jokingly tell them off, and show them my paddle blade.

By nightfall, I have covered forty miles, a satisfactory progress. I reckon that until the moon set at 3am, I will have enough light to paddle in reasonable speed, and to make sensible progress. I am fighting against tiredness with "creative" songs, rhymes of my daily experiences on popular folk tunes. Thank God, no one is hearing me out here! The moonlight disappears two hours too early behind thick clouds, and fog sits right on the water. The wind picks up, and so do the waves. I have nearly forgotten the inevitable result: I am getting sea sick! I cannot see the horizon to give me visual stability, and my kayak is dancing on the waves. Seasickness is not a new sensation for me, and usually, a good vomit will sort me out. I do not get weak or dizzy. Tonight, my dinner is refusing to come up, despite a finger down my throat, and I continue to suffer. Visibility improves a bit at times, and with it, my seasickness. By 4am, I feel vile again, and I still cannot eject my dinner. I am counting the hours to sunrise at quarter to six.

By 9am, the tide turns, and the real fun starts! The forecast was for waves of largest three feet, but now, it blows at a rate of twenty knots following wind, with a strong tidal current against it. Twelve to sixteen feet tall standing waves develop. I whizz downhill on such a wave at ten miles per hour, or more, but I am still only covering three miles per hours of distance. This wide tidal race usually invites to an exciting surf-play in the waves, but after twenty-six hours on the water, I am too tired, too seasick, and I am paddling a fully laden kayak. Should I not be able to see land soon? My nerves are stretched to the limit.

I might be taking some risks, but I am not suicidal. When I prepare, I do everything to minimize the dangers. Still, I cannot reach my food in these waves, and I barely get my drink bottle to my mouth. I am only able to refill it from my water bag behind my seat, if I manage to keep my balance. I try to use my female urinating device as usual, but after collecting two whooshes of sea water into the open zip, I do not care anymore. For the first time ever, I let it run right into the dry suit. Now, it is a wet suit... Why doesn't the warm body fluid at least reach my icy feet? There is no call from number two, but frankly, I would not give a shit if it does. I have tethered myself to the kayak since quite some time, and I can feel my concentration fade.

Anyone, who cannot develop superhuman strength in such conditions, should not start such adventures. I am glad to be only responsible for myself, and not having to worry about a partner. No rescue boat would be able to ride out these waves, and to fish me out of the soup!

Eventually, I reach calmer coastal waters, but there is not much time to relax. I must paddle another six miles along the coast. Alejandro has sent me a message to my satellite phone, telling me to land more to the west, as the rangers patrol the area around the lighthouse, where I was planning to land. Due to my shortcut across the Golfo San Matías, the special permit to camp in nature protected area has not arrived. I have no idea what the coast looks like, and prepare for an unpleasant landing. Shore waters are calm, and having passed a little reef, I can get out on a steep pebble beach safely - after 120 miles and thirty-two hours of ceaseless paddling. My legs tremble, and I am tired and fully knackered.

Peninsula Valdés is famous for its diverse wildlife. Every yard of coastline is occupied either by Magellan penguins, sea lions, or elephant seals. The south capers, a type of baleen whale, arrive every year to calve in the two sheltered big bays. The access for tourists to the nature reserve is carefully regulated. Only a few yards off my secret camp site, I can study a colony of elephant seals, the massive fat giants basking in the few rays of sunshine. The bulls are up to ten feet long, and three and a half tons heavy. As they age, they develop a distinctive nose, which hangs like a trunk past their mouth. The cows only grow to seven feet and weigh under a ton, and have no trunk. Strong bulls can gather a harem of up to twenty cows, which they violently defend against other marauding males. I better move my kayak out of the danger zone of a bull in mating mood, because, who knows… Should I get too close to them, loud grunting tells me, they are displeased.

I accept nature's primacy, and like to leave this wonderful area, before my unannounced presence becomes a problem. During the night, I get the idea, I could try a five-mile portage across the land bridge, instead of paddling without permit around the peninsula. The wildlife gathers mostly on the outer shores. Inside the bays, I am less likely to upset any creatures. The wind is still blowing from the north east, and my necessitated camp shortens the way through the bays. The forecast for the second next day says rest. I decide to carry on tomorrow, although my body screams for a break after this stressful long overnight paddle.

The trip towards Golfo San José turns out to be pure delight. Wind and tide push me leisurely along the coast, and I hardly paddle. My aching body relaxes, while I enjoy the sight of thousands of little penguins, seals, and sea lions of all types and sizes. Their heads pop out of the water everywhere like little jack-in-the-box. I can make out the various harems on the beach. From about fifty feet, I can hear the cows and calves grunt, howl, and squeal, interrupted by the imperious barks and snorts of the oversized patriarchs. A fifteen-mile strip of cliff gladdens my sea-kayaking heart, and I steer closely into each nook and cranny, inhaling deeply the scent of algae and mussels. I feel intensely connected to the sea with all my senses. Such moments are the reward for all stresses I must endure!

It is October, high season for the whale watching expeditions. Five larger boats are in the southern bay, stacked high with about fifty tourists, all of them armed with cameras. Who knows, if an overzealous ranger might still want to stop me? I quickly paddle past. From one boat, I hear my name being shouted. "Maybe, I need to be a whale for them?" I laugh to myself, as my electric bilge pump can produce a high fine jet as the spout of a whale, if my cockpit is flooded. But I better get to move on, pay no further attention to the boats, and enjoy my own whales further out, jumping around just for myself.

I count more than fifty animals, but I can only enjoy the sight of these powerful marine mammals in passing. I must watch my GPS, as I want to take a direct line out of the southern bay to the northernmost point of the mainland. On the satellite pictures, I have spotted a wide beach to camp on; my chart says "dunes" on that end. My ETA would be an hour after sunset, but the alternative would be a detour, and camping once more on the peninsula. Wind, tide, and my progress are all good, and the moon is meant to shine brightly for the first hours of the night. I decide on a night landing, which should be no problem in this calm water with good visibility.

The wide beach I intend to land on, turns out to be one of those unpleasant, forty-five-degrees steep pebble walls. The strong wind sends a dumper crashing up the steep beach. I hope, this dumper becomes less powerful further away from the land spit on the inner side of the bay, and paddle an impatient two miles to the west. But I do not dare to land anywhere on this stony steep wall, despite the bright night, and decide to go back to the land spit. The "dunes" marked on the chart must be somewhere? I can spot them with my strong flashlight high up above the pebble wall. But between them and me, there is the unsurmountable barrier of this single high coastal dumper. It is 11pm by now, and I am still working my way towards the tip of the land spit. Once I have moved around the dumper, I simply keep on paddling southbound, and in the right direction, until I can find a good landing spot. If I cannot land, I will just carry on, as I have done many times before. What is the problem?

The moonlight reveals a few lines of whitecaps at the spit, and I take a wide berth to avoid them. The wind is noticeably picking up, but is thankfully following. I am not comfortable anymore out here in over twenty knots, and I am chilly. A broad bay shows up on my GPS, offering shelter to land amidst this northern wind. White foaming breakers in the pale moonlight dictate another wide berth. I fight two miles backwards into the wind, before I can enter the bay. But it feels better to face the "enemy" than to have it creep up from behind.

An unexpected breaker in the bay entrance nearly wipes me out. It is almost dark, and I can barely slide from the whitish breaking peak sideways down its back. That was close! There is some shelter in the bay, despite the threatening cliff face and the daunting steep pebble beach. My exhaustion dictates I must risk it all. The single dumper sounds moderate, and with a deep breath, I let myself get washed up the beach. Thank God, I am ok. By now it is 1am, sixty miles will do for today!

Shining my strong flashlight about the place, I notice I have become a new member of a colony of elephant seals. "Budge up, guys. Here come two added members to your harem, my kayak and I!" If I keep enough distance, the animals are not aggressive. My most heroic act in front of the looming cliff face is an ice-cold naked shower in the darkness, curiously watched by my neighbors. They smell strong enough with their continual burps and farts, a bit of freshness will not go amiss here. I climb three steep ledges up to the top of the beach, and find a free space for my tent between two groups of these primeval animals.

I get a pleasant surprise in the early morning, a little baby elephant seal has snuggled up to my kayak, an orphan searching for a new mama. It is heart-warming and heart-breaking at the same time. Does my boat really resemble a female elephant seal? Or was it the tuna oil I poured out of my tent last night, close to my stern? It is sniffing and snuffing on the stern of my kayak, trying to suck on what mother nature provides to feed a baby. But there is nothing to be found...

I spend the next strong-wind day relaxed on the beach among my elephant seals, observing their X-rated activities. Suckling babies are everywhere, and new ones are in noisy production. To copulate, the massive bull grabs the small cow from behind with his front fins, and if she is not keen, his weight leaves her no choice and unable to move. Due to such brutal copulation habits and the many fights of the bulls, females and their calves are often casualties. If one bull rises to his full height, the females and babies dash back instantly to their groups. The bull cannot let them stray too far, as the neighbor would be glad to offer them sanctuary.

The tidal range is getting higher each day, and I find many tidal races with standing waves around the headlands. Not too bad just yet, but further south, the effect of these wave actions will become more challenging. I will have to pay careful attention to what time I go around these exposed dangerous spots. Several wrecks sticking out of the water denote the hidden reefs along this coast.

At Cabo Raso, I accidently land among a large colony of Magellan penguins. These funny guys in their dinner jackets are only about a foot and a half tall, and very shy. I sit still among them, and watch them return from their daily fishing trips up the beach in what looks like conga lines. Their nests are in sandy hollows further up in the shrubs, well hidden under low hanging branches. When I have a little peep, they duck and look like they wish they were invisible. I restrict my curiosity to a few photos, and leave them to their evening activities, but they will not let me sleep with their tweeting and chirping.

Next morning, a few of the gentlemen are lining up behind my tent, waiting for me to get out of their path, like English breakfast guests in front of the still closed buffet. I hustle and clear out as fast as I can. Once on the water, I watch them fish, often alone, but sometimes in groups of up to twenty animals. They leap out of the water like dolphins, a beautiful vista!

Punta Tombo offers a strong tidal race against me, and despite powerful paddling, I can only reach a speed of one or two miles per hour. Thank goodness, even amid the tide, the standing waves are still moderate. An enormous colony of gulls is populating this cape, thousands upon thousands of birds live here. I take the opportunity of a sheltered natural harbor to land for a short break, while the gulls rise around me like a big cloud. They disperse over the next hundred yards into the air, water, and among the boulders. The rocks are coated white with their acrid excrement. Their sparse nests, consisting of only a few bits of grass, are crammed into every available niche. What a life! My kayak in my tiny harbor is starting to float up on the incoming tide. This wild nature distracts me so much, that I nearly forget to keep it in sight. I can barely wade in and catch it, before it sets off without me.

Around 1800, Cabo Raso was an ancient fishing village of about hundred inhabitants. Today, it is being renovated by Eduardo, an inventive young man turning the ruins of the old houses single handed into a holiday village. Today, I find him at work on the buildings, after he met me the night before at the outer reaches of his territory. Unfortunately, I am not able to increase the turnover of his little shop, but I do admire the attention to details, and the skills he applies to the restoration. In summer, he is already looking after guests, and he is covering the function of hotelier, bar keeper, chef, handyman, shop keeper, policeman and mayor of his little kingdom all by himself. The guests are here to admire something that impresses me also: Beyond the cape and on an island off the coast, I find a sea lion colony exceeding in size everything I have ever seen. Thousands upon thousands of animals are lounging on the rocks, grunting and snorting, swimming in the water and following my kayak with a splash, whenever I traverse the narrow channel between the island and mainland. It is unbelievable, almost unreal, to be part of this nature spectacle.

The coast itself turns into a highlight, I savor my journey along the rocks, and poke into every tiny bay. I land on the narrowest sandy beaches, climb up on the cliffs, and delight in the view of this beautiful coastal paradise. This is what I love about sea kayaking: You never know what you see around the next corner, or what happens the next five minutes! It could be a dead boring straight coast with nothing but sand or gravel, or rugged, every corner inviting to explore. The landscapes could change beyond a land spit, or the weather and tides are turning. You must manage all this with technical skill and mental preparation, and must be well prepared not only for the next day, but much further ahead. Or, suddenly, you are stuck without water, food or a forgotten or broken essential piece of kit.

My camp site today offers plenty of plastic storage boxes used on fishing trawlers, but it is otherwise relatively devoid of rubbish. Did a trawler lose its load in a storm? Various wrecks are telling their own tales. A herd of half-feral, shaggy sheep are demanding to be shorn. They almost disappear in their heavy coats. No one seems to be about to release them out of their woolly carapace.

I have a rest day, and I am exploring the coast on a walk. I find many beautiful green rock pools, discover the reefs at low tide, and enjoy the seclusion. With some difficulty, I light the first camp fire of my trip. In the end, it needs a spoonful of white spirits to kindle the damp drift wood. Now, all I would need is a strong shoulder to snuggle on this romantic evening. The satellite phone with my family at the other end must suffice. A delicious piece of meat to barbeque would also be nice, but I still enjoy the limited offering of my pasta dishes as my outdoor dinner. But most of the time, I prefer to cook inside the tent, nicely snug and warm inside my sleeping bag.

South of Camarones, the coast is strewn with idyllic looking farmhouses, lonely bays with fishing nets, and deserted sailing boats. A dolphin appears as a good omen for a quiet day. I am paddling close to the edge of a reef, and feel safe and relaxed. But I know, I should not take my eye off the open sea!

I am torn out of my daydreams quickly. The low swell manages to send me an unexpected breaker, created by a submerged rock, and I capsize without any preparation. Neither helmet nor hood protect my head, nor a PFD my body. I know, my only chance to escape the reef, is to quickly roll up again. I manage, but now, I am caught in the regular reef surf. Another roll gets me up again with effort. I straighten my kayak back out to sea, and notice I lost my helmet and all my headgear. But all I can think is: "Get out of here!" Neither my boat, head nor body would be happy about any contact with the sharp edges of the reef. I just manage to fish the helmet and visor out of the water during my sprint out, but two other scarves sink into the waves. It takes a while for my nerves to calm down, this could have ended differently!

Reefs can be an unfriendly territory for a small water craft with an unprotected passenger. I am pleasantly surprised I managed to roll up again, despite the ballast of a water bag on the back deck, and the PFD clipped behind me, in anticipation of an easy day. Now, both are hanging aside. I have not expected any kind of danger, yet it nearly got me. The Australians call these unexpected breakers in open water "bombies", and their southern sea is full of them. This morning's dolphin must have been my guardian angel! The handy water bag allows me to shower my freshly washed hair. I shake myself like a dog, and continue to enjoy the day. This was quite close!

I can avoid the strong opposite tidal flow around the next headland, by sticking close to the rocks in the eddy. Either, I go full power around tiny spits at the right time, and keep the kayak on course, or I would get washed into the counter current, and would not make any progress. I feel a bit sorry not being able to camp in all those wonderful bays I am passing, but it is still my goal to circumnavigate South America by kayak! I am already taking my time to enjoy this wonderful heartland of the Argentinian coast. Only one of these dream bays can serve as my campsite for the night. A dolphin greets me, is it the same one that held a protective fin over me this morning?

Strong head winds give me the gift of a day on land. I enjoy the break between many little rock pools, caves, and deep ravines to explore. Near the top of a mountain, I follow a dry river bed, and find many skeletons, cacti and huge piles with thousands of pearls of guanaco dung. Do these hygienic animals always use the same spot for their business?

Day fifty-seven looks like a perfect day! I am flushed at eight miles per hour through the narrows of Isla Leones and the coast, without having to lift the paddle. I am not too happy to pass so quickly, as there are so many interesting things to see! Stopping is no choice, as the tide would shortly turn again. Bahia Gil is the next highlight! My map shows a long channel at the end of the bay, aptly named Caleta Hornos. I can paddle a mile into the narrow gorge with the running up tide, and I have it all to myself. It is magic!

But the graffiti on the steep rocks show regular boat traffic. It seems like every captain who dares to enter the gorge leaves his mark. Is this necessary? At the end of the gorge, there is only mud, barely traversable. I see a phenomenon I cannot quite work out. Every two or three seconds, a fountain gushes up a good fifteen inches high, spaced only about fifteen inches apart. Are these submerged mussels? Or does the mud work with the tide?

I can land in a shallow bay of the gorge, the takeout spot for dinghies of yachts at anchor. Some people before me have tidied up here, a box with all sorts of miscellaneous items is hidden behind a rock. I climb up the ravine, and enjoy a beautiful vista. On the other side, a guanaco calls me with an odd bleating sound. Guanacos love to stand on the highest points, and scout the landscape like a Native American. Condors, the South American vultures, soar above, looking for cadaver. They will not get mine!

I leave the bay with the outgoing tide, and enter a few tiny narrow channels with handrailing on the walls each side, only to exit backwards. This is nearly cave paddling, but without the worry of getting squished to the ceiling by sudden waves. This area is one of the finest sea kayaking destinations ever. One could spend weeks here, exploring the bays, and camping in the most wonderful locations. But nonetheless, I manage today to cover thirty miles. Exhausted from the surfeit of natural beauty, I snuggle contentedly into my sleeping bag.

From now on, I must choose my landing spots with more care and attention to the five-yard tidal range. Where the water retreats beyond a reef, my exit may be blocked. I can see the bottom of the sea through the calm clear water, and I feel like I am on an endless snorkeling trip. The landscape is becoming gentler, not as spectacular as the last two days. But there are still beaches inviting for a little stop over. Thankfully, high tide these days is in the morning and evening, and it is easy to land and launch.

This morning I forget to close the pee zipper of my dry suit. As I quickly hop into the water to pull out my stuck rudder blade, the cold shower from below feels like lightning under my rear. I was never faster at getting back into my boat! But I do not allow myself the luxury to land again, and to change my underwear. Instead, I paddle merrily into the new day. It is now day sixty of my tour, I am more than two months en route, and I have covered 1,250 miles. Only 15,500 to go...

Chapter 3
OFF TO THE CAPE!

Argentina, Part 3: Puerto San Julian to Puerto Williams
November 19th - December 24st, 2011

I have reached Puerto San Julian. The coast guard is so kind to collect me from the river delta, which forms a natural harbor. My kayak is slung diagonally across the pick-up truck, the front sticks by a yard out of the driver's window, the rear hangs by another two the other side off the back. The Argentinian officers seem to consider this mode of transport as normal, but I do not. Nervously, I follow the driver maneuvering our over-width load around the few bends of the small town to the coast guard station. For the return trip, they revive an ancient trailer. The two days of my break are quickly gone with chores, and I am on the water again. The remaining miles will not pass by standing still!

My next landing is one of those dreaded steep pebble beaches. My kayak is so fully laden, that I am unable to pull the heavy boat up the beach. I slip back on the loose small stones repeatedly, and there is a danger of the boat getting ripped out of my hand by the next dumper washing high up. I hang on to the bow of the boat like a counter weight, and I am somehow helpless. I manage to reach the front hatch, open the lid, and fish out a few bags, to throw them high up to the levelled section of the beach. Any time, a wave could slosh into the hatch, or the kayak could slip out of my hands. I shimmy carefully to the cockpit, wiggle out three heavy water bags and start the electric bilge pump. Bathed in sweat, I finally manage to pull up the kayak. My gear is saved! Hopefully, the beaches will become a bit less steep soon.

The gradually increasing tidal range is keeping me occupied. Nature is not concerned about my ideal paddling and landing times, so I often must improvise. The high-water line, normally easy to recognize, is wiped out by heavy rain, and I must move camp higher up twice. It is not fun to be soaked by the spray of the breakers in the middle of the night. My most recent location on the edge of a dry riverbed is not horizontal, but I will at least stay dry from below. My night is short and restless. I keep my dry suit on, and feel a bit trapped. If there will be more rain, the unstable cliff above might break down, or a sudden deluge will come down the dry river bed? I check on my kayak several times, which I must leave on a higher ledge. If the wind becomes the next hazard after high tide at half past ten, my kayak could be blown away. I better fill it with heavy rocks. By four o'clock in the morning, the weather calms down, and I can relax.

By about 10am, the mud at the top of the cliff has dried enough to reach a dirt track, where I see a house in the distance. A serious storm has been forecasted for the next two days. I secure tent and kayak against storm and water, and start my trek toward civilization, armed with my satellite phone and GPS.

I can camp by the house, and wait two days, until the forty to fifty knots of wind die down. At low tide, I can wander about the beautiful rocky coast line around Isla Monte Léon. It feels like I am in a giant dry pool, garnished with many caves and arches. Due to the fragility of the chalky rock, one of the largest arches, thirty yards high and twenty wide, collapsed about two years ago. But the continual erosion of the strong tidal range already created new ones. I would have missed this impressive natural spectacle, if I had just been paddling past at high tide!

I wait for a higher water level until 9am, before leaving next morning. Soon, a thunderstorm with thirty to forty knots winds comes up. As hard as I paddle now, I still drift back at a rate of a mile or two per hour. I spot a tiny chance to land, and let myself drift backwards into a gap in a reef. The cliffs behind me are steep, and there is no place to camp. I must decide to start again, or I will be stranded by the outgoing tide. With heroic effort and partial unloading, I drag my kayak across a quickly increasing sandbank. Thankfully, the weather calms down again, but my landing time this afternoon at 4pm is half an hour prior to lowest tide. I pick a spot where the beach does not seem to be too far, but still I must walk 850 yards for a dry camp spot.

On my return trip from the first luggage run, I suddenly cannot see my boat anymore against the background of the white spray of the waves. Has it drifted off? I can only see it when I get close. It is easy to pull it across the slippery surface of the reef plateau, but the last two-hundred yards of this portage are challenging work, as the sand sticks to the kayak. My campsite in a dry river bed is also not ideal, as there is the danger of getting washed out by a sudden flood wave, if the rain continues to become heavier. Landing at low tide like this can hardly be a bigger effort.

Same situation the next day. I decide to only paddle six hours around the high tide time from one river mouth to the next, to avoid further long portages. I pull my boat to the nearest sandbank, get in, and wait for the incoming tide to flood me. I am not going to pull my kayak one yard further than I must! At lunch time, I put in a half hour break in a dilapidated tin shack under some threatening dark clouds.

Back on the water, I spot my targeted river mouth by the depression of the high cliff, and hope my ETA of three hours before low tide will still let me land with reasonable comfort. The weather is getting continuously worse, and the thirty knots wind is blowing from all directions, finally from front right. The tide still pushes. It is amazing how the little shore waves turn into foaming breakers, each one like a little shower, and I can hardly see. Can I just drag the kayak for the last two and a half miles in the continuously receding, knee-deep water? It would be a pleasant change from all the paddling!

Unfortunately, the coastline now changes, the steep section ends, and becomes a gently sloping shelf, which is dry at low tide. After a further half mile around a stony reef, I can paddle in high winds with significant effort. If I stop now, I am still 500 yards off the coast. To continue, and to wait for the water to rise again, would give me a very long paddling day, and the strongest wind was expected in the late afternoon. There is no better landing spot, and the water retracts from my boat. So again, I begin pulling, carrying and dragging for miles - why did I not bring a kayak trolley? It would be most welcome right now.

After the first luggage run, I pitch my tent, and tie it stormproof down. On the way back, I know I should take some of my broad sand pegs along to secure my empty kayak when I must leave it for the second luggage run. I know a light boat on this exposed sandy and rocky reef flat is a welcome target for the storm. I have seen how empty kayaks have been rolled across beaches by strong wind, but I am already halfway back, and could I not fetch the kayak first, and then the bags?

"The wind is not that bad …, it is letting off…, and the sand is so sticky…" All excuses for not turning back.

To make dragging the boat a bit easier, I empty it completely. Only the devil knows why I then really set off with both bags first. I only turn the bow into the wind, and leave it unsecured behind. Several times, I turn around and check if it is still where I left it. Heavy-laden, I lean into the strong wind. After two-hundred yards, I look back again. Damn it, my baby really is off now without me! In the off-shore gusts, it is half bouncing, half flying across the sand towards the open sea. In a panic, I dump the bags off my shoulders, and try to break the world record for the 200-meter sprint. I hope my kayak takes not off over the open sea! I can run faster than I can wade or swim, so I speed up further, as I know, that with each bounce and roll, the kayak can sustain some severe damage. Upside down, it comes to halt about fifty yards ahead of me. Fully out of breath, I throw myself on the stern and rest for a while, before I dare to check it closer. The helmet under the net behind the cockpit has protected at least the spare paddle in its bag on the back deck, also the main paddle I have stuck under the bow bungees. I get busy quickly collecting from all over the wet sand my pieces of gear which were stowed loosely in the cockpit.

Thankfully, the loaded open gear bags I dropped in a panic did not turn over, as the various dry bag rolls would have been blown all over the open plain. I tie all bits of luggage together to a solid pile, and keep on dragging the empty kayak towards the tent. Hopefully, that one has not also taken off! It stayed in place in the lee of the high cliffs.

After a closer inspection of my kayak, I note an extensive list of damages. I doubt my repair materials and options here on the open beach with flying sand and rain are enough to make a proper repair, and hope for a transport to the nearest town of Rio Gallegos. Alejandro, my trustworthy friend and helper from Buenos Aires, finds a host family, and sends out the coast guard who collects me from this wilderness with a four-wheel drive vehicle.

Day 95, between Rio Gallegos and Punta Dungeness: As easy as the landing was yesterday, so difficult is the start this morning. What is the cause of the difference? For four hours after high tide at 6.30am, I am trying to get out. I finally must give up. During the night, the height and frequency of the waves has changed dramatically. Now, they are man-sized and follow in quick succession, creating a strong backwash. The layer of pebbles is thin, underneath is solid sand, and the running waves cannot drain away easily. I simply cannot get close enough to the waterline to push my heavy loaded kayak fast and straight enough into the water, to jump on after. Several times, I get washed, and once pushed a hundred yards along the coast before I can escape the wet stuff with the kayak in my hand. Thankfully, I get pushed in the right direction. It is impossible for me to leave this beach, sitting upright in my kayak. After a four-hour battle, my power is exhausted. My big repair job is not fully watertight, I must go over it again, and to free my rudder from the many stuck pebbles by taking it apart. There are problems to solve each day!

Once all repair jobs are done, the continuous rain sends me to sleep. After a snooze, the sea does not look any more inviting. Next morning, I cannot see it at all. This time, it is fog hiding the size of the breakers, even when looking from the waterline. According to the sound, they are a little less steep, but I really cannot see anything in this thick soup. Two hours later, I can at least make out the waterline from my tent. I study the breakers, and decide to have another go, visualizing success at the first attempt. But as soon as I am in the range of the backwash, the boat is ripped from my hand. I straighten it out, and spot another gap in the breakers: "Now, or never!"

The cockpit fills with water, and the next breaker turns the boat over. There comes another gap! The next attempt I try differently. I push the kayak in, however it likes to swim up, and with the paddle in my hand and myself tied to the boat, I swim for my life. Despite getting drenched twice, the backwash finally pulls me out. I am free! I climb in, empty the cockpit with my helmet and the electric bilge pump, shovel out handfuls of pebbles, and gather myself in somehow quiet water. I still cannot see the breaker line in this fog, but at least, now I am on the other side of it!

My GPS helps me to keep a good distance to the coast. Up to Cabo Virgenes, near the entrance to the Magellan Strait, I paddle blind, and fear to become seasick. I am missing the horizon line to anchor my sight. Turning around the cape, the fog lifts like a curtain in a theatre, and like a ghost rider, I turn from the dull fog into the bright sunshine. I am close to the infamous narrow between the Argentine mainland and the great southern isle of Tierra del Fuego. A magical moment! To my right is a broad friendly-looking sandy beach, there is not much swell anymore. A few Sunday trippers enjoy their fishing, and no one seems to wonder, where I could suddenly be appearing from. I give a cheerful wave, sing Johnny Cash's "Rider's in the Sky", and feel relieved of the pressure of the fog. My goal for today is the southernmost tip of the peninsula by Punta Dungeness near the Chilean/Argentine border, where the crossing of the Magellan Strait at twenty miles is the shortest.

I am now hundred days into my trip. For a complete circumnavigation of South America, I could paddle through the Magellan Strait. It would be easier, and I am making my own rules for this journey. But without reaching the infamous Cape Horn, my journey would not be complete!

I am passing an impressive two miles long penguin colony with thousands of animals, and land a short mile off the border near a house with a blue roof, thinking this must be the station of the coast guard. Wrong! An oil refinery has spread itself here, and disturbs my well-earned sleep with their noisy machines.

At 1am, the strong glare of a flashlight shines on my tent, and I hear steps crunching on the gravel. I am relieved to see only the over-eager men of the coast guard, whose station is not far away in the cliffs. They have found me like a Geo-cache from the coordinates of my "I'm OK" message, but they still feel like they need to check on my well-being in person. I think they are just bored, curious, and keen on a signature card.

Visits like this after sunset, when my tent is dark, and I am obviously sleeping, particularly after midnight, are not one of my favorites. I am quite grumpy. Had I been able to speak the local lingo, I would have told them my opinion quite unmistakably. Idiots...they return at 10am, I am feeling more cheerful, and they get the cards they are after.

The strong wind enforces another rest day, which I spend with a long walk to watch the penguin colony, and to visit the idyllic red and white Chilean lighthouse on the border. Even the next day, I hesitate to tackle the 20-miles crossing of the Magellan Strait. The forecast is for fifteen to twenty-five knots from the north, with waves of three to ten feet. It would be a nice paddle with following wind, but in combination with those waves, these are tough conditions over my limits. I settle down for another two days next to the oil refinery. When I can hear a helicopter flying to supply the many outlying oil platforms, I feel encouraged to set off anyway. The wind cannot be that bad, if they are flying?

The tide goes with me, the sea is calm in this sheltered side of the coast, but further out are many white caps. I still like to keep on going. The following ride in high wind and waves is not for the faint-hearted. Wind and tide give me a hefty push towards Tierra del Fuego, but where shall I land? I see the two little houses of the Argentine/Chilean border on top of the cliff. On the right seems to be a river mouth promising an easy landing spot, even at low tide. But that's already Chile, and a reef is blocking my way. I manage to find a narrow continuous gap, and with a pounding heart, I paddle towards quiet and shallow water. Every reef has one or more narrow gaps without breakers, but when you go through the narrows, and hear the water crashing all around you, you can just pray "Please let me through...please let me through...". One hour after low tide, the reef is still shallow, and I decide to wait. I am chilly, but relaxed, and am hanging on the shallow reef until the incoming water takes me to the left, to the Argentine section of the cliff.

Two paddling days later, I meet up with my friend Alejandro in the Paddle Club of Rio Grande, where he and his friend Juan Pablo are preparing their kayaks for their circumnavigation of Isla de Los Estados. We had vaguely considered doing that together, but as we never managed to paddle together before this challenging trip, I better let the guys do their job themselves. The two guys will come towards me in the Beagle Channel, when they start in Ushuaia in a few weeks. Three busy days are filled with the standard city duties, one of which is to repair my life-supporting dry suit. I hop into a river while wearing it, to see where the wet patches are coming in. Even the best Gore-Tex suit cannot withstand ten-hour paddle days without starting to show signs of wear. A new suit was on the way, but has by now been completely swallowed up by the Argentine customs. After this pit stop, I feel well prepared to soon reach Chile, and to circumnavigate Cape Horn!

About a week later, my path leads me along the easternmost coast into the furthest reaches of Argentina. A few other paddlers had to give up their quests to go around Tierra del Fuego, and were evacuated by helicopter. There is no road access in this remote corner of the world. The endless desert of the mainland becomes green, interspersed with little rivers. A delight for the eyes, after this long dusty and arid section. I can paddle close to the coast, which is protected by thick fields of kelp in quite a few bays.

One evening, I slalom through a minefield of tiny reefs to a wild beach covered in bones. I discover a seven-yard-long, overgrown whale rib bone. A horde of young bullocks is running feints at my tent, and I remember holding up a gas burner against water buffalos in Australia. No animal likes fire!

As I stick my head out of my shelter next morning, for the second time on this trip, I cannot see anything. Thick fog curtails my vision. By 8am, the veil lifts a little, and it feels safe enough to paddle out over the reef, navigating a sharp rocky headland. By midday, I float again in the pea soup, encircled by hundreds of birds flying overhead. Together with the reflecting waves off the cliffs, plus the incoming waves, I feel I am in a three-dimensional carousel, as I handrail my way along the coast. Best conditions for sea sickness! At the entrance of Caleta Falsa, breakers develop, and the water is getting wilder. Only guided by my GPS, I paddle blind further out to see. I feel uncomfortable to paddle in these conditions, but there is no alternative. At least, the birds circling me are not vultures, and three miles ahead of the dominating Cabo San Vincente, the fog is lifting. I am in the middle of the running up tide, which is the worst timing for the tidal waves marked on my chart around the Cape. The current is going in the right direction, but behind the headland, I meet the biggest tidal waves of my paddling career! I am used to paddling in swell waves of three to four yards high, but these are five to six yards! They feel just massive, and bring my adrenaline pump to full power.

I concentrate, and ride down each wave at top speed, but I am relieved when I reach calmer waters. At the time of the tide change, this exposed area might be flat as a millpond, but due to the fog, I am arriving three hours too late. At least I would get to Cabo San Diego, six miles away, at tide change. I aim my bow in that direction, and take care to avoid yet another field of kelp in the bay. Just after about a mile, the rising wind defeats me. It would blow straight into my face after getting around the next cape. I do not feel ready to cope with further challenges in uncertain conditions, and find shelter in Bahia Thetis, a bay used by the seal hunters dozens of years ago.

In a tumble-down building, I find a massive pile of old seal pelts, stacked up like carpets. Half preserved and half rotten, they are witness to the ample catches of the 1950's. Today, the bay is deserted, and shows only the historical buildings. Trekkers or horse-riding tourists use a newer, simple wooden hut in the area.

I prefer to spend the night in the familiar environment of my tent. A nosy fox disturbs me in the darkness by licking out an almost empty box of processed cheese I forgot under my deck net. Neither shouts nor lights are stopping him, so I take the tub, and throw it far off into the shrubbery, with the fox following behind.

The closer I get to the infamous Cape Horn, the greater the mix of anticipation and tension. It is a dream for every sea kayaker! Cape Horn, they say, is not a given!

One of the last days along the Argentine coast leads me past wonderful rock formations with many arches, towers and caves. I dawdle, always in the lee of the rocks, and cannot get enough of the multitude of beautiful vistas. The first real "Gaucho", an Argentinian cowboy, rides with a lead horse past my kayak, wearing colorful clothing. I look at him with as much amazement as he does at me. A smile and a wave overcome the cultural barriers. I pitch my tent on a small hillock that night, and two further Gauchos with lead horses are passing. It is a most pleasing view to my eye, when men and animals are passing across the green meadows along the stony river bed. I feel tempted to offer a temporary swap of transport!

Today is my last paddling day in Argentina! After a short stopover at the coast guard station of Moat, I am expected at the station of Almanza, just on the other side of Puerto Williams in Chile.

I am in the Beagle Channel, the narrows between Tierra del Fuego and the southern archipelago, whose southernmost tip is Cape Horn. I am greeted by clear and calm weather, and the mountains in the distance appear higher than before, now even snow-capped. As a match, the air and water are getting noticeably colder. I get drenched by a hail shower in the late afternoon as I am cruising through a labyrinth of small islands. The same evening, the Almanza coast guard takes me to Ushuaia for my exit stamp.

The next day, after crossing the Beagle Channel, a small boat of the Chilean Navy receives me. They escort me into the harbor of Puerto Williams, the waiting point for all boats trying to round Cape Horn. I move into a room of a small boarding house, and look forward to a few quiet days with a Christmas party with many international sailors in the "Micalvi" Yacht Club.

But in my mind, there is only one big question: When will I get a weather window for my circumnavigation of Cape Horn?

Chapter 4
THE CAPE HORN WEATHER TRAP

Chile, Part 1: Puerto Williams and the loop around Cape Horn
December 25nd - January 8th, 2012

"Cape Horn - is not - a gift - Cape Horn - is not - a gift - Cape Horn - is not - a gift". This rhythmic mantra goes with my strong paddle strokes. I am by now lying flat on the front of my kayak to have a chance against the ever-increasing winds. Thankfully, I am flexible, and I am determined to arrive before sunset "over there". But the wind is the enemy of a lonely sea kayaker. And Cape Horn has fierce winds...

I am at mid-point of the crossing to Isla Hornos, the very last island of the Cape Horn Archipelago National Park at the bottom end of South America. These latitudes are infamous for their unpredictable storms. On the north side of Isla Hornos is only one sheltered landing bay. It has a long, narrow and steep staircase, which is the only access to the rocky plateau of the island. This last stretch of six miles across open water must be doable in one and a half hours? It is half past three on this almost spooky, wind-free day. Is this the calm before the storm?

I have been on the water since four o'clock this morning, to make the most of this calm weather. The path through the small islands was easy, too easy. A twenty-mile crossing over water smooth like a mill pond, and then I am hopping from island to island in shelter. I am already envisioning myself going the same day around Isla Hornos with the "real" Cape Horn. What challenge is a fifty-mile paddle on a quiet day for an experienced sea kayaking goddess like me? I only must get the right weather window and zack, the infamous Cape Horn is ticked of my list!

But those leaning too far out of the weather window can topple out of it. I have been warned. Cape Horn is one part of the world that is most feared by seafarers of all sizes. Countless wrecks litter the sea floor, they have capsized, been stranded or simply been swallowed up by the stormy seas. The weather can turn in minutes. Predictions are difficult and very unreliable. What am I doing here, in this nutshell of a boat? And alone?

The Chilean Navy requires an escort boat in an extensive written application to paddle around Cape Horn - two horrible words for an independent and free expedition paddler like me. There is a sailboat to officially escort me on the loop from Puerto Williams around Cape Horn, the "Polar Wind" of my friends Osvaldo and Jutta, experienced Cape Horn sailors. But it is Christmas, and the predicted weather window is small, and the sailors will not need the three days head start to Isla Hornos that I do need.

I plan to leave alone early morning on Christmas Day, to be able to use the predicted calm and long-ish weather window for the crossing of the archipelago in two days' time. One must formally sign out of the harbor in Puerto Williams. I hope the officer on duty will let me go alone on this Christmas morning. I assure quite believably with some female charm, that the "Polar Wind" would be following in two days to join me on the "dangerous" twenty-mile open water crossing to the archipelago. And sure, they would be also with me for the "even more dangerous" circumnavigation of Cape Horn! For a kayak, the path to get there is along an easy coastline with plenty of landing options, sheltered from the dreaded southwestern winds. For that, I really would not need an escort boat!

The latter is correct. The former I am not too bothered about, as neither the "Polar Wind", nor I, are intending to float along in cozy harmony. Well, the paperwork has been done, and the officer, mellow from the holidays, believes me. I am off! Never have I jumped faster into my already packed boat. Cape Horn, here I come! And without the hated escort boat!

In the evening of 25th December, I land as planned in the little harbor of Puerto Toro, after a beautiful stretch of thirty miles along the sheltered coast. There is another Navy officer on duty, and this one also asks for my permit, and where my escort boat is? Everything takes too long for me. Impatiently, I listen to the, for me, incomprehensible phone calls. Again, we check the weather forecast, and it is good. I ladle on a hefty dose of female charm, and assure again that the "Polar Wind" would be following the day after tomorrow, to be allowed to paddle the next twenty sheltered miles alone. Had I known where and how I would be landing on the evening of December 27th, I might have been grateful had the officer stopped me in Puerto Toro.

And I stumble fully into the trap, into the infamous Cape-Horn-weather-trap! December 27th is, as predicted, dead calm. I am full of confidence I would reach Isla Hornos tonight, easily, and without any problems. I set off at a good pace, and make quick progress. A large boat of the Chilean Navy catches up to me on the twenty miles crossing. It seems they have become aware the "Polar Wind" is indisposed today. But they also seem to realize, an escort boat in these mill pond conditions is an absolute surplus requirement. After three hours, I am alone and free again! I arrive on the other side with no issues, and dive into the shelter of some islands.

Three different forecasts predict a rising wind towards early evening. About six o'clock, an uncomfortable southwesterly of twenty knots is supposed to draw in, getting stronger later in the night. But by that time, I will already be home and housed at the Navy station of Isla Hornos, I think, and continue my relaxed paddle between the islands. One final small crossing left for today! Only a measly six miles to Isla Hornos, the last island of the southern archipelago. I start to push my kayak at about 2pm out of the shelter of the gap between the last two islands before the final.

The first four miles are calm and easy. I can already see the safe landing bay with its steep staircase. I will be done in less than an hour. By half past three, a first breeze is coming, then the wind freshens up, and the swell is rising. The wind and waves are getting stronger and higher, finally smacking me cold and wet into the face. High winds already?

The wind comes from the southwest, and therefore, not only whistles into my face, but also pushes me sideways to the east, out of the strait before Isla Hornos. In that direction, there is nothing, only Antarctica. That is not where I would like to go tonight! "Pedal to the metal, girl! The wind is getting stronger. The waves are getting higher. But you have more power, you can paddle hard, you can do it," I tell myself and repeat like a mantra in the rhythm of my strong paddle strokes. "Cape Horn - is not - a gift - Cape Horn - is not - a gift - Cape Horn - is not - a gift..."

My GPS counts down the remaining distance, it is only a ridiculously short distance of less than two miles! High time to put on my PFD, which by now is hanging sideways off my stern in the water. The wind has literally blown it off the deck. When the weather is calm, I attach it with one bungee rope on the back deck, so I am forced to put it on when the conditions become more challenging. I perform a quick stretch to the rear, a momentary balancing act - hopefully my arm does not get caught when slipping into the life vest! The paddle is already tied to the boat, and to be on the safe side, I attach the carabiner of my bowline to my PFD.

In the worst case, my kayak is the best flotation device. If it gets blown away, should I capsize and must exit the boat, I will die out here within a few minutes, despite a floating dry suit, life vest, my personal locator beacon, VHF radio, flares, and whatever other "safety gear". My safety begins in my head! The only thing that can help me out here, is continuous hard paddling without considering I may capsize. If the waves are getting that high that I am in real danger, the open rescue boat sent by a large Navy ship would be in even greater danger, and that would not necessarily mean a safe rescue. I can react to the waves far better in my kayak than a little open motor boat can do, they would be uncontrolled bouncing up and down in the messy sea. Out here, I am only responsible for myself. To exit the kayak here would mean certain death from the cold, or to drown, or both.

I am used to paddling alone in high waves and rough seas. I love it. I love the sea. I have strong respect, but no fear, I am fully concentrated and stay cool. Only once have I capsized on the open sea, years ago in Australia, but I safely rolled up again. This stuff here, I shall also manage.

It is getting slowly serious. The wind whips already with thirty knots across the high waves. My safety bowline drags sideways in the water. Despite wind and waves, I take a fraction of a second to tighten it. "Don't drag - the reins - don't drag - the reins - don't drag - the reins". I have a new mantra.

On my GPS, I can see the distance to safety counting slowly down, but another number is moving frighteningly faster: The degrees to the landing have changed from 180 at the start, to, by now, 245! I am blown out of the strait at an unstoppable pace. To adjust the angle deliberately a few degrees to even out the drift is impossible.

At some point I reach the level of the landing bay, but the distance is not getting shorter. Meanwhile, the number for the degrees of the bearing is racing upwards! I am simply blown past, and now would have to paddle straight west into the continuously increasing headwind to make the bay. Only half a lousy mile! The lee of the island would have to shelter me by now! But the wind is howling ever stronger, the sea is seriously uncomfortable, and I must realize for the first time in my paddling career, I will not be able to make that last fucking half a mile! Despite mantras, highly polished paddling technique, a well-trained body, and an iron will. Turn now, girl! Before it is too late, and all you can do is to greet the penguins of Antarctica!

For three seconds, I pretend I can relax now, and shake my maltreated extremities. Three seconds, in which I drift with the wind, and just have to balance, when the waves are rolling over me from the stern. But I am still getting unstoppable pushed out of the strait! Now, I must fight even harder, or once more, I will get blown past my destination, instead of managing a safe retreat into the narrow, protected channel between Isla Herschel and Isla Deceit - where I set out from three hours ago.

My strength is waning, and with it my concentration. Now, do not make any mistake! I must make landfall somewhere before dusk. It would be my certain death to float around out here in these winds and waves in darkness. To my horror, I realize, despite all my powerful paddling, I am drifting merrily past the safety of the sheltered channel. Good God, is there anywhere to land at all?

The southwestern coast of Isla Deceit, which is my last hope of a landfall, looks fully unprotected, dark, rocky, and very threatening. There is hardly a flat space and no sandy, or at least pebble beach. Despite the waves, I am trying to read the chart on my GPS. I zoom in as close as I can, and hope to spot something resembling a sheltered bay.

Another possibility comes to my mind: Can I reach the eastern, protected side of Isla Deceit? A quick glance to the southeastern tip only reveals spray high as houses, with waves crashing on a long submerged rocky headland. If I can give the frayed rocky land spit a wide berth, and withstand those waves and the wind, but still were to get pushed south east, instead of reaching the lee of the island, I would have no chance to get to safety tonight. After that spit is no other land until Antarctica.

I must move along the southwest coast of the island, searching for a take-out spot, and to reach it without being blown out to sea before. Concentrating on my new goal renews my energy. At the very end of the island, I discover a bay about hundred yards wide, and it seems to even have a patch, on which the rocks are only sized between a foot- and a tennis-ball. Unfortunately, the waves are breaking on this "beach" with evil power. It could have horrendous consequences to make an uncontrolled landing in this high surf, and to get thrown alongside onto that rocky shore. I am hesitating, paddling back and forth, still full of concentration not to capsize in the now about sixty-knots wind and four-meter swell. I MUST land here, somewhere, NOW!

Desperately, I seek shelter close to a huge boulder about ten yards high, standing to the left side of the bay thirty yards out... if shelter is a word to use in the thunderous hurricane and gigantic breakers in this rocky desert. Beyond, I see a field of arm-thick strands of kelp going up and down with the swell. Some of them reach up to the rocks, and offer a marginal cushion. Should I dare to land there? I have no other choice. The breakers here also hit the rocks with violent force, but occasionally, a set comes a little lower. This is my very last chance!

I put on my helmet already as I was closing in on the coast. I cannot remember how I unclipped it from the net behind me and put it on, without taking my hands off the paddle and the eyes off the waves. The helmet is essential in such a risky emergency landing!

As good as it goes, I am waiting for a lower wave set. I take a deep breath, and paddle with my last energy on the backside of the breaker onto the thick slippery kelp bed on the boulders. I throw the paddle high up the shore, rip off the spray deck, jump out of the kayak, slip and fall. The next high ice-cold breaker takes my kayak and myself further up the rocks, directly onto my beloved paddle. Somehow, I end up underneath my heavy-laden boat. I struggle myself free, adrenaline ensures I do not notice pain nor my surroundings. All what counts is that I am alive, intact and not ripped to pieces. My paddle is broken in half, and the kayak sustained severe damage. But I have no broken bones! The fat hematoma on my legs really does not count.

I quickly secure the boat and the sad remains of my broken paddle, as wind and sea show no sign of letting up. With my satellite phone, I send a quick message to my friends, family and the blog - some might be worried about me in this sudden hurricane. "I have landed" I write, "More later". I cannot do more, I am still in shock after the stress of this emergency landing. This will have to be enough for my loved ones at home and the Navy. I later find out, the Navy officer and his family living on Isla Hornos have been watching my odyssey with binoculars, and have rightly been very worried.

At the time of my landing at half past eight, a full sixty knots wind was measured at the Navy station of Isla Hornos. By 10pm, it was an unbelievable 106 knots, rising to 120, and then 130 knots until midnight. This is Cape Horn! But I am alive, not injured, and still have all my gear. I have a damaged boat that is repairable, an undamaged reserve paddle, and food, water and batteries for several days.

Where have I landed? This rocky shallow strip of coast in the bay of the last corner of Isla Deceit is strewn with big sharp boulders, and less than ten yards wide. The steep rear cliff wall behind is looming threateningly close above me, and I fear falling rocks may come down on my head, kayak or tent at any time. The breakers smack on the rocks with a thundering primeval force. To escape on foot is impossible. Despite all that, I thank God, He let me land safely!

Is it even possible to pitch a tent? On a somehow levelled spot behind a two-yard high rock is the only choice, and the rock even gives a bit of shelter from the storm. I need to hurry to set up my night abode, it is nine o'clock, and soon it will be dark. The hurricane howls stronger and stronger, and tears at my fragile cloth shack. I pile big stones on the bottom sides of my only three days old Hilleberg Staika dome tent, tie additionally Kevlar strings to the six corners, and attach them with heavy rocks to the ground. At least there is no shortage of those. Sleep will be out of question!

Most of the night, I lie like a beetle on its back, all four extremities stretched into the four main corners to strengthen the tent. The split reserve paddle supports corners number five and six. I hope to preserve my precious shelter from broken poles or tears in the fabric. A typical Cape Horn hurricane fights around me at 120 knots.

Next morning, I evaluate the situation. The bottom sides of my tent are looking quite holey from the friction on the rocks, but thankfully, the great rip stop fabric prevents further tears. One guy line has rubbed through, but I can fix it. No broken poles. I have a somehow stable protection from the wind and weather, without which my involuntary asylum on this beach would be exceedingly uncomfortable. Who knows how long I must hang out here?

The heavy rain of the night is easing off, the wind still blows at twenty knots. The whipped-up sea sprays salty water over my campsite. Thankfully, I do not need to worry to get flooded high up here. But the weather must first calm down further to think about repairing the kayak, and to escape this rocky hell.

After two nights, Thursday is starting dry and less windy. I have a closer look on my kayak. The side seam has split over a length of several yards, a bunch of holes need patching, and the broken rudder fin must be replaced. With my limited repair materials and abilities, I think I can make my floating castle sea worthy, but the broken paddle I can only give an emergency repair with an internal splint. I will have to use my spare blade. I hope the resin of my repairs can dry in these wet and salty conditions, and my boat will not disintegrate into its component parts once afloat.

Via satellite phone, Peter reaches me with shocking news: Alejandro has drowned! My friend and reliable helper from Buenos Aires has paddled the same day, in the same stormy winds, and in the same latitudes along the Staten Islands at the most southeastern point of Argentina. His friend Juan Pablo could rescue himself with his kayak into a high cave, but for Alejandro, all help was too late. His body was salvaged two days later by the Argentine Navy, his kayak never found.

We had thoughts about paddling together around Cape Horn, or if I might have liked to add Isla de los Estados to my circumnavigation. What would have happened if - I do not like to finish thinking. When we last met in Rio Grande, we were joking both about our upcoming 50th birthdays, and what amount of life we may have remaining. "I won't live long, I do too many dangerous things", Alejandro said laughingly. Well, so do I, but I know I will have a very long life. But as much as I am mourning Alejandro's fate, I have little time to stay inactive. I am sitting on an inhospitable rocky island, and must find out how to get away from here in one piece.

I notice a tiny waterfall on my daily restless walks across the rough boulders of this narrow strip of shoreline, and fill my water sacks. As a precaution, I shorten my food rations, and use the batteries of laptop and satellite phone sparingly. Who knows when I will get the next calm weather window to break out of this drab prison? A rescue boat cannot land here, if it is too bad for me to start. There is no place for a helicopter to land, and climbing up to the top is also impossible. All I can do is wait, wait, and wait again until I can paddle off myself.

Three to four yards high breakers are crashing without stop onto my shore. It is a continuous enervating noise, and a gruesome sight when you are stuck. I need strong nerves. The threat of falling rocks, the tent at break point, rationing of resources, the message of Alejandro's death, and the uncertainty of my launch from my unwanted asylum - I need to take it all.

New Years' eve 2011, I spend alone on my dark narrow rocky shore, the fifth and hopefully last day of my enforced sojourn. My phone call with Peter, who is partying with friends in Denmark, leaves mixed feelings. I feel lonely, but I celebrate my survival.

As I watch the breakers over the tide changing the past days, I ponder where it might be the best start position for my launch. I decide on the furthest corner of the pebble beach, the forecast for New Year's morning is favorable. The evening before, I carry my kayak 300 yards to the corner. It is a dangerous balancing act over the slippery rocky boulders with my empty, but still fifty pounds heavy kayak on the shoulder. No slipping, slapping my freshly repaired kayak onto the rocks, or breaking a leg. On New Year's morning, I realize the breakers in that corner still roll in too heavy, and a start at exactly the opposite end of the bay seems to be safer.

Thought, and done! I shoulder my heavy gear bags, walk back, and once more, I must do the dangerous and sweaty climb with the kayak on my shoulder, just to the other end of the bay. Finally, everything is in place and loaded. The boat sits high enough not to be caught by the larger breakers, wedged between a few big rocks covered with kelp. They give a lumpy but slippery starting ramp. To pull a heavily laden kayak across uneven rough rocks is pure stress to hull and seams. Hopefully, my repairs will hold!

Helmet on, PFD on, I have only one chance. If I pick the wrong moment, and my start from the slippery uneven boulders goes wrong, the worst danger is to get washed backwards onto the rocks. If a high wave grabs the kayak too early, and I cannot jump on in time, or one of the still scary breakers comes at me wrong, my one and only chance of a break out is gone. The consequences of that - I do not want to think about.

With heavily pounding heart, I wait until the biggest waves pass, and carefully push my kayak into the danger zone. With the smallest wave of the set, the heavy boat comes afloat. I jump astride, my bum falls into the seat, legs still out, and I paddle like hell out of the danger zone. Thank God, I have escaped without problems! My hands are still trembling, I stuff my legs inside, and snap my spray deck on within a second. New confidence comes with the relief of my successful ride through the breakers of the launching site. I must cover the seven miles to Isla Hornos without drifting too much to the left, and I will be able to recover in the shelter of the Navy station. I have briefly contemplated the alternative, a direct retreat to Puerto Williams. But should I give up the chance to paddle around the "real" Cape Horn, just because I once got the weather wrong? Especially now, that I am so close?

This time, the chosen weather window with fifteen knots wind holds up long enough for a safe crossing. Even though I get pushed out sideways by ten degrees, with bad memories of my failed attempt to reach Isla Hornos, I arrive after two trembling endless hours in the sheltered landing bay.

The hordes of people dumped the same moment by a cruise ship pass me by unnoticed, as I sit in a corner of the steep wooden staircase. After this devilish ride, I am in no mood to be a tourist attraction, and to pose for souvenir pictures. I hope no one tries talking to me. I prefer to call my family with relieved New Year wishes. My mood changes between joy and tears, I thank God that I am here and healthy, remember Alejandro, and consider how close I came to a similar fate.

The next two days, I enjoy the loving care of the Chilean Navy officer Cadiz and his wife Paula, who are living all year round on Isla Hornos. No hot shower has ever felt better. Paula bakes fresh bread, and serves an opulent New Year's meal. I am relaxing, but wondering how the final southern highlight of my trip will be? How will the eighteen-miles circumnavigation of the Isla Hornos compare to my experiences on the way down here?

The weather for January 3rd promises to be relatively calm, with fifteen knots wind and two to three yards of swell. I choose to go anti-clockwise. The Navy officer amazingly is letting me go alone without issue, he does not even mention an escort boat. And I certainly will not!

But still, should I not consider it after my recent experiences? No, an escort boat does not make any sense for me in this swell. Far more important is the cooperation of the weather. I do not want to rely on the help of others, or even to endanger my helpers. I like to rely on myself, and my ability to keep calm and to show strength in marginal situations. If I doubt myself, I should not go.

After a calm start along the sheltered northeast and north coast, the western end is showing up on the wild side. Due to the prevailing southwesterly wind, the sea is rough and whipped up. Once more, I put strong demands on my concentration to stay upright, and to look only ahead. I cannot let go of the paddle, not even for a second, to take some pictures, to pause, or to admire the landscape. It is a pity, as the steep rock formations at the western tip are truly breathtaking, but my safety has priority over photos.

With one eye, I try to enjoy the scenery, with the other, I watch the fat breakers rolling over the scattered rocks. At some point, I spot with the right corner of my eye a larger ship of the Chilean Navy. It better keeps a good distance, as closer to shore, where I can still paddle, there are many submerged rocks which cause problems to larger ships.

Finally, a helicopter circles above me at watch. For more than an hour, the pilot is distracting my concentration. Or is he waiting for me to capsize, and to start swimming around Cape Horn instead of paddling? I dare to give him a cheerful wave with one hand a couple of times, but cannot afford to look up. Did the Chilean Navy sent a TV team after my spectacular start, to record further escapades or the world famous daring sea kayaking lady? But other than two half-hearted selfies, this challenging circumnavigation of Isla Hornos must be undocumented due to safety concerns.

I am back for a relaxed brunch in the sheltered landing bay by 11am. I have conquered the infamous Cape Horn solo! The circumnavigation demanded all my advanced paddle techniques, but as the weather window stays open, I set off for my return trip to Puerto Williams. In the sheltered quiet waters of the archipelago, I now have the close escort of a Navy ship, but here, it is surplus to be around. After a fifty-miles day, I pull into Isla Wollaston for a weather stop. I spend two relaxing days at the Navy station, and the officer's wife Pamela spoils me with freshly baked lemon pie. Delicious!

The last two days along the sheltered coast via Puerto Toro to Puerto Williams, I can paddle alone again. At the suggestion of the Navy officer at Isla Wollaston, I sign a statement releasing the Chilean Navy from being responsible for me. Such a paper I could have signed when I entered Chile, easily, and with little "burro-crazy", rather than fighting those endless permit battles!

The reception by the international sailing community in the Micalvi Yacht Club of Puerto Williams was overwhelming, with a great party the same night. But only my friends of the "Polar Wind" I tell of the embarrassment in the harbor office upon my arrival. I intended to collect my exit stamp to paddle over to the Argentinian Ushuaia, but a Navy officer dared to confiscate my passport! I first must receive a lecture from the district commander about my "solo trip" ...and of course, he would not be free until Monday 11am. This means, I will be missing the calm weather window on Monday morning to cross the Beagle Channel back to Argentina. Unfortunately, no officer is interested in that problem.

"You have been naughty!" is the greeting from the commander, trying to look like an angry Daddy. Only it is not his fifteen-year-old daughter, but a grown up forty-eight-year-old adventurous woman. I try to look penitent, but cannot keep down a smile. And as I see the creases in the corners of his eyes, I realize the dreaded lecture for my solo trip is already over. Now, the commander just likes to hear about my experiences, and to congratulate me on my success.

But who was sitting in the helicopter that day before, who did his best to distract me? Turns out it was the commander himself with his wife, on a tour of his offshore Navy stations. Now, it may be my turn to tell him off re the unnecessary distraction!

On the internet page of the Chilean Navy, the enforced "lecture" by them holding back my passport, was described as "The commander received the exceptional athlete to offer his congratulations to her achievement in the southern chilly waters." I was, of course, always accompanied by a Navy escort boat. The helicopter was a "safety measure" and not a day out for the commander and his wife. Got it.

Chapter 5
THE ONLY WAY IS UP

Chile, Part 2: Puerto Williams to Puerto Eden
January 9th - February 25th, 2012

The first great milestone is behind me: The conquest of Cape Horn! I am alive, healthy, and quite proud. After the successful circumnavigation of the southernmost tip of South America, I could adopt the old sailor tradition of wearing a small golden ring in the left ear. Though usually I do not make do with second best, I prefer silver jewelry. I rarely wear ear decorations, so I decide to insert a sparkly red ruby into the cockpit of my silver kayak pendant, which I am always wearing as a talisman, instead of wearing a golden earring.

The only way of the next months is up. Quite literally, the general direction of my paddling is north, after going west for a section first. I plan the route to Puerto Montt by taking the shortest distance through the canals of the most beautiful fjord and island landscape of western Patagonia.

The character of my trip changes. There is hardly any more a difference between low and high tide or powerful currents to be aware of. I am mostly protected from the swells of the open sea. The main issue is the continuously strong southwesterly wind, but as soon as I stop travelling west, it blows to my advantage. I am looking forward to a few relaxed months. Will this become reality?

With the just dried exit stamp of Chile in my pocket, and befogged from different aftershaves stuck on my cheeks from the good-bye kisses of the many Chilean Navy officers, I am finally underway to Ushuaia, somehow late at 1pm. This time, I accept the brief escort of a Navy boat as a guard of honor, rather than an intrusive safety measure. To reach the most southern town of Argentina, I need to cross the windy Beagle Channel. After I have done my chores, I will return to the other side, and be back to Chile.

I shop for three weeks of food, and re-stock my repair materials, as the next opportunity to do this will be in Punta Arenas. In between is only wilderness. No town, not even a village, only three lonely Navy stations, happy to receive rare visitors. I do not need to worry about carrying a lot of water, as there are plenty of clean sparkling creeks along the way.

The Argentinians also give me an escort of honor out of their waters. See you again in Buenos Aires!

I was fighting against the need to have an escort boat for this further stretch in Chile, and I am finally allowed to carry on travelling solo. After having survived the inferno of Cape Horn, they seem to think I am sufficiently capable to paddle alone in the mostly sheltered channels of Patagonia. With an escort boat, the lonely wilderness adventure would only be half the pleasure. I feel well equipped with satellite phone and PLB signal to make contact, should I need help. But my best insurance is my experience, a careful choice of equipment, common sense, and good nerves.

After finishing a kayak adventure, I am often asked why I put myself to such strains. My first answer often is a "Why not?" I suspect the question is only asked because I am a woman. When men climb high mountains, thunder across salt lakes at hundreds of miles per hour, or explore the arctic with a dog team, people are not surprised, but admire the explorers. Perish the thought of me getting such ideas.

By now, I am underway for 140 days, and it is mid-January. The next days, I delight in the intoxicating natural beauty of the glaciers of southern Patagonia, sometimes stretching directly into the Beagle Channel. With this background, this pleasant weather and favorable currents, paddling is a sheer delight. I am stopping at the first glacier flowing down near Caleta Olla, and make camp early by 3pm, to walk up as close to the tongue as possible. The view is too beautiful and tempting to just paddle on by. Some sailors also stopping in this bay show me the start of a path to the glacier I might not have found on my own.

I ramble through beautiful flower meadows, damp moors, and past lichen covered rocks and cliffs on which stunted trees cling. I cannot quite get to the foot of the snow-white glacier and its wide sparkly lagoon, but have an incredible view - and wet feet, as my trainers are not suitable for hikes in the muddy mountains. My GPS leads me in the right direction, and at the end, the path is everywhere.

The next day, I start at a spooky night time hour of 4.30am. A glacier tongue glowing brightly keeps on calving throughout the night large bergs.

With my fragile kayak, I keep a respectful distance in a sea of bizarrely formed ice sculptures. After an hour, I enter the milky lagoon of a glacier with its not too attractive gray-black tongue. The sun has melted it, and the color of the dragged soil is predominant. I get out of my kayak to take pictures of the odd shapes the rocks have been ground down to, and to admire the powerful nature. By mid-day, I spot a waterfall rushing down a dark glacier tongue, something I have not come across before. What a sight!

In a smaller arm of the many branches of Calleta Olla, Fjordo Pia, there are more glacier tongues. I decide to take a little detour, and to travel up three miles. Three sailboats anchor in a quiet bay, but I intend to reach the end of this fjord arm, to explore the glacier tongues. I can get close to the non-threatening shallow edge of one of them. The glacier tongue at the very end, I can only reach by crossing a lagoon with larger lumps of ice, which are getting closer and closer together. I must niftily slalom around smaller ice floes and yard-high bergs. My kayak is unfortunately not solid like an icebreaker!

Suddenly, I hear a low motor sound, and a continuous dull "clong, clong, clong". A sailing boat pushes its way through the ice, and due to its size, it cannot avoid all collisions with smaller floes. The French boat is heading to the breaking edge of the glacier tongue, and disappears behind a big berg from my sight.

What would happen if the glacier calves a big berg of ice now? The more lumps in the lagoon, the more active the glacier. The wave caused by a house-sized berg braking off would cause havoc, swirl all the swimming lumps about, and squish my fragile craft. I better skip and miss the last mile to the edge of the tongue. I have experienced enough glaciers over the past two wonderful days!

With some effort, I work my way through thick kelp beds towards Timbales. In the middle of the channel, the wind is blowing into my face with twenty knots. It is bothersome to hook into the long stalks of the tough plants with my bow hopping up and down in the waves. They get stuck on my toggle, and I must reverse to let them slip off. It feels quite like stabbing and poking rather than paddling swiftly, when my paddle hits the thick kelp and not much water.

My journey through the fjords and channels of the beautiful deserted southern part of Patagonia leads me on a westerly track for another week. I must paddle directly into the predominate wind, before I can take a wide berth. First east, and finally I head northwards towards Punta Arenas.

With at least fifteen knots into my face, I start at the junction of some channels north of Isla Londonderry. By early afternoon I enter a small inlet, only navigable during high tide. I can barely walk and drag the kayak in. Entering the damp living room of dozens of ducks, I find a small, flat and grassy hillock covered in duck droppings. Is this a sign it will not get flooded? Or is all this the result of one tidal period? Those ducks can count themselves lucky I will not eat them for dinner. At night, I stay awake for an hour around high tide, and peek outside to see the inlet slowly filling with water. All ducks are afloat, but I stay dry!

There is some heavy rain on Friday morning, but winds are calm. Packing wet is not much fun. By dawn, I pull my kayak with the outgoing tide past a few larger stones to deeper water. I do not like to suddenly sit high and dry while I pack! The water is lumpy, can I find a bit of shelter in the kelp bed near the coast?

It is arduous work making progress between the islands and fjords. It is very tiring to fight headwind, and clinging loops of kelp in the near constant rain. It got so cold by now, the rain feels like hail. Some days, I only make a few miles headway, and stop for the day early afternoon, if I spot an inviting place to land. Those are quite rare here!

On day 150 of my tour it is rain, rain, rain! Luckily, the next day, I can enjoy paddling dry. It stays calm until 5pm, the sky is half blue, and I can see as far as I have not in weeks. When I reach Canal Cockburn, I am presented with mirror smooth water and an amazing rainbow. Thus motivated, I paddle forty miles, and only decide to stop at Isla Prowse as it starts to drip again. The beach I select for the night is anything but ideal. I must pitch my tent on top of stinking kelp washed on the beach, with a generous helping of rubbish. I lay out some large green leaves in front of the entrance of my tent, to simulate a bit of cleanliness.

The next days are again like I have hoped for, easy and pleasant. The landscape is becoming mellower, the mountains are less rough and rocky. I find a beautiful campsite on Isla Capitan Aracana, a slightly elevated section between two beaches and bays. I can hear water from both sides. Last night, I went to sleep listening to a river, a day before to the whooshing gurgle of a waterfall. Nature spoils me!

At the pit stop in Punta Arenas, I treat myself to the luxuries of fresh fruit like bananas, avocados, cherries, grapes and plums, they all find a space in my kayak. I have an added sack of groceries clipped to the back deck, and load ten liters of drinking water.

The first half of the day, I can paddle in the lee of the coast. The Magellan Strait is getting narrower, and I am soon facing the north straight. The bits of kit I received in Punta Arenas improve my sense of well-being a lot: A new dry suit, a new tent, and a second laptop.

At least my equipment is back in top form, as the paddling is harder than I have expected. That first stage to Bahia Woods is the easier one, with moderate headwind and shelter in bays. Passing Cabo Holland, it changes rapidly. The west wind is picking up, and there are only steep cliffs up to 1100 yards high, without bays to find shelter. Today, with these challenging wind conditions, I make at least thirty miles, but decide to stop for the day on a small sandy beach. The forecast is not good, I must stay here for another day.

It turns into a two day stay. I use the opportunity to rest my aching muscles, and to eat, read, and sleep a lot. On the second day, the weather is getting even worse, though a few rays of sunshine break through the cloud cover. A fox with her two youngsters is my only company. Not shy at all, they come close to my tent. In Germany, I would be worried about rabies, as they are not bothered at all about this strange big animal in its red burrow sharing their living space. The mother barks shortly at me to mark her territory. I ready my paddle and a few stones, just in case, but they are gone quite soon.

The severe weather forces me to have more breaks over the next days. The rain is so heavy I have difficulty just looking outside. If I open the tent door, I might get a big wallop of water into my face. Not exactly inviting!

As I leave the Magellan Strait, it presents its roughest part yet. The wind picks up to thirty knots and the opening to the Pacific Ocean lets the swell roll in this far. I fight for every yard. Facing these high waves, I even consider returning to my earlier launching spot. The only chance to make headway is to cross the bay to the mainland. After three miles of very tough paddling work on this crossing, my day is not yet done. I drudge another 500 yards along the mainland, and another two miles to go past Isla Santa Ana. Between the next two islands, I have some shelter from wind and waves, but can only get around the tip with last effort. The earlier six miles took me more than four hours. Only after another four, I find an acceptable place to stop in Bahia Clift.

The beach here is of strange texture: Sharp black stones are washed over a carpet of sea grass. When I walk on it, I am swinging like on a trampoline. In the distance, I hear a river running, and close by, I discover a grassy dry meadow offering a wonderful place to pitch my tent. The place is sheltered from the wind, I can hardly hear the surf noise, and I have a fresh water source. What else could I want, especially as it looks like I will have to stay another day, at least due to the poor forecast. With this slow progress and the many breaks, I start to worry about my supplies getting low, and if my gas canisters will last all the way to Puerto Montt.

The following days, I make a bit more headway with an average of thirty-five miles per day. I mostly have shelter from the uncomfortable strength-sucking west wind. A few dolphins and an occasional idyllic waterfall brighten my spirit. The landscape is becoming more delightful with a picturesque mosaic of bays, canals and small islands. There are 300 miles left to reach Puerto Eden, a tiny village of 200 people, only accessible from the water. The next day's forecast is for low winds.

I make a disastrous mistake: Due to an imprecise sea chart, I mistake Isla Baverstock, which I just passed, for Isla Rennel. I must paddle ten miles into a dead-end channel, which was not recognizable as such on the charts. I assume I would be heading back in a northwesterly direction. But suddenly, I am stuck! Now, I have two options: An 800-yard portage over land which I briefly checked out on a walk, or back-paddling all the twelve miles to return to Canal Cutler.

As the wind is not too strong, I decide to paddle back. Trying to make up the lost time, I only settle at nine o'clock in the evening. Now I know that the passage shown on the chart between the two parts of Isla Rennel does not exist. To get to the main channel north, I must go around Cabo Dispatch and Isla Piazza. What an odyssey!

I enter the main channel after three days of detours, and I am so relieved I use the satellite phone to give Peter in Denmark a call. Normally, I am stingy using the batteries of my electronics, but now I am so glad to be back in "civilization"! I see lighthouses, and occasionally a fisherman's motorboat zips past. The animals increase in variety, I see whales and dolphins, and one night, the buzz of a Colibri wakes me. I must share my campsites with ducks, which point out my presence with loud chatter and spread wings. Now, I am only 150 miles away from Puerto Eden!

The sandflies inhabiting these warmer regions of the fjord lands are becoming a plague. I already had to learn in New Zealand's fjords how to quickly pitch a tent, dive into it, scrape off the hundreds of flies from the inner tent, and to stay inside all the time to wash and change. These beasts will keep me company for the next few weeks. All activities take place indoors - cooking, eating, brushing teeth...even having a pee. All into one pot, in that strict sequence obviously. For the big business, I have plentiful supply of small bio-degradable trash bags. In the morning, I can easily clean the soaked multi-purpose pot in the sea, and it is sterile clean and non-smelly. Shocking? No, it is just very practical. No dishes to clean in the evening, no scrubbing in the morning, and you boil your water anyway for the next dinner.

Even though I always pay the most attention to how high the tidal water may rise on my campsites, I wake one night with the feeling of lying on a water bed. Half an hour before high tide, the dry meadow in this inlet is fifteen inches submerged. I decide to lie still, and to float up on my inflatable sleeping pad like in a pool. The floor of my tent is near waterproof, and all gear is stowed securely in waterproof packages. It is a strange feeling, but the tide goes down soon, and I simply fall asleep again.

New night, new inlet, the phases of the moon have lowered the high water at night - this meadow will stay dry! Again, I wake half an hour before high tide, stick my finger on the tent floor in expectation of some dry grassy soil underneath, and feel something wobbly once more. Heaven, not again! But I can laugh aloud, as I realize my finger pokes on my half empty water sack!

It is getting warmer on my way north, and I make satisfactory progress. Most times I paddle without gloves, and rarely pull my hood over my head. It will not be long before I will start yearning for cooler temperatures when near the equator! No break until Puerto Eden, only hundred miles, three paddling days. I still do not know if a nice local is able to offer me a warm and dry accommodation, as I have no messages on my request via internet. This village is totally cut off!

Chapter 6
BEYOND EDEN

Chile, Part 3: Puerto Eden to Puerto Montt
February 26th - March 30th, 2012

Fifteen miles before Puerto Eden, I notice the first signs of civilizations. Smoke rises in the bush, I see a fishing boat and men chopping wood, and huts of people harvesting mussels. Behind a rock, I see a boy standing in a fishing boat, it looks as if he is using a small engine to pump water out of his leaking boat, but he makes ok signals as I am passing. Later, I learn that divers under the boat were working with air hoses served by the compressor. Soon I see Puerto Eden, a small fishing village with two hundred inhabitants. There is no road access to this hamlet which lies at the end of a wide fjord valley. To me, it looks like paradise, but no one takes notice when I land!

I unload my kayak, and carry the heavy bags to my camp spot at the end of the jetty. A friendly local helps me to lift my kayak. Workers in a nearby hostel allow me to charge my batteries, and to take a hot shower. The lady next door volunteers to do my laundry, and in no time, it flutters in the wind. All is well!

It is high time to stock up my provisions after four weeks in the wilderness. My path leads a mile along a wooden boardwalk to the only shop in the village, the "Super Mercado Eden". I ring the bell, and an old lady opens the shop door, where the stock seems to be at least as old as herself. She allows me behind the counter to pick out the few things suitable to my needs. I buy spaghetti, a lump of cheese, some sweets and potato crisps. Most of the rest of her stock is alcohol. No oats, muesli, powdered milk or crackers, I must go on half rations for breakfast. I still have ten portions, but there will be twenty days to Puerto Montt. For dinner, spaghetti will suffice. The offer of fresh veggies or fruit, other than wrinkled potatoes, dry onions and two lemons, consists of a few raisins. An artificial fruit flavored powder for my drinking water will hopefully quench my craving for some vitamins.

By 5am, the clucking of the chickens in the nearby coop rudely wakes me. For a long time, I paddle on the east side of the channel, with only a few landing spots on offer. When I finally spot a white pebble beach, I am proud of myself for passing by, but the next one is too tempting. Dry, level and clean campsites are short here, so I cannot resist. Later, I find out this site is only to be enjoyed with earplugs inserted. Passing boats make waves which wash noisily through the pebbles.

But I will learn to treasure pebble beaches! Soon, hardly any decent places for the night are to be found. Some nights, I just stay on top of a large rock. It is hard to drag up the kayak above the high tide mark without damage, and to secure the tent in strong wind.

The next demanding section will be the crossing of Golfo de Penas. I ask Karel, my weatherman in Israel, for the forecast for the next five days. A friendly start, then headwinds of twenty knots. Not good enough for a full crossing, I can expect be grounded for a few days in a row. Taking account of my limited reserves of both food and energy, a small detour of an added fifteen miles to the nearest Navy station of Isla San Pedro seems like a sensible move.

But first I must spend a night on a rocky beach in Canal Puddeman. The Navy station can only be spotted after Isla Penguin. Two and a half hours before I get there, I announce my arrival via VHF radio. They must have understood me well, but with forty minutes to go, they once again check on my ETA and current position.

I can make out the house and jetty, but where is my "reception committee"? No one is to be seen. The jetty is only equipped to land larger boats, and there is not a flat beach to land a kayak.

I wobbly unload at a very high jetty, and nearly lose one of my dry bags and a gas canister. I must jump in after. I am glad I am wearing a dry suit!

With some effort, I pull my emptied kayak up the wooden ledge of the jetty, and pile up my luggage. Yet, strangely, there is still no soul to be seen! I will have to go up to the house to meet them. I take my most important bits of kit, and walk up to the house along this wonky jetty which is not exactly in a great shape. The door is open, so I assume someone is expecting me! But the nearer I get, the more I feel spooky. The house, looking so intact and homely from a distance, is a ghost house! Who did I have a radio conversation with? This is Isla San Pedro, the only jetty, and the only house I can see!

I call again, and must learn I am at the old Navy station, which has been out of use for a long time. The new building is north east, and the jetty becomes a boardwalk leading past the house. I would be welcome to stop in and to re-provision. In the designated direction, I see some aerials beyond a hill. Heavily laden, I make my way over to the new building. For another mile and a half, I must walk along a rotten wobbly boardwalk, I hope it will be strong enough for my weight. Around the next bend, I see the new station, hear the throbbing of a generator, and know this one is not a ghost house.

A young man comes out of the building, but he is not a smart officer in a snazzy uniform, as they normally live in these stations with their families. This is an all-men's cave! I feel a bit funny, have I entered the lion's den?

On closer inspection, the "lions" turn out to be four very nice and well behaved young chaps. The boss, Juan, seems to have a good hand for discipline and cleanliness. I try to have a conversation with my "Spanglish", and check the forecast. It does not sound good at all: the next few days, wind from the north with at least twenty knots is predicted. I guess I will have to spend some time here, even if I am keen to continue my journey! But here, I have food, electricity and a hot shower. As there is no family life with wife and children, the guys have different leisure activities: A well-equipped bar and TV, soccer, ping pong and pool table, and even a small fitness studio - boys' toys!

The predicted rainstorm hits overnight, quite as strong as I had in Cape Horn. But this time, I am well sheltered in the Navy station - thank God. I am just worried about my kayak all night. Will it still be undamaged in the morning?

It is, but the storm will not calm down, and I tie it even tighter to the solid jetty. I can see the roof of the old station nearly flying off, to continue my journey is out of the question right now.

After five days on the Navy station of Isla San Pedro, I can get back on the water. Juan and José help me hold the kayak, so it is easy jump in and paddle away. The first few miles, I still fight three to four-yard-high waves. At tide turn, the favorable current and a wind from west help me to make good progress at four and a half miles per hour...until I get into a counter current, and my speed drastically reduces. The visibility reduces also, and I can feel the first signs of seasickness. I am no longer used to the swell of the open sea! Instead of moving away from the cliff with confused and reflecting waves, I stay as close as possible to the coast - a decision which does not alleviate my seasickness.

All landing bays are proving to be everything but sheltered. I will have to pick one of them, despite the large boulders strewn about. I have no other choice but to pitch my tent on a narrow wobbly platform I have created out of washed up fishing crates and planks. During the night, it falls apart, and the wind whips the wall of the tent into my face. The sounds of the sea and wind prevent sleep for a long while.

Day by day, the coastline is becoming friendlier and less mountainous. It looks like one could go on great coastal hikes. One little bay lines up to the next, and the high mountains are now well in the background. With easy winds, I make good daily progress at about thirty-five miles per day, but I am expecting to have to make a portage at the next river delta soon. Blue sky and a multitude of bizarre chalk stone formations full of arches, caves and waterfalls put me into a good mood. The bays and beaches are the way I love them, clean pebble beaches, without kelp and rubbish, sheltered from the surf, and pleasantly calm and sunny. I even enjoy a swim in the cold sea, and let the warm sun dry me off. I am a good distance off the stinking lump of meat that once was a whale, which I discover when I leave this paradise.

Up to Bahia Kelly, a spooky atmosphere hangs over the landscape. Black and deep violet clouds seem to predict the end of the world. Weird sounds come from the many caves: Either the boom, boom, boom of the waves, or the barking of two hundred seals living among the arches. The vultures circling overhead increase the feeling of being somewhere magically spooky and bizarre. They are living in a strange symbiotic relationship with the seals, cleaning up the dead and fecal matter, which holds undigested goodies. I see trees growing on top of other trees, and many penis-shaped rocks. Is all this real, or am I too long on the trip?

The next challenge is the historical small boat portage to Laguna San Rafael. A GPS spot marks the entry in the river mouth where I will have to transport the kayak a mile overland to make progress north. Despite my GPS point, the entry is not easy to find! Repeatedly, I get stuck on sand banks or enter dead ends, and the spot is still a mile away according to the chart. I must find the main current of the river, it looks like I am too close to the side of this wide delta. After a few more detours, I decide to take the left fork, and seem to have found the right way. I paddle through a forest of dead trees with black water and absolute silence... until I hear voices. Have I gone mad?

I listen, but nothing. Then again, but this time, there are two people talking! Two guys in folding kayaks are heading my way. They are Italians, who started from some small village ten miles north of here, and intend to paddle into the glacier lagoon of Ventisquero San Quintin. These folding kayaks could be walked along the shore, but both look as if a little bounce would be enough to tip them over. They are heavily laden, with bags tied to the deck. They say they are not really paddlers, rather mountaineers fancying a different type of adventure. One of them recognized me as the woman who paddled around Australia. It is a small world!

On the way to the takeout spot, I glide along the river on a mirror smooth surface. I feel almost drunk, as I see everything in duplicate. The turn off into the side branch of the delta I can find easily, someone has marked it with a piece of blue cloth. I turn in, and I am now close to my GPS spot! 150 yards ahead, I see a kind of trail with trampled down long grass, the two guys must have passed here two hours ago? This path has lots of water holes, and the swampy ground is giving in on many spots. I use my paddle as a hiking stick. Suddenly, shit happens: My right leg is sucked into a swamp hole up to over my knee! It looked so harmless and safe to walk here. But this is a mud trap like in a horror film. Desperately, I try to free my leg, I am thinking I may have to sacrifice my sandal, soft rolling boot and neoprene sock to the swamp hole, or having to cut the lower half of my dry suit leg. I cannot reach my knife, and eventually manage to free myself with a massive effort. Had I slipped into this hole with both legs, I would have had it!

Very carefully, I continue to fight my way along the trail, and eventually find the real tracks of the Italians. It looks like I went fifty yards too far, and now need to move both gear and kayaks to the correct spot, the real start of the safe portage trail. I unload my three gear bags, and move each to a slightly elevated section, always using the paddle as a hiking stick. Then I can pull the kayak up. In the same manner, I move all my gear to the next dry spot hundred yards along, and then another 300 yards along the trail. By then, I am done in and exhausted, so I decide to set up my tent at the one and only larger dry spot, obviously used as a trail campsite ever since. It was strange to see my kayak here in the middle of the green jungle, with no open water far and wide. I just finished pitching my tent, when it starts to rain. Perfect timing!

There are better ways to spend a Sunday, and the second part of the portage is still ahead of me. I feel like I am part of »Jungle Camp«, or like being in a slapstick version of Crocodile Dundee, but it is no one's but my own decision to take this route. Today, I do without my dry suit, it is just too warm to wear it with these exertions. For the next stage, I shoulder my gear bags and get going. I need to walk to the lagoon a total of five times, through water holes, muddy paths, small ditches and thick jungle. I even empty out my water bags, and later melt a lump of ice from the glacier. Fascinating, I am drinking water that is a million years old! My poor kayak gets dragged across many rotten logs. By pulling it over the last tree trunk, the bow toggle breaks, and I take a big leap backwards to land on my rear, nearly in the lagoon. But I have done it!

Laguna San Rafael impresses in the sun with its shimmering icebergs and floes, and a strong tidal current pulls me out. After the tide changes, the same current reverse stops me later from paddling round a land spit to a beautiful beach camp. But I reach my goal with a little portage through a rock arch, and pull all my kit over a few lumpy boulders.

A few days later, I see something on the horizon I cannot name. A salmon farm, or some other kind of platform for the fishing industry? For a long time, I cannot work it out. Suddenly, a helicopter flies over the surrounding island, and lands on the mysterious platform. This must be one of the larger ones, if a helicopter supplies them! As I get closer, I realize it is not a platform, but a large ship. On its deck park two small bright red helicopters. Is this a ferry, or a marine research vessel? I dare to get close, and suddenly a man's head peeks over the railings. Fernando explains this is a private ship, an expedition boat for rich folks who are after a luxurious fishing and outdoor adventure trip. The kit like the two helicopters, many rafts, jet skis, kayaks, and loads of fishing gear matches the purpose. The ship is set up for twenty-eight guests with thirty-two crew members. "Fancy a look around?" Fernando calls. Of course, this is too interesting!

Fernando thinks the same, when he finds out the reason of my trip, and about the distance I have already covered. He is asking me to hang around, until the owner and his guests have returned from their day trip. If I would like to stay the night, and tell about my adventures?

What a question! Of course, I like to stay! Soon after, I get to know Andrés, a wealthy Chilean banker whose expedition ship "Nomads of the Sea" is at home in Puerto Montt. He introduces me to his guests and crew, and there should be no obstacle to an entertaining evening!

The only thing is: The "Nomad of the Seas" is on the way back to Puerto Montt during the next two nights. If I stay, I would be hitchhiking for a few miles, and skip a section - and I have always been paying strict attention that there are no gaps in my South American circumnavigation! But I set my own rules, and the stay on board here is just too tempting...see what happens! I let them pull up the kayak, inspect my luxurious cabin, and look forward to a nice evening. Today, there are only six guests on board, all personal friends of the owner, and all of them members of the worldwide "YPO - Young Presidents Organization", a network of successful young entrepreneurs.

76

While I enjoy a hot shower, the men spoil themselves with a little helicopter trip to the glacier for a few sundowners. As soon as all are back on board, we enjoy some drinks together, waiting for dinner to be ready. But now, I notice something I do not like at all: As the ship gets into the open ocean, I become seasick! I just manage to hang myself over the toilet bowl, and my stomach rolls just like the sea. I must lie down, and feel quite desperate, as I am in no shape to offer interesting company. Only once the ship gets into more sheltered waters around the Isla Grande de Chiloe, I can get up for an hour, and entertain the gentlemen at least for dessert.

Even during the night, the ship does not reduce its speed. Full of horror, I realize that I should paddle back again for each mile we are now covering in this ship. What did Fernando say about how far it was to Puerto Montt? Seventy-five miles? When the ship stops at 6am near Caleta Leptepu, we would have already covered 150 miles! How am I meant to get back to the point where I got on board at Bahia Tic Toc? Could the helicopter take me back? With the kayak strapped to the skids? Quite a fancy idea!

I talk to Andrés about my situation, and a solution is quickly found: After landing in Puerto Montt, the "Nomad of the Seas" is heading south again, with a new load of guests. It is always a three-day trip: On the first day, they do a kayak trip through the archipelago, next they will watch penguins and seals with the jet boat, last is a trip to the glacier like I saw yesterday. The second day - today - a rafting trip is on the schedule; the guests are flying out to the start point by helicopter. After a wonderful breakfast, I get a free ride in the helicopter, but unfortunately, the raft is filled up. Just as the guys are back, they straight away head off to the next item on the itinerary: Fly fishing on a nearby river. That is not interesting for me at all. For the evening, a barbecue dinner is planned on a meadow near a hot spring, and once more, the helicopter comes into action. I could get used to that mode of transport - quick, effortless, warm, comfortable, dry - and expensive... Just the opposite of how I usually travel! The barbecue is amazing: At a log cabin, a whole lamb is roasted, we also grill a few chickens, potatoes and salad. There are only eight people to feed! To top off this wonderful evening, we all have a dip into the hot springs - of course with a glass of champagne served by the staff. What a life!

In the last bit of daylight, we fly back to the ship. We enjoy a short sail through the exceedingly narrow Fjord Estero Quintupeo. We anchor, and the captain uses a few strong flashlights to magically illuminate the rocks and waterfall. Later, the men withdraw to a confidential business meeting with cigars, and I use the time to update my blog entries. Tomorrow, we will be in

Puerto Montt. This is where this group of friends with the owner will leave the ship, and a new group of paying customers will come aboard.

For me, this means I need to move in with the crew, as the next group occupies all upper cabins. As the only space in the "girl cabin" is on the floor, I can re-acclimatize myself to the harsher camping conditions. But it does not get that far, a bed is found, but in a three-men cabin. One of them is absent all night, the other is on a bridge weather watching half the night, and the last one watches me. I find it very interesting to see life on board from this perspective. As a little thank you to Andrés, I go with the group out kayaking for a few hours, before I set off again, exactly from the point where I got on board! Only four days to Puerto Montt! I paddle through a maze of salmon farms, where more fish, fish food, and fish poop are floating around than water. From Puerto Montt, I go another four weeks to Valparaiso, where I will have a break for three months before I get back home to Germany!

Chapter 7
SPRINT TO VALPARAISO

Chile, Part 4: Puerto Montt to Valparaiso
March 31st - May 2nd, 2012

Finally, I am back on the open sea! After a stop in Puerto Montt with lots of work and recovery, I once again experience a challenging sea kayak day with high swell waves on the unprotected Pacific coast. I am lucky, the tidal current sucks me out of the last channel with over seven miles per hour. Later that evening, the sea comes up, and the swell reaches four yards in height. Additionally, I must deal with the reflecting breakers from the reefs and rocky coast. I am aiming in a straight line from Punta Pupelde to Punta Puga, and see with concern the line of white caps in front of the mainland. I have no chance of landing anywhere, so I carry on, getting past Punta Puga in the process. Nature's wildness impresses me; the mainland is strewn with many huge boulders and small islands. I must give a large cluster of rocks on a headland a very wide berth, before I can turn in for a relaxed safe landing from the rear on the beach of a sandy bay. This is an excellent choice for today!

Safe landings - that will be the most critical issue for the next few days. As impressive as the scenery may be, the breakers and surf are mostly so scary that I wish I would not see them at all.

My weatherman, Karel, sends me a forecast that makes me stay for three days exactly where I am, in Caleta Quedal. A fresh following fifteen to twenty knots wind from the southwest, alongside a swell of up to seven yards high is not a good combination. My limit is four yards. The sheltered fjords are over!

I am getting a visit from one of my only two neighbors, the local small lighthouse keeper and gaucho, Cecilio. He invites me to have a trip up to his hut the next day for a great overview of the area. When he leaves me, he easily grabs one of the free-running horses, swings himself on its back, and rides up a steep path into the bush. The horse finds the way back to its herd on its own. Will I have to do the same tomorrow? I trust him to follow, and enjoy a guided hike steep uphill through rain in stunning nature. Cecilio bakes fresh buns for us, and even though we are barely able to understand neither Spanish nor English, communication works somehow with a mixture of "Spanglish" and body language.

The next day is not good for paddling. It has been raining the whole night, and the sun is coming through the foggy clouds only slowly. With such poor visibility, I know, I will become seasick, as I always do when I cannot see the horizon. I have intended to eat my breakfast on the water as usual, but as I am crossing Bahia San Pedro in four yards of swell, I feel sick.

Behind Punta Condor, I discover the first good landing bay since the crossing, but I have only done fifteen miles, not enough to already stop for the day. The swell calms down, and my stomach does the same. I manage to eat an apple and some carrots, although the small reflecting waves close to the cliffs still confuse the water uncomfortably. A bit further north, I see a river mouth which offers a sheltered landing. I select the right side, but from the sea, you always underestimate the surf!

I put on my PFD and helmet, unhook my safety line and paddle leash, and the fragile GPS disappears below deck. I approach the beach cautiously, but the one breaking wave catches and throws me over. I must roll, and manage only on the second attempt. I am feeling weak with an empty stomach. To make it worse, I notice the rudder is stuck to one side. I am at the mercy of the next wave crashing on top of me. Already close to the beach, I feel too weak to roll again. I bail out, and a few smaller waves wash me and my kayak ashore…separately.

Why must there be people on the beach right now? Four locals watch my inelegant arrival, one of them even poses like he was ready to save me from drowning. The situation was not life-threatening, but quite embarrassing. Their respect increases, when I tell where I come from and how many miles I have paddled already. They help me to carry my boat and gear up to the dry section of the beach. I reject their friendly invite to stay at the local school, as I like to be off again early morning. First daylight is at 8am on this side of the earth, autumn is starting!

The further north I paddle along the Chilean coast, the mellower the landscape becomes. After the high rough cliffs near Puerto Montt, I can now see shallower broad beaches. The swell is rarely above four yards. Past Punta Galera, I continue in the direction of Bahia Bonifacio. It is day 225 on my trip. I see many pelicans flying around me, and a few penguins. How much longer will I be able to see those little gentlemen in their black and white "dinner jackets"? An increasing number of fat jellyfish is populating the sea. They are up to a yard long, pink and white in color. Do they sting? I do not dare to touch them.

The nights are cold and damp. My sleeping bag does not keep me warm enough anymore. If I want to leave before 8am, I must pack a soaking wet tent. In the afternoon, I should land quite early to have at least an hour of daylight to get my tent and gear dry in the last sun rays.

A large Navy ship from the "Gobernacion Maritimas" in Valdivia shows up, crewed with twelve men. That must be a fair-sized bill for the Chilean tax payer! Their only day's mission seems to be to check on the kayak lady. It should not be that difficult, seeing that I post my GPS position in my blog entry every night. I also post my regular departure time and average paddling speed in calm seas. They put a skiff into the water, and three men ride over to my kayak. I seem to be a welcome exercise object!

"Is all ok?" they ask. "Yes, of course" I answer, "the sea is calm." "How do you feel? Are you well?" How do I feel? Great, or I would not be out here. "Do you need anything?" No, thanks, I am well sorted, as usual. "Where are you heading to?" "Bahia Bonifacio," I answer. And the next harbor? Sorry, not Valdivia where they come from, but Talcahuano, and then Valparaiso. "Can we take a picture?" "Of course, not." Baffled faces ensue, until they see I have just made a joke. I thank them for the mutual entertainment and set my mind on the trip to Valparaiso. It will take another three weeks.

The way there has its challenges. The weather, impenetrable fog, and, in some parts, life-threatening landing conditions make me spend a night on the water between Bahia Nihue and Quidico. As I stick my head out of the tent that morning, it is so foggy I cannot even see the water, even though I am camped less than a hundred yards away. Despite the limited visibility, I feel capable to start with low tide and low surf, but for the next 60 miles, I cannot find any protected landing spot on my chart. Puerto Saavedra would be more than a day's distance away, and its entrance is questionable. Additionally, the swell increases from a moderate two yards to over four. In those conditions, an open beach landing would be dangerous. Starting or staying? If I wait for too long, I could be stuck here for over five days. I really would love to skip this section! But I have not missed a single mile of my trip, and I was not planning to do so now. By 11am, the fog is lifting, and I manage a dry launch. I hardly dare to look at the surf along the coast, as an uncomfortable landing lies ahead.

Or should I continue through the night and land in Quidico? I have not prepared for a night paddle when I left. With another layer on my body and enough food in reach, it should be doable!

The sky is clear; stars and shooting stars sparkle at the beginning of the night. As it overcasts, I entertain myself by watching the lights of Puerta Saavedra. At midnight, I see the lights of a ship, and it serves me as my personal lighthouse, until it disappears into the darkness.

By 4am, it is completely dark, no moon, no stars, no lit houses or cars on the beach, only the dark gray sky. I stay far out to not hear the threatening surf. It starts to rain, and I shiver.

If I was driving a car, a sleep of a few minutes would be fatal, but here on the water, with calm conditions, I can allow myself to do so. I need to pay attention not to drift too close to the cliffs. Dawn is close, and it is still fifteen miles to Quidico!

I need to find a safe landing spot. The surf piles up high, and rolls in a half circle into this wide bay. In four meters of swell, the waves need more than one corner to calm down, before you can call it a sheltered landing. I am not sure what to do, until I see a small boat crashing through the breaking waves. Is this the coast guard? No, even better, a few local fishermen are coming to my aid. They know the local conditions best, and therefore, they also know the best way to land here. They guide me away from the dangerous surf towards their open boat and gesture for me to come on board. After twenty-five hours on the water, I do not need a second invite, and swallow my pride which says, I should have to do everything by myself. This morning, I am not keen on a trashy surf landing! After some balancing acts, the three guys manage to pull my heavy kayak on board. With hair-raising speed, they hop, skip and jump in front of each breaker to the beach. To land my kayak here would be life-threatening! The bush drums of the local fishermen have alerted other folks. Gina and her sister Cecilia invite me to stay at their house. Many thanks!

After two days of rest, I need once more the help of the fishermen. The surf belt looks as scary as the worst ones I have seen in Australia. Without their help, I would be unable to reach the open water. We load my kayak into their open fast boat. They are waiting patiently for the right time. At the highest speed, they shoot diagonally through the breakers. The bow rises vertically, and I am glad my kayak is securely tied to the boat. With the slow speed of my paddling, I would not be able to break out here! Thankfully, those guys really know what they are doing, and we quickly reach the open sea where the waves do not break any more.

The next section will be about forty-five miles, so I am likely to land at Lebu at 1am. The Navy likes to send an escort boat for the last night hours. I have switched on my VHF radio since 5pm to announce my position, but there is no reply. By 9pm, I spot a ship, but still, no one has called me on the radio. Twice, I announce my position, but no answer. An hour later, I spot navigation lights behind me, and they help me to keep direction. The men on board cannot resist to deploy all their "toys". The finger of a strong searchlight sweeps the sea, and blue and white strobe lights are flashing. I imagine I am the object of a naval exercise, and they pretend I am a smuggler's boat. Would they also like to practice to "rescue" me? But how could that happen in a real emergency without lowering a small skiff? This boat does not have one!

When we reach Lebu, I almost feel I am in a discotheque, with all those lights after the darkness. The fishing boats, the stars, the lighthouse, the illuminated harbor walls and the town itself, everything is brightly lit. The men in the boat guide me close to the main harbor wall along the rocks into a small safe landing bay.

The next few days, the Navy guys are both valuable help and quite a surplus distraction. While I unload my gear, and pull up the kayak to a dry area, a Navy officer follows me and keeps asking the standard questions about my plans for the next days and my physical condition. I cannot help but answer a bit techy and with sarcastic humor. But ok, they have their orders!

When I arrive in Constitution and am just happy to see no uniforms, they pop out of the woodwork, armed with notebooks and the same questions as yesterday. Fed up, I answer the familiar questions, but faster than the officer is asking them. That confuses him so much, that he must call his boss to discuss his problem. He wants to talk to me personally, and asks once more the same questions. Finally, he requests kindly if I have any other needs. Hmm...is this the phone order service of the Chilean Navy? Jokingly I said, a bit of fresh fruit would be nice to have. Lo and behold, the next morning I have a delivery of fresh fruit!

If everything goes to plan, I will be in Valparaiso in less than a week, around May 2nd. The only issues, other than the Chilean Navy's overzealous efforts, are the daily starts and landings. Two more times, I must accept help to get on and off the water. Once, the heavy fishing boat laden with my kayak is dragged into the water with a team of oxen, the tractor of ancient times.

My arrival in Valparaiso happens late at night and in darkness, against my plan. But the next day, I get an official reception with many Chilean Navy boats to escort me in and four-striped officers to congratulate. A Navy marching band plays to my honor, and entertains the crowd and dozens of press people with notepads and cameras. A small pre-taste of the "real" arrival back in Buenos Aires in two years? It is May 2nd, time to have a break!

For statistics lovers: From Buenos Aires to Valparaiso, I paddled 4,733 miles. I used 247 trip days, of which I paddled for 167 days. The first section of the trip is behind me. The second one will take me from Valparaiso to Georgetown in Guyana on the Atlantic side of this massive continent. In between, there are the coastlines of Peru, Ecuador, Colombia, the crossing of the Panama Canal, and the dangerous Caribbean coast of Venezuela. The first four months, my partner, Peter, will be paddling with me. I am excited to see how we will work together as a couple on this trip!

Chapter 8
PADDLING PARTNER PETER

Chile, Part 5: Valparaiso to Arica
August 25th - October 19th, 2012

Back to work! After three months at home in Husum, I start the second major stage of my circumnavigation of South America. Additionally, I have planned a Christmas stop at home, as in my short summer break between May and August, I had to move my 87-years old mother into a nursing home. She is still quite fit for her age, has gone with me to TV and radio interviews, but who knows, how many more years we may have to celebrate Christmas together?

The tickets have been bought, and all preparations are complete. 17th of August, Peter and I are flying from Hamburg to Santiago. Many people say, travelling together twenty-four/ seven will be a stress test for our relationship, but I am sure we will be fine.

I am truly curious to see what challenges we will face as a couple. We will be using a large four-person Hilleberg Keron-4-Tunnel tent, so limited personal space will not cause a crisis.

Will it be easier as a twosome, and is paddling safer? I think with two paddlers it is twice the problems and twice the opinions. But on the other hand, paddling as a duo would give us more fun, insights and good chats.

For this new stage, I get a brand-new kayak. A new manufacturer has offered to build a kayak according to my specifications—and named it "Freya 18" in my honor. Now, even two of them will be floating on the Pacific! But it took what felt like hundreds of phone calls and emails, before we were assured, the kayaks were safely on their way from China to Santiago.

Christian and Ignacia, the kind hosts who looked after me in Vina del Mar on the last stop before going home, receive us with great hospitality. In their apartment, we can immerse into our last preparations. I function as a load master, and Peter is the IT expert. I pack our supplies into zip-lock bags, and Peter sets up the various programs needed with our electronics. It is a sensible case of labor division: I am the brawn, he is the brain.

At 7am, we are ready to start. Our host, Christian, takes us to the harbor, to the same spot I landed on May 2nd. We have a wooden pontoon to fill our kayaks with the many bits and pieces we will need. As load master, I am in my element, and like magic, many dry bags disappear into the boats. A Navy officer is ticking off our equipment against a list of requirements. I almost missed those gentlemen! When the officer asks where our anemometer is, one of the requirements of his list, I put a finger into my mouth and hold it up into the breeze. I think we are ready to go now!

A gentle push puts our brand-new kayaks off the pontoon, we jump in, and off we are! It is a strange feeling to paddle next to my "old" kayak teacher, with whom I started paddling eight years ago. My career in sea kayaking is quite short! A Navy boat escorts us out of the harbor, and does not lose sight of us in the next few hours.

Paddling in my new "Freya 18" feels great! The seat position is perfect, and the pedals and rudder react to the slightest touch, even though the boats are heavily laden. We just need to pay attention not to get too close to each other, as it could be fatal with these wind and wave conditions. We must deal with four yards high swell with fifteen knots southwesterly wind on top, which is physically and mentally demanding after such a long break. On this exciting first day, we prefer to land in Quintero at half past three, instead of reaching Zapallar as originally planned.

The beach we are heading to seems to be calm, but my gut feeling says to watch the breakers carefully and to wait for the right moment. I agree with Peter, who says he would wait for me to land safely, and then follow my lead. I wait for the lowest wave, and paddle on its back quickly and safely to the shore. I throw the paddle high and dry up the beach, jump out of the kayak and pull it quickly off the surf zone. Now it is Peter's turn. He also gets well through the waves and throws his paddle up the beach, but he cannot get his long legs out of the kayak in time. He stands up to the hip in water, getting his trousers filled. Ah well, we are still practicing!

This beach at Quintero is a total gem. It has white sand framed by a few impressive rocks, and it is devoid of people, besides our friends from the Navy. "No, thank you! At the end of our first day, we really do not need fresh water or food." I make it quite clear, we also do not need an escort from tomorrow onwards! It was a good decision to stop here. Peter's wet pants and socks get a chance to dry in the sun, and slowly we get used to our camp routines. Other than the Navy officers having fun with their jet skis in the bay, and a drunk fellow knocking on our tent door at 8pm, nothing disturbs our peace. When the Navy guys realize we are really spending the night here, they disappear. With so much attention, we feel a bit like a well watched prisoner! A frog concert lets us quickly fall into deep sleep.

Next morning, we get another visit from the Navy at 7am. Two cars speed along the beach, and eight men decamp to complete their paperwork. Peter, as a morning grump, is even less happy than me about so much attention early in the morning. I do the communication and explain again that, please, we really would like to do without an escort boat from now on!

A shark fin briefly glints on the surface, there are still many penguins and seals to watch. The weather is so pleasant that for a while I can paddle just wearing a shirt. I hope, I do not catch a sun burn! We take things easy, and are relaxed as we get closer to our stop just after Punta Ligua. Even at this pace, we manage to cover 30 miles, and are lucky to find a pretty beach for the evening. There are a few holiday houses, is this a restricted beach? We do not have to wait for long, before three ladies approach our tent. One of them is the owner of this beach. She explains, there is no serious difference between private and public beaches when arriving by sea. I secretly hope it is no problem to camp here for a night. The best part: There is no Navy officer anywhere to be seen!

The coast with its rocks and boulders is a true sea kayaker's paradise! But – we have already received a Navy call and a visit, spot a helicopter overhead, and several blue and white vehicles on land as we come around the headland of Pichidangui. We just wave briefly, and continue our journey to Ensenada Tortoralito. Anyone who thinks we could now avoid further contact has underestimated the efforts of the Chilean Navy. Three young officers in an inflatable raft race up behind us, and ask for the sixth time today the same questions. The prospect of breathing their stinky exhausts for the next ten miles while they are escorting us causes me to gesture to them with some anger that they really should get lost now. I hope the boat behind us will fall back and turn into one of the bays! Did they finally get the message?

Oh, heck no! Yet another one of their ilk! Up until just over a mile before our chosen beach, another Navy ship follows us. As they see we are landing here, they disappear. This must be it for the night, right?

But as soon as we have finished pitching the tent and are cooking dinner, Navy team No. 8 for the day appears, this time with innovative ideas and rules for our trip. "You should have to call in every four hours!" "No, that was not agreed, and we are not changing the rules just because a new boss may now handle our control. Since Cape Horn, I have followed the instructions, giving my position every evening when I land, not every four hours. Are we also secretly escorted by a submarine? We are finally requesting to be able to paddle during the day without constant supervision and molestations!

At our next stop at Punta Huentalauquen, we decide to take a day's break. Wind and waves do not allow a safe start nor a safe landing. Also, Peter and I both feel a cold coming on. We spend the day eating, sleeping and reading. As usual, the Navy shows up, but to our surprise, they are not after us but are talking to one of the local fishermen. We almost feel neglected, have they delegated the job to the fishermen?

I use the day off for a small repair, as I biffed my bow slightly on the last landing. The local fishermen engage in the repair, bringing various bits of tools and materials to mend the small damage. Next day, I hitchhike back to Vina del Mar to pick a spare rudder part I think we might need in future. I better be prepared with the new kayaks!

It takes four days for us to get fit again to be back onto the water. We make considerable progress until the following wind turns at 10.30am. Our speed decreases from four miles to two and a half miles per hour. We have hoped to reach Puerto Oscura, but by 2pm, we decide to stop. After four days of sickness, twenty miles must be enough for the day.

The night is not as quiet as we had hoped. Three dogs, two strong males and a puppy turn up and chase each other all night up and down the beach, barking at full voice. We find the puppy curled up in our outer tent vestibule next morning, obviously happy to have found some shelter from his rambunctious mates. Is he looking for a new home? Peter feeds him some left-over sausages from last night's barbecue the locals made for us, and we hope he will not vomit in our tent.

Sadly, we must leave the cute fur baby, and start our new paddle day with fifteen knots headwind. Next night, a rooster ensures that we cannot get any more sleep after 4.30am. I cannot decide which sounds are harder to cope with, the croaking frogs a few nights ago, the barking dogs last night, the crowing roosters, or Peter snoring his head off at night and singing along to the songs on his MP3 player by day. I was having such a quiet, peaceful trip by myself! It takes a bit of time for me to get used to having another person along on my journey. But there are so many positives, and I am looking forward to our shared experiences!

On the 10th day of our mutual trip, we have a wonderful encounter with a massive school of at least a hundred grey speckled dolphins. Peter, who has not seen any dolphins before, nearly freezes. "Are you sure they are not sharks?" he asks me with worry. Hahaha, of course not! As if to confirm, they gambol playfully all around us, jump high out of the water and fall back with a loud splash, turn onto their back and show us their near whale-like rear fin when they dive down. Wonderful! All in bright sunshine, which brings a glow to the tips of the mighty mountaintops above the low hanging clouds.

From the distance, and on the satellite images, the beach of Caleta Hornos looks like it should give an easy landing. But as we get closer, we can see rocks with a nasty surf break. We decide to try the concrete launching ramp used by the fishermen. It is a risk, but both of our timing is good, we suffer no damages, and together, we carry the boats high up the beach. We set up camp in a corner of the harbor right behind the fishing boats, which is fairly buried in rubbish. Tomorrow, we only want to cover a small distance of fifteen miles to the harbor of Chugungo, as a swell of over four yards is predicted.

In these conditions, it is not certain if we can make it to the next possible safe landing on Isla Damas. On this Pacific coast, stopping just anywhere is impossible, the swell is crashing on the shore in uncontrollable breakers, it must be a well sheltered bay or harbor to make a safe landing.

Via Isla Tilgo and Punta Tortoralilo, we reach Chugungo. Unfortunately, the whole wonderful safe harbor is encircled with a four-yard high wall! No chance for kayaks and smaller boats to get out of the water here. Larger boats use a boat lift. We must try our luck at the nearby beach, but the surf is big, and a few rocks are to be seen, so we secure ourselves with the helmets. I land first, and wave Peter in afterwards. My timing is fine, the landing works, but it is difficult to pull the heavy boat out of the water.

Peter is waiting, and barely notices a wave is gaining height just behind him. Frantically, he paddles backwards, just over the crest of the wave. But he is still in a spot where he should not be: Too close to the beach to wait for a lower wave. Now, all he can do, is sprint forward, as it is too late to go further back. He side-broaches into the breaking wave which carries him towards the beach. His high brace is not strong enough, he is thrown over, rolls up again and is already close to the dry sand line. But the next wave washes him closer to the rocks in my direction, where I can do nothing but hold onto my kayak in the surge. "Jump out" I shout. He must regain control over his boat, or it may be crashed! Finally, he can get out to grab the bow toggle and pull the kayak up the beach, away from the threatening rocks. That was close!

We only leave at 10am next morning, as we must take care of a few repairs on the rudder system of the prototype kayaks. A test pilot of a newly developed design must be prepared for some teething problems.

In a straight line, we cross over to Isla Damas, which looks like a little paradise. We are looking forward to our own lonesome bay, without fishermen, tourists, yapping dogs and Navy officers. As it is only 4pm, we explore the island on foot, walk along wild beaches and bizarre rock formations, exotic shells and flowering cacti. Vultures are circling above us. We are no longer used to walking long distances, and dead tired, we slip into our tent.

As we continue towards Cabo Bascunan, the landscape changes. The mainland is less rocky, there are more dunes, and the inland is getting flatter. If only it would not rain all day!

The sea is calm next day, and our kayaks glide through the water with pure joy despite the heavy loads. By midday, the wind totally dies down to a spooky silence, only disturbed by the paddles entering the water.

We see a triangular fin piercing the smooth surface, was it a shark? In the afternoon, Peters first whale shows up...and down again, only to spout an incredible water fountain shortly after. To round off the maritime show, we enjoy watching the large sea lion colony of Punta Alcade.

Our expedition life together works well, we bicker little, and if we do, it is about trivial things like whether to sweep out the tent before packing it, or how much sand should stick to the luggage before it is loaded.

In the Yacht Club of Caldera, we get an indoor campsite just for us, and the kindest hospitality from the locals; but we suffer three days of noisy disco music due to a Chilean bank holiday. High time to move on!

With a headwind of fifteen knots, we aim for Chanaral. As there are no town chores to do, we pitch tent just outside town at a coastal road rest area. Unfortunately, the BBQ pits are covered in mountains of rubbish. Just as we settle in for the night, I switch on my Chilean mobile phone, and it rings already. This number is not available to anyone other than for the Navy, who, as usual, ask us for our schedule. I at first do not want to take the call, but Peter is curious. Patiently, he explains once more that they can find our position each night on my website. That was not good enough, and half an hour later, they turn up in person to ask the same questions. I do not even get out of the tent.

Tomorrow, we like to reach Punta Taltal to fill up our drinking water. From there, it is five days until Antofagasta where we want to stop for a longer break. We enjoy a peaceful night, and an easy start into a wonderful day with lush winds – paddling life can be so beautiful! Dozens of sea lion colonies litter the headlands. At Taltal, we stop only in town to fill up the water bags at the bathroom of a restaurant—the city beach is dirty, ugly and narrow.

On the satellite images, we discover a much prettier white sandy beach close by. Peter has read somewhere there should be a Club Nautico, and we easily find the single free-standing building on a small artificial white sandy beach. We find a sheltered spot on the wooden veranda of the deserted club house. At night, the wind is blowing cold from underneath through the gaps of the planks, but I have spent nights in worse places! At least the floor was leveled and dry.

As we are crossing the bay of Punta Grande, hundreds of sea lions and sea birds entertain us, trying to steal each other's food. What a spectacle! I am excited to see whether the beach we are aiming for really does look as peculiar as it looks on the satellite images. The scene really does look morbid: Black sand, white crosses and behind, a narrow strip of desert sand with a few salt pans created by the incoming sea water. It will do for one night!

We reach the Yacht Club of Antofagasta on September 30th. This time, we are not dealing with the Navy, but with the flying units. Pedro, a local dentist, lives with his family in a beautiful house on a site of the Air Force, and offers us his home for the night. His two little girls give us their room, and we joke about how Peter, at well over six feet, would fit into a kiddie bed.

Next morning, we sleep in, and are surprised about how quiet it is on an Air Force base. We need to go to Arica for our big food shopping. Until midnight, we apportion and pack the supplies. Why do we think we will be able to start next day, when a head wind of twenty knots and four-yard high breakers are predicted?

Pedro takes us from the Air Base to the Yacht Club, and one glance at the harbor exit confirms my concerns. Wind and waves pin us down for another day, but instead of being taken back the twenty miles to the Air Base, we set up tent on the lawn of the Yacht Club. This lawn, the only bit of green anywhere, we find way more agreeable than the dry, monotonous desert around the Air Force base. I doze in the tent when it starts to rain: A free shower courtesy of the automatic sprinkler system!

The visibility next morning cannot be worse. Combined with swell of up to four yards, these are once more the best conditions for me to become seasick. My stomach cramps, why can I not throw up? I am overheating, and stow my jacket and socks below deck. We go around the next headland in a north-east direction, the waves come from behind, and my seasickness disappears.

On October 4th, day forty of our trip together, we head to Punta Mejillones. Peter once more plugs into his MP3 player, and blocks all communication. I cannot really say I like paddling next to a deaf person, and decide to paddle close to the rocks of the mainland. Peter does not like to follow me there anyway. As we turn into the bay of Punta Mejillones, a twenty knots headwind smacks us in the face. As we would rather like to cross the wide bay tomorrow, it is not worth it to go into town, and we land on the nearest beach available.

Without getting hit by rocks falling off the cliff behind us, we continue our trip after a brief visit from the Navy. They were only shooting a few pictures from the far distance, and turn away quickly. They have learned to leave us to our freedom! An incredibly noisy sea lion colony is a pleasant distraction of the day. Via Caleta Michilla and Caleta Atala, we work our way to Topocilla. An ugly industrial town is not an inviting place to spend two weather days, but we must head for land to fill up our water supplies. A fat wave catches me when I land, and for the first time since paddling with Peter, I must roll, and do not like to continue paddling in this dripping wet state. We surrender to fate, and pitch tent on the ugly black sand town beach.

On the way to Iquique, we come across a field of pretty yard-long colorful jellyfish! If you are a fisherman, you will curse at those creatures blocking your net.

On a high headland near Punta Paquica, we watch some strange climbers. The massive cliffs are covered in a thick layer of white bird shit - guano. A handful of young men scrap off the precious nature product into large bags, and in Europe, we buy it as a fertilizer!

Via Punta Arenas, we arrive at Punta Comache. With low swell, it is no big problem to manage the distances of 40 miles per day in between two safe landing spots. The Humboldt Current, together with the southwest winds, is pushing us an added mile per hour. On tonight's landing, Peter is showing off an involuntary example of "bridge building". Just over a mile before Punta Comache, we spot a lonely mini beach we like better than the next large town beach. It is a narrow, four-yard gap with lurking white sand. After this long and exhausting day, I cannot be bothered to reach out for my helmet and PFD? Luckily, I get swept through the gap elegantly ashore.

Peter has not the same luck. He is also waiting for a gentle wave to push him through the gap, but unfortunately, his bow hits a submerged rock. The next wave turns him 90 degrees, and washes him up with bow and stern onto each side of the rocky gap. If not so dangerous, it would be seriously funny! The kayak looks like it is going to tip off the rocks any moment, but head, rocks and kayak together do not get on. Sprinting in to save my partner is more important than a funny picture, and I try to lift the bow off the rocks when the next wave comes in. I manage at the second attempt. The nose of the kayak is severely dented, but thankfully, Peter not hurt. With his weight and the heavy load, the kayak could have broken in half sitting free in the middle with bow and stern locked. And yes, one should always wear a helmet and PFD when landing among rocks!

Thankfully, we can fix the damage with the materials we carry, but there are better things one could do after a long, demanding paddling day other than a repair job. During the night, I check several times on the drying process. All is well, and next morning, we are off again to enjoy a large area with jelly fish, some sea lion colonies and a few little penguins.

Soon, there are no birds and no seals, just airplanes and container ships. The harbor of Iquique is home to the most important fishing fleets of the country, and the activity around us is matching. Suddenly, we meet quite a lot of civilization!

Robert and Monica, our hosts in Iquique, have contacted us via internet, and offer a stay in their apartment. We take our time in these two days for a rare trip back-country. Robert takes us to a nearby mesa, where daring hang gliders throw themselves down into the valley. We continue to Monte Pintura, the "Painted Mountain" with its near 1,500-year-old rock paintings. Until today, no one knows who or why they did this.

Returning to the water, we are looking forward to being back in nature and untouched wilderness, but our next stop in Caleta Mejillones leads us straight into a rubbish dump with mountains of burnt trash. Even though there is no road access, some fifty people scratch a living here and the soundtrack of the night is supported by three electricity generators. Let us get out of here!

Skipping several landing options, our goal is Caleta Vitor. By now, the heat is starting to become a problem, and I remember sometimes in Australia where even the sea was no longer refreshing. The equator is getting closer, butterflies are everywhere, and little dolphins show their fins.

In Arica we meet Abraham, the guardian of the local Yacht Club. Proudly he presents us the guest book. The earlier entry is over a year old, there is not much visitor traffic in this final corner of Chile close to the Peruvian border.

With Abraham's help, we contact the local Navy, and a friendly officer turns up, willing to help us with our exit papers even at the weekend.

At about 6pm, a car picks us up, but does not take us to the expected "Policia International" to receive our exit stamps, but first to the Navy office. We must have a permit to leave Chile with the kayaks, and to enter Peru in the same manner. After an hour, they send us on our way, having given a promise to return in two hours. They need to contact the offices in Peru.

In the meantime, we have a fancy dinner in the restaurant of the Yacht Club. By half past ten, we get a phone call from Abraham. We should be ready at 9am tomorrow to receive our paperwork. This would mean, we must stay another day! The planned route of forty miles cannot be done if we leave only after 9am. Just as we are about to digest the news and disappear into our tent, we get new directions: The Navy will pick us up at 6am to give us the required permits, and then take us to the police, where we would get our final exit stamps. Many thanks!

After a short night, we must sign four copies of various papers that say nothing more than two people in kayaks make their way to Vila Vila in Peru. In the emigration office, we finally get the exit stamp we were longing for.

By half past seven, we are packed and off, in time to reach our next destination in daylight. As we are crossing the bay of Arica, we meet the Chilean Navy for the last time. Are we missing a document, are we not allowed to leave? No, they just want to say goodbye, and wave from a distance. Thank you, Chilean Navy, for the many things you have done for us. And thank you Chile, for your hospitality and the many amazing people we could meet. Now, Peru is waiting!

Chapter 9
LOVELY LIMA

Chile/ Peru: Arica to Paita
October 20th - December 12th, 2012

The closer we get to the Peruvian border and leave the endless Atacama Desert behind us, the greener and warmer it gets. On the northern half of the globe, it becomes colder the more north one gets! We can still see a few little penguins, but for how much longer?

In our first Peruvian harbor of Vila Vila, a car of the "Ministerio Del Interior" and representatives of the Peruvian coast guard are expecting us. We barely land on the beach and already receive our entry stamps! Forms to fill out? Chilean exit papers? Who needs that?

The time difference to Chile is two hours. When we get up next morning at 6am Peruvian time, it feels like 4am. The distance to our next destination Puerto Grau is only fifteen miles. The distance to Ilo on the day after is forty-three miles, an ambitious distance!

A short day works nicely for our lower energy levels. By mid-day, we reach the inviting pebble beach of Puerto Grau. It is hot on shore, and I take my first swim in Peruvian waters. There is no doubt, we are moving closer to the equator!

We are getting up early next day to make it to the nature sanctuary of Punta Coles. It is packed with seals, sea lions and seabird colonies, but also serves as a military reserve. As there are no warnings or signs saying "Forbidden!", we decide to stay, as we will be gone by early morning. In this new time zone, we must get up at 4am to use the daylight between 5.15 am and 5.45pm.

When we crawl into our tent dead tired by 7.30pm, we hear some voice an hour later shouting with a bossy tone "Hallo! Get out the tent, quickly!"

Peter, with his earplugs on, does not make any move. I take my flashlight, open the zip and say a friendly "Hallo." Again, all I hear is "Get out, quickly!" I was about to ask him if this is his customary manner towards a lady. Next to him appears a man in civilian clothes, who is politer than his companion. He is the commander of the military camp, and asks, if he could help us in any way, such as giving water, food, or a more comfortable place to sleep. Thanks very much, we need nothing other than our undisturbed sleep! He takes off with a signature card and my passport – just for a minute!

The minute becomes an hour, and there is no sign of the commander. I am about to drop off again, when our tent is bathed in the bright light of car headlamps. Is that the commander with our papers? No, it is the harbor master of Ilo, who has been alerted and wants to check out what is up. I explain to him that all we want is peace and quiet – and my passport! He takes off, keeping the headlamps on our tent, and returns after ten minutes with the commander and my document. Now, he needs to check the papers for my male companion...for just a minute. And this time, it really does not take longer than that. They stole us an hour and a half of our precious night rest. We both insert ear plugs, and hope that this is it for the rest of the night.

Next morning, we start under the supervision of two very curious soldiers. They take countless snaps of our packing process with their smartphones, and we pose for a few more. Two signature cards finally satisfy them, and they let us go.

After an uneventful night in Caleta Yerba Buena, we are on the way to Mollendo. There should be a nice harbor we can use for a pit stop. The even shape of its walls looks a bit suspicious on the satellite images, and on closer inspection, it turns out to be a trap. The whole harbor bay is encased by a massive wall, and the beach is garnished with large boulders. No chance to land here, and the two gents from the coast guard on duty at the harbor entrance confirm. They suggest trying the next bay of Playa Catarindo. We lose no time to leave this paddler trap behind.

Half an hour before sunset, we arrive at the suggested safe beach, and are well received by the coast guard and a couple running the local beach restaurant. They bring out a small table with several snacks and drinks. Many thanks! A lady coast guard officer does the translating, and we are offered a campsite behind the restaurant, and a shower in the private quarters of the restaurant owners. We look forward to a quiet night, watched by video cameras and guard dogs.

After a quick trip to Arequipa to meet with sponsors, we return to discover with horror, that the sleepy little coastal town has transformed into a Saturday Night Rave event. Lights, fireworks and hammering disco sound everywhere throughout the whole night.

Quite tortured, we make our way to Caleta Quilca. We enjoy the many fascinating rock shapes, arches and caves along the way, passing a bunch of sandy little bays ideal for landing. We pitch our tent on the wooden veranda of the harbor master's building. We are warmly received and curiously watched by the locals. Peter must get up several times during the night because of diarrhea! Montezuma's revenge? Next day, we paddle again, but he is still not much better. By the afternoon, it has gotten me too. What did we eat or drink that was wrong? I remember, we got told only drink water from sealed bottles, and no tap water like we used in Chile. We will have to do this from now on. But how can we relieve ourselves from the kayaks, as it is necessary now in our current condition? At least, it is easier when there are two of us. One is to hang the naked behind overboard, while the other stabilizes the kayak, which is impossible to do alone!

After a night's stop in the idyllic Caleta La Linca, we can once more watch the harvest typical for this region: A guy prepares his small open boat to go out to sea near our camp, laden with many empty sacks, a long nylon rope and an inflated truck inner tube. A bit later, we see his boat bobbing up and down in the waves next to a majestic rocky arch, bare of the man. Once we look up, we can see him moving around on top of the arch, collecting guano. We have seen this job a few times on the mainland, but never just a single guy in such an inaccessible location in the middle of the whipped-up sea.

The swell around the rocks is an easy two yards high. We are wondering, how will he be able to get the heavy guano sacks down into his boat at anchor, ten yards away from the rocks? How will he get himself back into the boat? I can see the up to forty-yard long rope reaching all the way up to him on top of the rocks. Barefoot, wearing only T-shirt and underpants, he starts to stack the sacks on the edge on top of the arch. He throws the tire into the sea and jumps down, landing on all fours on the tire, with a burning cigarette in his mouth. With the flat tool he was using for scraping the guano off the rocks, he paddles over to his little nutshell of a boat. That was impressive enough, but how is he going to get the sacks into his boat from the tip of the rocks? We do not have to wait long. He has tied the sacks to the rope in such manner that all he must do is give the rope a pull and they tumble like dominos into the water next to him. With a few heaves he pulls them aboard, and the show is over. He smiles quite flattered, when he sees my thumbs up. I am obviously the first "gringa" watching his acrobatics!

The color of the water changes to light milky green near the mouth of the river Chuli. On this background, the many sea lions frolicking and fishing in this water are easy to recognize. Their elegant jumps and dives remind me of dolphins. It is quite impressive, when several dozen shoot out of the water in a coordinated maneuver, and scary, when a considerable number gangs together and comes close. They are checking out what kind of "orca" in our black and white kayaks has entered their colony, and urge us with their means to leave their territory. We cannot get enough of the spectacle. This is one of the best sea lion performances I am lucky to see on my journey!

After these beguiling natural delights, we unfortunately must camp both in La Planchada and Puerto Atico on dirty narrow beaches in industrial areas. We sleep directly near a reeking harbor basin surrounded by pipelines, piles of rubbish and concrete walls. Only in Puerto Viejo are we at peace with our environment again. The locals give us a nice reception, and there is great laughter when the mayor himself grabs a broom to clean a corner of the paved local soccer field from the trash for us to camp on.

After an uneventful paddle morning, we reach the historical harbor of Puerto Inca by mid-day. We have a swim in the sea, and enjoy sightseeing the famous Inca ruins. Next day, we plan a forty-five-mile paddle to reach the safe fishing harbor of Puerto Lomas, hopefully still in daylight.

It seems like we were longingly awaited there! A veritable welcome committee has gathered at the harbor entrance, consisting of coast guards and local families. We have barely landed, when dozens of hands reach for our gear and help to move everything over to the coast guard building. I nervously watch one guy carrying my kayak with one hand without securing it with the other, as a fish is more important to hold on to. The priorities here are obviously different. Like a caravan, everyone follows us to the backyard of the station where we can set up our camp.

This place will stick in my mind as "chicken village". Already at 2am, their loud clucking and crowing wakes us from deep sleep. During the rest of the night, I can even recognize their different voices: Sopranos, mezzo sopranos and tenors. We have no difficulty getting up early, to leave in time for dawn. On the way to Playa Hermosa, massive bird swarms move across the sky in straight lines like laser beams. Seals and seabirds are chasing the same prey, and try to steal noisily from each other.

In Puerto Caballas, we must pause for two days. The surf prohibits us to continue, landing here was like a ride on a cannonball. Our weather man Karel is predicting swell of over four yards. We are quite undisturbed here, there is only one man around collecting seaweed, who thankfully can share some of his drinking water with us.

Via Caleta Lomitas, we continue in the direction of Isla Indepencia. Suddenly, two whales surface right in front of us, one ginormous, with the other a bit smaller. It might be a mother and child, or a male and a female. The larger one lifts his fins, and like in a ballet, they both show their fluke simultaneously. We try to follow them, it seems like they are waiting for us. At least, they seem to know where we are! We come so close, I could touch the larger ones back with my paddle. It is a bit spooky being this close, and I try to give them more space by paddling backwards, but I am not scared to be around them. After ten minutes, the show is over, and we paddle over to Isla Indepencia. Our goal is the outer, northernmost bay, which unfortunately seems to be a graveyard for seals. It is difficult to find a spot without the odor of the carcasses.

The weather follows a regular pattern: Windy in the morning, dying down at lunch time, and picking up to a fresh breeze in the afternoon. The Humboldt Current still exerts its influence here, and keeps the sea cool, while the land is getting heated up by the strong sun. Near the National Park of Paracas, we meet up with the Peruvian Navy. The harbor master himself went out on a large coast guard ship to give us some gifts. We try to find a sheltered corner in twenty-five knots headwind to make the handover a success: They manage to throw down a sack full of delicious treats, and two baseball caps of the Peruvian Coastguard. Peter especially has use for it, as his old cap got lost while landing a few days ago.

The closer we get to Lima, the snazzier the holiday houses in the bays we pass. Marco, our host in Lima, suggests in an email that we should meet up at Punta Hermosa, which leaves us with only twenty miles to paddle. That suits us well, our tired bodies have been asking for a rest the past few days. On the way, we are enchanted by the picturesque harbor of Pucusana, with its partly futuristic, partly traditional architecture, and its hundreds of fishing boats with beautifully painted and decorated bows. We are watching the fish market from our kayaks, and cannot get enough of the colorful buzzy scenery!

Punta Hermosa is one of the best areas in Peru for surfers. For us, it means pure stress to get around the breakers at the headlands to search for the safest landing spot in the many different small narrow bays. If only our host could see it from our point of view! It is a significant difference to maneuver a heavy kayak through a narrow unbroken line, and to land safely on a steep beach, or to surf on a board over the breakers and just hop off in the shallows. No surprise, that a surf world champion has settled here. We can stay in the beach house of Sofia Mulanovich for the first night of our stay in the Lima area. We hope to stay here for a few more days, but our sponsor Thule has different ideas: They plan an official arrival in Lima for 10am next morning. But how are we supposed to do that? This would take at least seven hours from Punta Hermosa. It is a full paddling day with our average speed of 3.5mph, and even longer, if we have headwind. We decide to let Sofia's team drive us to the Club de Regatas, just over a mile off the intended landing beach. We can set out from there, well rested for a fake arrival, to meet the press with a friendly smile.

Our sponsor provides us a pleasant hotel in Lima, and spoils us with delicious food in selected restaurants to keep us smiling for the many TV and press appointments.

I have often wondered how much journalists prepare for interviews, and what they know about the person they are going to meet. Often, they seem to know little to nothing. An example is this interview, which consists of five questions:

"So, you are the first woman going around the world in a kayak?"

Sorry, I am not circumnavigating the world, only South America, and I am not the first woman to do this, but the first person.

Next question: "How do you like Cervice?" Well, this Peruvian specialty of raw fish I get served daily in my kayak, therefore I know it so well…

"And what do you think of Peruvian soccer?" I am German, but I am an avid kayaker. Soccer is not the activity I pursue, neither myself nor as a spectator, and I have no idea about nothing!

"Has anything exciting happened on your journey?" ANYTHING exciting? Every day, there are dangerous or at least exciting occasions…where shall I start?

"Which continent will you tackle next?"

I am not even half way round my second one…is the here and now not interesting enough? I am not a continental factory!

This kind of journalism I find difficult to take seriously, no one wants to know how many miles per day I do, how I eat on the water, what the waves are like, and what I demand from myself.

After Lima, the water becomes yucky the second time of my trip: The sewage works north of town must be broken, as it disgorges its stinking broth unfiltered directly into the sea. It is a soup made of soap and urine, garnished with poo and condoms. Not exactly pure joy to paddle through that! In Punta

Salinas, the locals help us pull the kayaks up the beach and to make camp. Peter is the more social one of us today, they think he is the one doing the circumnavigation of South America. Mistake: The hero in this tale is a heroine, the senora!

But even heroines are not immune to another Montezuma's Revenge. The contaminated water after Lima must have found a way into my body: For the whole night, I cannot get rest, and it was the same culprit which plagued Peter three weeks ago: Diarrhea and nasty cramps. But where do I find private relief on a brightly lit town beach with plenty of people? Either, one digs a very composting deep hole in the sand of the vestibule, or one could use a plastic bag with a good seal and must find a rubbish bin next morning to dispose it. I lie on my back, try to sleep, but need to get up three times in the night. Even though I feel knackered and limp in the morning, I decide to paddle. I want to leave this busy town beach behind. All night, there was a car from the coast guard parked next to us, keeping watch.

Even though we have a break every few miles, this day's paddle is a fair torture. My stomach is still rebellious, and like Peter a few days ago, I often need to hang my rear overboard. I manage to down a few bananas, an apple, a few carrots and a mango, at least something. Luckily, we are glad to have a good following wind. Even when we take a break, it pushes us several hundred yards along. It is hot, Peter protects his bald head with a soaking wet hat to cool down.

For the entire day, we are paddling past high dunes with ugly looking breakers. Only close to Punta Salinas, our next intended overnight stop, is it possible to have a relaxed landing. It is close to a nature reserve, with only a few solitary houses and promises a quiet night.

Sleep is often the best medicine, and this also goes for me. My digestion is still not right, but I feel I am getting stronger to do another long paddling day. It is hot on the beach, and I prefer to be on the water during the day. We need to protect our tent from the direct sunshine with sleeping bags and blankets to keep a bearable temperature. The Humboldt Current helps us to cover forty miles, and we expect to land by 4pm on a busy city beach. Thank god, we find a private corner on this Sunday afternoon. All fishermen are busy launching a brand-new boat. To reach our camp spot, one would need to climb under the jetty.

Chimbote is our next stop to fill our water bags. We have forty-five miles to cover in daylight between 5am and 6pm. We have a half day pause on the beach of Punta Huaro, and enjoy a swim in the sea and a lovely walk across the island. We are well motivated, and manage to arrive in the last daylight after thirteen hours of paddling. On the way, thirty fishing boats line up like in a race. Is the fishing ground really that attractive where we came from?

Next pit stop is Huanchaco. In calm seas, with pleasant winds from the back and a helpful current, we make good speed. If only it was not so hot! Peter often douses his hat with water to keep his skull cool. I have a "Blu Bandoo" gel-filled visor band on mine, and suggest to Peter, that if he were to catch a jelly fish of suitable size and keep it in his hat, it may have the same effect! The ugly stain from the rusty cap button on top of his bald head would also disappear...

Close to Huanchaco, we discover a craft of the past: A local paddles up to us in a floating device made of bundles of reed. It has a high-pulled-up prow, and he is paddling it with a bamboo stick split in half. Caballitos de Totora - Little straw horses, these simple, up to five-yard-long boats are aptly named. They have been built by the local fishermen since centuries. Here in Huanchaco in northern Peru, they are very popular tradition, with dozens of crafts vertically on the beach to dry off. While we should put on PFD and helmet for a challenging surf landing with our heavyweight kayaks, the local fella seems to fully trust the stability of his lightweight construction. Two large fish he caught lie unsecured in the hollow of his "straw horse", and the signature card I gave him ends up in the brim of his hat, since that was the only dry place he knew.

The cold Humboldt Current is still pushing us, and the small Humboldt penguins are still around. It is hard to believe we are approaching the sixth latitude just before the equator. The water is as cold as in Valparaiso, with temperatures in the higher fifties. Once the current disappears, the penguins will also be gone.

We need to be prepared for all eventualities on such a trip. We plan to paddle forty-five miles to a beach past Cherrepe, but extreme surf makes the landing on the spot we have selected from the satellite pictures impossible. I was about to have a closer, careful look, when suddenly a monster-high rogue wave rolls in underneath, and breaks in front of me in a mess of foam. Peter has already turned his kayak, and I see him sprinting out to sea. As I did the same, one more of those monster waves lifts me five yards up to the crest, and I crash down on its other, safe side with a loud bang. Just get out of here! Out of this massive surf zone, before one of those monsters breaks on top of me! In our hasty retreat, we climb up several towering rogue wave mountains. How do they manage to appear so suddenly? We are shocked. This moment was one of the scariest of the whole trip!

Just be gone, far away, without a look back! Any attempt to land here would be too dangerous. Whether we like or not, we now need to carry on through the night to reach Pimentel. We have a planned night trip after Pimentel, as we would be passing a seventy-mile sandy beach with no shelter to give a safe landing. Now, we must do two consecutive night paddles!

As dawn fights through the fog, we see the first fishermen working in the rising sun. Some of the little "straw horses" are dancing on the waves. One young straw horse rider, barefoot, uses a cut open bin bag as wind breaker. We ask for directions to a safe landing spot. He points us to a swimming pontoon at the end of a long jetty jutting far out over the surf. I have my doubts that this would be the best exit point. The pontoon floats up and down in the waves of the heavy swell, and pulls on the rotten looking ropes holding it to the dilapidated jetty. But better here, then in the foaming, unpredictable and endless surf belt!

I carefully come along its side, clamber quickly onto the pontoon and pull the kayak over the wobbly edge. With good timing and a favorable swell, I drag my kayak over the edge, though I do not like the nasty crunchy sound it makes as I drag it along. I kneel for stability on the wobbly floating platform, and help Peter up the pontoon. To reach the beach, we would need to balance with our gear bags and kayaks across a tangle of unreliable planks, and decide to make camp directly here on the end of the jetty. We tie the empty kayaks onto the pontoon, and pick a place where the planks are close enough together not to lose any bits of kit falling through the gaps. Should that happen, they would be lost to the foaming sea, never to be seen again!

Despite the noise from repair construction works all around us, we try to sleep, after paddling twenty-four hours through the night. Later this afternoon, I see twenty odd "straw horses" go through the massive surf belt without any issue. Those light boats have some advantages here. If one of them tips over, they do not have much to lose other than their catch and their pride. Our hundred-kilogram battleships are in far greater danger.

Next morning, the workers start a generator at 8am, and we sit bolt upright. We still feel worn from the last night paddle, but favorable weather is demanding for our departure. By 10am, we are on the water, this time we have planned to arrive by sunrise. Another seventy-mile leg!

In this night, cool temperatures are not the issue, but my tiredness is. I need to have short power naps in between the regular hourly breaks. I lean forward with my head on the cockpit rim, elbows tucked in, and the paddle blades about fifteen inches above the water. If one blade is catching water, I will notice it even during these micros sleeps. I am aware if a wave threatens to capsize me, or I start to fall sideways out of the kayak. Even when Peter is annoyed and wants us to make progress, I insist on my naps. From earlier night trips, I know what my body demands. Last night, we have passed the long paddling time by taking turns to sing songs to each other, but this night, I cannot think of any. Better Peter watches the starry sky or takes a nap himself, instead of being annoyed!

Other creatures out here are also looking for some rest. Peter rams a sleeping seal, frightening the living daylight out of it, and he takes off with a mighty splash of his rear fin. Massive flocks of resting seabirds lift out of the water with noisy screeching. A slowly increasing swoosh makes us listen up, is a heavy rain squall closing in? No, it is a clear and starry night. Shore surf? My GPS says differently. As the moon and my strong flashlight light up the water around us, we can see the origin of the spooky sounds: A massive school of dolphins of several hundred animals is chasing through the night! It is incredibly beautiful!

Isla Lobos de Tierra should be near...but, where is it? In the gray morning light, fog is hampering visibility, so we can see barely 500 yards. The roar of the breaking waves on rocks and the barking from the sea lion colonies show the island must be near. Suddenly, the fog lifts like a curtain in the theatre, and we realize, the island is just in front of us! Thank God for the GPS. In the main bay, several boats are at anchor. Men dive with long oxygen hoses to the bottom of the sea to harvest mussels, powered by noisy engines. They give us friendly waves. We need at least one full rest day after two nights of paddling, and decide to take the next, smaller bay. The water here is clear and warm, and for the first time, we see turtles floating instead of penguins riding the cold Humboldt Current north. A clear sign, from now on, currents and the animal world would be different. We have nearly reached the tropics!

Isla Lobos de Tierra is a nature reserve, many pelicans with colorful beaks are nesting on the beaches, and cute little blue-footed Boobies present their partners their feet in a mating dance. We pitch tent at the beach section least likely to upset the wildlife, that is if we need to camp here at all! Our sleeping bags covering the tent for sun protection, are soon spotted with bird shit. A good sign, we really should not be here! But we must have a day's rest!

Two rangers are not excited to see us camping here this afternoon. Once we explain, we would always stay near the tent, and are not upsetting any nesting animals, they are ok about it. Looking at the massive quantities of plastic bags and rubbish spread all over the island, I cannot help but wonder why the rangers are not in charge to help free the birds' nesting places of the civilization trash?

The calm weather dictates a fifty-miles leg to the quiet beach after Punta Shode, where we have another rest day. Thereafter, we hope to do forty-five miles to Foca. We have only fifteen miles left to cover to reach Paita on our last day, before heading to Germany for Christmas break. If all goes according to plan, we will arrive in four days at lunch time in Paita.

We leave next morning at 4.30am, passing the river mouths and bays of Punta Tur, Punta Nac and Punta Falsa pass on our way. The further we are getting, the more the beaches are facing north, even northeast. Heavy surf and dreadful landings are history!

Just before Punta Nonura, we discover a wide quiet beach with a few buildings. Is it the twenty-knots wind that makes us oversee the yellow warning sign? It is military area, and an excited chap sprints down to us at record breaking speed. Nothing we can say changes his mind to let us stay for just one night. His superior's voice squawking out of the radio ensure his compliance. We should instantly pack our bags again and go to a beach just around the headland. It is rare that the military does not welcome us!

Peter is launching with anger and impatience, takes three waves frontal, and loses his last hat. It is the one he got from the coast guard in Pisco, and he really needs it to cover his bald head. He curses loudly. I delay my start, hoping the hat will get washed ashore, and luckily, I am able to fish it out of the surf. Followed by a boat full of soldiers ensuring we really leave this bay, we paddle two miles to the designated beach. Thank you! This beach is even more pretty and secluded than the last one.

The beach is populated by thousands of little red crabs coming out of their sand holes. They seem to have a magical attraction to the intensive scent of Peter's sandals in the vestibule. They screech and scratch around our tent all night. Regardless, it is an ideal place for a windy rest day and to slowly let this stage drift to an end. It will be Peter's last relaxing beach day. After the Christmas break, he will stay in Europe. We are selling his kayak in Peru.

Just prior to the landing in Paita, a rocky arch near Punta El Ajureyo is inviting us to paddle through. According to a legend, it is a good omen and a sign of good luck. Different to many other arches, this one looks suitable, no tricky rocks blocking the passage, and there is hardly any swell. Even though Peter will not go through, I do it on my own. I cannot miss a lucky omen!

In the large bay of Paita, a coast guard ship is coming out to meet and guide us to a large Navy boat with many men staring curiously down to our kayaks. They point to a rope ladder we should use to climb on board. Dozens of hands pull our boats and bags to the top. On land, the harbor master greets us, and offers a room in the Navy's guest house. We accept gratefully, and have an extensive shower, not just ourselves, but all our kit needs to be freed from sand and dirt. In the hot tropical sun, everything dries instantly.

Happy and at peace with the world, Peter and I finish this last mutual day of my expedition. Christmas is in three weeks, and tomorrow, we fly home!

Chapter 10
ALONE IN ECUADOR

Peru/ Ecuador: Paita to Esmeraldas
January 9th - February 6th, 2013

I am four weeks into my stay in Husum. For the next section, I need to deal with the bureaucracy not only of one, but of a handful of countries. My next trip will take me through Ecuador, Colombia, Panama, Colombia again, Venezuela, a little detour to Trinidad and on to Guyana. I need to get vaccinations against yellow fever, tetanus and hepatitis A. I will take only stand-by products against malaria, as it is unlikely I will be in danger in the coastal regions.

Somehow melancholy, I arrive where I left off with Peter. I am back on my own again. I prefer it this way, despite the smooth paddling together.

The water temperature has increased to the higher seventies - the cold Humboldt Current does not extend this far. I get my first sunburn on the forearms, despite I am using a sun blocker. Taking a dip in the evening after a long thirty-five-mile day does give limited refreshment. The equator is close, the penguins are gone.

After a night with dogs, policemen and intrusive locals lighting up my tent with their car headlights at regular intervals, I am ready for a rest day. The jet lag takes its toll, an early start does not pay off. Only a few miles after Cabo Blanco, I find a beach that promises seclusion and undisturbed rest.

I must get used to the warmer temperatures. Butter and cheese are off my menu, they melt way too easily. I need fat in my diet, so I buy a bottle of olive oil and a re-sealable sachet of mayonnaise. White chocolate is a different issue, I would rather eat it molten than not eat it at all!

I must take care of my skin in the tropics. One sunburn is one too much. I must watch not to get any serious skin issues from the heat and humidity. My rear end is showing first spots, I need to make sure it does not get as bad as it was on my Australian circumnavigation!

After two peaceful nights, I am well rested, and paddling is fun again. The weather in this region is quite stable and temperate. The strong off-shore winds at night calm down in the morning. Later in the day, there is an on-shore breeze. The water is warm enough to be pleasant, I am not getting a cold shock anymore, when a wave licks into the boat. I wear a fleece shirt with a hood to protect myself from the sun and leave my arms covered up. Fleece keeps both warm and cool, and does not rub on the skin, even when it is wet. I do without a PFD altogether, as my skin would not last being rubbed up.

The sand dunes and hillocks show little green specks. Holiday season is full on. I am surrounded by kite surfers and jet skis pulling tourists on banana boats. Deep sea anglers and horse riders pass me by, but most holiday locations do not look overfilled.

I paddle close to the shore, but far out enough neither to get caught by reef breakers, nor by high-spirited teenagers who throw themselves into the waves in "Bay Watch" style and try to swim out to my boat. I do not want to find out what would happen, if I had a large group of them hanging onto my kayak. Instead, I keep a discreet distance, like a queen in her carriage. Accordingly, I practice royal waving. Sometimes, I hear the surprised whistles of men on shore playing football or standing on their surf boards, as soon as they realize it is a female paddling past.

I pass the last holiday village and the last fishing boats at anchor, and reach an area devoid of humans. After a few miles, I will leave Peru and enter Ecuador. Puerto Pizarro, the last Peruvian town, is behind me. Thanks again for the manifold kindness and hospitality I received in Peru!

After a quiet night in Punta Payana, I am ready to enter a new country. My fourth country flag, of Ecuador, sticks on both sides of my kayak.

Some fisherman in the channel close to Isla Jambeli offers me food from his cooler boxes: Watermelon, milk, mango, a bread roll, and a freshly caught crab. Are these gifts, or am I meant to pay? I am not sure - I am also not sure of the meaning behind the bible he shows me when I leave. Language barrier...

The entrance to the channel is hard to find, there are loads of little sandbanks, and it looks like the German Waddenzee with its tidal creeks and mud flats. At the entrance, a small motorboat cruises until the water rises and allows passage. I do not need to wait that long with my kayak, I get washed across a little sandbank to the next deeper pool, get out and drag the kayak into the deep-water channel. The sea ground here is not mud, but firm sand, which is easy to walk on. Inside, it has plenty of water to continue with easy paddling. The atmosphere in this mangrove labyrinth is a bit spooky. After a few miles, I turn from the little side channels into the main canal, and see on the horizon the harbor of Puerto Bolivar. Close to a small maritime museum, I pull my kayak up the wooden pontoon, and search for the office of the harbor master. I should have an escort boat go with me over to Isla Puna, as there may be pirates in the bay of Guayaquil. They are mostly after the outboard motors and the catch of the fishermen, but who knows, what they may think could be attractive about me and my kayak?

I ask the men in the coast guard escort boat to please stay far behind me, so I do not have to breathe in the exhaust fumes of their engine and listen to its constant noise. In this manner, I might easily forget that there is an escort boat at all. Pirates? What about the pirates?

I have not to wait long for those! They show up just after the escort boat says goodbye to take care of another matter. I am about ten miles before Isla Puna. "You can do it," the coast guard guys shout as farewell, "it is not far now", and they peel off. I know I can do it, but you are not here to take care of my limited condition and paddling capabilities!

After two miles, a small open boat with three guys aims directly for me and pulls alongside. It is nothing unusual, as I gave them a friendly wave as I would any other boat. But those guys I do not like...they are not fishermen. I know how fishermen look like...I keep on paddling, fully unimpressed about their presence.

"Are you alone out here?" one of them asks.

"Si". It is an obvious answer, and I carry on paddling in normal speed. "Where are you going?"

"Playas" I say, as I am not in the mood to have a long chat in my broken Spanish. Their boat circles around me and they shout something like "Olas grandes", high waves around the headland of Isla Puna. Today, at that location? I shrug to show it does not worry me. But something else does worry me. They stop their motor and shout another sentence of which I only understand one word: "Piratas!"

Their provocative manner, the broad grins, and the way their t-shirts are knotted about their heads - the modest fishermen I have met previously behave different. And these guys are not any of them.

When I hear "Piratas", I laugh out shortly and shrug my shoulders again. "No hablamos mucho Espanol, no entiendo." I call back. I do not speak much Spanish and do not understand. I do not stop at all, and simply carry on paddling, pulling with even, strong strokes without turning back to see what they are up to now. "Go back home to Mama, boys!" I think, and hope that they lose interest.

And really, they stay away. I take a deep breath, as I realize that this encounter could have ended differently. I would have no chance, if three guys in a motorboat want to empty my hatches. For quite some time now, the GPS disappears below my deck as soon as a boat gets close. A local may not be able to fathom what and how many valuables I may be carrying with me.

Later, I tell Peter on the phone about this, and I am glad to hear that he has received an email from the German Embassy. The Colombian Navy will be looking after me twenty-four/ seven, once I arrive there in a few days. I felt safe in Argentina, Chile and Peru, and most of the few escorts were more of a nuisance than I was grateful for their existence and protection, but Ecuador already feels different.

One can estimate the dangers from the weather and the animals, but bad people are a different matter. For security reasons, I now post my blog entries with a two days delay. You never know who reads it.

After a quiet night, I am almost relieved, when a Navy officer arrives in a motorboat to check if I am still alive. But he is not able to escort me for long. No pirates on the sea today? Eighteen miles before I reach Playas, another small motorboat approaches my direction. I tense up, but thankfully it is only the Navy coming for a look-see. But six miles before I make landfall, they turn away without giving me further instructions, and I am on my own again.

As I am fully self-dependent, I search for a suitable landing spot. I decide on a section of the beach with fancy houses, hopefully showing an area to offer some security. I have just pulled my kayak and luggage hundred yards up the hot sand, when a Navy officer turns up on his roaring quad bike. They have other plans for me than camping on the beach.

The quad biker loads my luggage, and tells me to go another three miles in my empty kayak to Playas. I obey him, and paddle to a safe site within the fenced area of the harbor master's office, where I can camp. For tomorrow night, a place within another harbor masters' office of Chanduy has been arranged for me. I have also received an email from an officer in Punta Salinas offering further overnight accommodation. I am now passed along daily from one Coast Guard station to the next. On one hand, it is comforting, but on the other, it is contrary to my ideas of paddling with freedom. Being sensible can be such arduous work!

I have been offered a room in the harbor master's lodge, but I only use their shower, and camp out in the back yard. I like to get a bit of a breeze, and the four walls are my own. My tent is free of mosquitos, the hot room without air condition they offered me was not. Paddling into a continuous head wind is tiring. My damp body has been sitting in an ongoing draught, and that cannot be healthy. I am aching everywhere, and need this Sunday to recuperate.

I do not belong to any church or faith, but out of curiosity, I take part in the mass in the village church. I do not understand a word, but the friendly peaceful atmosphere of these simple people, dressed up in their Sunday clothing, touches me. Peaceful people with faith like these cannot be bad, can they?

As I reach the small coastal village of San Lorenzo, I create a stampede. More than hundred people are running to the beach. With so many spectators, I really cannot afford a mishap when I land in moderate surf. I wait for a low wave, and get washed right into the crowd. I worry I will hit someone with the heavy boat, but I barely have landed, when dozens of hands pull me out of the surf zone. I am the highlight of the day, if not of the week or even longer. Everyone is friendly, but none of my movement goes unobserved. To have a shower outside is out of question, I need to wash and change inside the tent.

Next to my tent is a beach hut guarded by a watchdog. He comments on each of my movements with a warning growl. In the tropics, animals always surround you, whether you like it or not. I fall asleep watching a gecko outside on my inner tent, and wake up with cockroaches and small, mean ants all around my sleeping mat. Not to mention the toad in the entrance. However, on the water, seals, dolphins and whales are getting rarer to find. Since the Humboldt Current has turned away from the coast, there is not much left to watch.

The wind is following since I am going eastbound towards Manta. It is a lively industrial harbor full of stink and noise. I paddle to the jetty of the harbor master past the endless marina wall with many ships and boats. Strangely, there is no boat in sight to receive me. Once again, I call the office, but the officer who answered knows nothing and will get back in touch.

I could also ask for shelter in the nearby Yacht Club. But with this stinky noise all around me, I decide to quit town as fast as possible, and plan to paddle two bays further into the wild nature. It is only 3pm, the wind is calm, the sea is calm, just let me out of here! On a beach just past Jaramijo, I find the peace and quiet I am looking for. I prefer the sandflies nearly eating me alive while I set up camp, over the noise of the industrial harbor.

Today, I will cross the equator! It is day 378 of my journey. I noticed yesterday that I was entering a northern current with cooler water, which gives me a bit of a boost, but it also creates shore break which makes landing difficult.

The equator only shows up on my GPS like a jackpot full of zeros. There is no sign on land, but somewhere should be a special monument. I call my family to celebrate with them. My father, the late marine biologist Dr. Heinrich Hoffmeister, crossed the equator on a whale trawler as a young student. The mariners marked the occasion with all sorts of pranks and games. The initiates received new names on a funny "equator baptism". A certificate confirming crossing the equator, with his new name, "Walross", hung for decades by my father's desk. Now, his daughter follows him, but with less ceremony. I am back in the northern hemisphere!

I catch up with my baptism a bit later, although less voluntarily. As I head towards the Navy station of Pedernales, the surf looks lower from the low view point of my kayak than it really is. I have neither counted on an unprotected landing, nor am I mentally prepared. My timing is poor, the first breaker capsizes me, and sucks me out of the kayak. I do not even have the possibility to wait while hanging upside down, until I can roll up again. My left sandal nearly slides off my foot, but my head gear swims off. I keep hold of my paddle. Wave upon wave breaks over me, and I swallow a hefty dose of water. Luckily, I see my kayak being washed up the beach without taking too much damage. Two men on the beach hold on to it, while I swim ashore coughing and spluttering. Thank God, not more spectators saw this embarrassing arrival.

Next morning, I get ready to start again. Skeptically, the men are watching me. They do not know that this sort of a crash landing was the exception. Today, my timing is right and the way out to sea is free. I hope they remember me this way!

Extensive sandy beaches and palm groves without any mountains mark the further land. No more holiday resorts and tourists, only a few local boys and cowboys guarding herds of cattle are giving me a friendly wave. It is hot, the sun burns down without mercy, and I must fight a headwind of fifteen knots. I manage just over fifteen miles today, and I am happy to reach the beach of Galera without problems.

I need to stay at the lively city beach, but friendly greetings from the locals give me the feeling I will be safe and welcome here. Unfortunately, two young guys are over the top with their curiosity. Just as I sank into a deep recovery sleep at 10pm, they thought they had to come to visit me.

"Senora, por favor, palabra, conversation..." I hear while already half asleep. I wake up fully, an am in a bad mood.

They say, they only want to chat. I stop them quickly from sitting on top of my kayak, which I have as usual placed as a barricade in front of my tent. They settle down on the other side, and start to talk to me with placating deep voiced Spanish. As I do not think I am missing anything important, I explain: "I am tired, I want to sleep, please leave now". The angry tone of voice hopefully spoke for itself. They continue to talk at me, and drum on top of my kayak. I settle on a more rigorous approach to get rid of them: I open the zip of my tent, shine my strongest torch directly at their face and hiss "Fuck off!"

No result, instead once again they retort, "Senora, por favor; senora, por favor; senora, por favor..."

I try to stay calm and switch strategy: No further reactions, in the hope they will get fed up, rather than become violent. I am not afraid, only annoyed about my disturbed night's rest. Eventually, they give up and go away. This persistent manner might be successful with the local ladies, but not with this seasoned, grown up German! Despite everything, I sit bolt upright two hours later, hearing some strange noises. I am worried they have returned, with a few more men in tow, who would not only call "Senora, por favor". Just in case, I fetch my signaling whistle from the kayak into the tent. I listen to every little rustling in the bushes around me. It is only animals - or a few lost souls from the nearby cemetery? Were the guys a few of the undead? Were their pupils not deep black when I shone the torch at their faces? Whatever was creeping around my tent that night, it has ruined my peace and rest.

I start next morning tired and listless. I leave Galera at dawn without meeting further locals. Dark clouds draw across the horizon; it is not just a little shower, but a real cloud burst with headwinds of twenty knots. I fight it, I do not want to give up and turn back. The visibility is poor, but I make the decision to carry on until Atacames. That is half way to my next longer stop in Ecuador, the town of Esmeraldas, and if I do not take on the prevailing head winds now, when will I do it?

Staying in the Coast Guard station of Atacames is a tempting offer after the experience of last night. The village is a popular holiday resort, and the base is directly next to the well-populated city beach. What should I do? Safety has preference over an undisturbed rest. The Navy chaps are happy for the distraction, and I move into the room of an officer on holiday.

At the beach promenade, ice-cream and fruit vendors are lined up cheek by jowl. One can buy sunglasses and beach toys, and there are many ways to have fun on the water: Kite surfing, body boarding, paragliding and riding on banana boats behind a strong motorboat in tow. I walk past countless bars, restaurants, souvenir and tattoo shops; loud music is pounding out everywhere. But I am not on holiday here, even if I must stretch my stay to two days. After the last stressful paddle leg, I need some rest, and my skin is grateful for the chance to regenerate. My strained muscles get pampered with a massage on the beach, although the one or other grain of sand finds its way between the masseuse's hands and my skin. I also can shop for food better here than in Esmeraldas. In the big city, I only need the exit stamp to legally leave Ecuador in the direction of Colombia.

I try to enjoy the lively beach life and savor fresh mangoes and coconuts. I let a woman plait a few little Rasta braids on one side of my head. Twelve of them cost four dollars. But they do not stay in for long, two hours later, I undo them again. They are a bit painful, and make my gray outgrown hair too visible!

Two days before I arrive Esmeraldas, I paddle past the first of the infamous large river deltas with their hidden drug farms and kitchens. I am glad, the Colombian Navy is ready to escort me soon along this coast!

The penultimate day in Ecuador leads me to Rio Verde. Two fishermen guide me through the confusing waves into the calm delta. Dozens of people wave to us as we paddle past them on the right shoreline. Looking at the many dark-skinned people sorting the catches on shore, I wonder if this is South America or Africa? This northern area is a melting pot of the most diverse cultures' skin tones. I am getting a reception by the mayor, and I am spoiled with a free hotel room. Many thanks!

On the way to Rio Verde, the driver of a three-wheeler motorbike takes great pains to stow my kayak safely. He fixes it on a few thin planks of wood running along the side. Just before we get to the beach, it happens: One of the planks becomes loose, and squeezes the stern. I hear a nasty crunch and crackling gel coat. I am cursing roundly, and luckily a few pedestrians jump into action to support the stern before it breaks any further. The damage is annoying, but easy to repair. Dozens of curious eyes watch me mixing up some two-component fast-curing epoxy glue, and apply it to the damaged areas. No big deal, but I am getting a bit behind schedule. Since half past seven, my escort boat has been waiting at the end of the river delta, and it is now eight o'clock before I manage to get going. For three hours, the boat stays unobtrusively near me, but by eleven thirty, they are bored and turn away. Two hours later, they are back, but my request to keep a bit of distance, that I do not have to smell their exhausts, only leads to them disappearing completely. Later, I see them again, escorting a handful of small boats from the direction of Colombia. I wonder if they are drug smugglers?

Before I manage to reach La Tola, I get stuck in shallow water. I ask a fisherman to help me pull the kayak hundred yards to a place where the river is deep enough for me to paddle. Without talking, he does as I ask him to do. I thank him sincerely, but I can see in his face, he wonders what the stupid "gringa" is doing in his waters, and even getting stuck! It is another 500 yards of pulling and walking until I get to deeper water, and I hustle to paddle towards the wide visible area of the Navy station of La Tola. It is already dark when I arrive, and I find lots of helping hands. Two sailors carry my luggage to the Navy station, and the locals care for my kayak. The helpfulness I have experienced in Ecuador, carries on to the last hamlet. La Tola is my final stop in Ecuador.

Chapter 11
COLOMBIA'S DANGEROUS COASTS

Colombia to the Panama Canal
February 7th - March 13th, 2013

Colombia! Ahead of me is one of the trickiest sections of my circumnavigation of South America. I have often been irritated in the last months by the overbearing care of the Navies, but here, I do not mind being escorted all the way. I have heard a lot about pirates, drug smugglers and the FARC rebels of this region. The danger is real. I am on my way to Cabo Manglares, the boarder of Ecuador and Colombia. The first small motorboat speeding towards me turns out to be harmless. But with the next two, which rush past me at their highest speed late in the afternoon, I am not so sure. With unfriendly faces, they carry a stack of jerry cans, as petrol is used in enormous quantities when making drugs.

No Navy boat is yet to be seen. They were supposed to wait for me since noon at the exit of the river delta. Neither radio nor satellite phone text manage to reach the boat or Commander Delgado in Buenaventura. Only after multiple contact attempts by Peter in Europe, the Colombian Coast Guard vessel is on its way. They have expected me further south. It is half past four in the afternoon, and I am glad to see the four guys in their open boat, equipped with three strong engines.

We discuss how to continue. It is safest to spend the night on board. The men stay there anyway, and no one has planned for me to spend the night ashore. I hop across, and they pull my kayak on board.

There is a tiny cabin at the bow of their boat with a mattress, but I do not want to steal the bed of any of the guys. I lay out my camp right next to my kayak. It is not looking like it will rain, and it is warm enough for my sleeping pad and a blanket to suffice. In a sheltered corner, I light my small gas stove. I will have two of those cheap Chinese noodles squares, the men eat their cold military rations. Had I known I had just lit my gas stove on top of twelve barrels of petrol, I might have also decided on a cold dinner. I continuously have the smell of petrol in my nose, and the rolling of the boat does not let me sleep. It feels as if someone is constantly shaking me to wake up.

Most of the night, I lie on my back with my eyes open. I listen to the guys chatting for a while, watch the stars and the lights of the mainland, and admire the bio-luminescence around us. Soon, three guys jump in hammocks tied to the frame of the sun roof, one guy is on watch and keeps the boat away from land.

At 6am, we get back to the precise GPS-spot, where I last night entered the boat. We have been drifting off eight miles. I have not slept well, now fighting boredom, strong river mouth currents and a fifteen-knots headwind. Paddling is tough, but landing at Tumaco is still doable just before dusk. The Navy boat keeps a good distance all day.

It takes a bit more exertion before I reach the first large town in Colombia. A line of river mouths and strong tidal waves make me paddle far off shore. I must zigzag past the little islets close to Tumaco, lined in front of a thick tropical rainforest. The Navy station comes into view. It stretches over the whole tip of a headland, and is a village itself, like in Esmeralda and Puerto Bolivar before. It should be safe there! After five paddle days, I will have a two-days break.

My room offers some comfort with a nice bed, fridge, TV and air conditioning. I must get my entry stamp for Colombia, change money and buy a Colombian phone card. A moderate earthquake next day makes the phone system crash at times, it is difficult the get the card activated.

The town itself looks much cleaner and friendlier than I had been led to believe. Many policemen and soldiers give a feeling of security. When I have lunch in the canteen of the station, I can see live, that smuggling drugs is a real issue. In a small bay are rotting many confiscated smuggler boats, among them are several small self-built semi-submarines, and a large boat with four engines and dozens of petrol barrels. The coca farmers need the petrol to make cocaine from the plant material.

Commander Delgado has previously told me of a big upcoming event, a Naval parade! He asks me to take part in my kayak, but on rest days, I really do not want to get wet! I would rather be a passenger on one of the Navy boats. I am awaiting a dignified military parade with uniforms and marching bands, but must have misunderstood. What I get to see now, is very much different: It is carnival in Tumaco!

I could not have chosen a better time to experience the Colombian joy of life on the Pacific side of the country. There are no tourists anywhere, the high crime rate keeps them off. But all I see today are happy faces! For these days, no one wants to think about the dangers of a life in Colombia, and only likes to party. And party they do everywhere: In the stilt houses on land, and on the many larger and smaller boats with their typically sharply raised bows. Thousands of colorfully dressed people buzz around. Musicians of all kinds gather on the boats, many of them are well overloaded. For the fun water battles ahead, all boats are armed with foam spray, water guns and buckets. Three Navy vessels, a police boat and the Coast Guard make some efforts to keep the procession in line.

I am trying to imitate one of the young carnival queens, shaking their tight little bums in glittery hot pants and high heels, but even the drag queens make a better job out of this than me! On the close to shore parading boats, half naked flesh is heaving, the noise is indescribable. I take hundreds of pictures, and I am happy to watch the spectacle from one of the Navy boats at a safe distance, rather than to be in the middle of this boisterous dancing, sweaty crowd!

Felipe and Dario, my Navy bodyguards, take me next day to an amazing beach restaurant. We indulge in "carne asado", barbecued meats with yams, potatoes and grilled plantains. Delicious! Admiral Nero gives me a goodbye present, a great multi-function knife with the inscriptions "Joint Forces against Narco Traffic". Tumaco, at least for me, presents its best side!

Heading to Mosquera, I am flushed out of Tumaco bay by the current, and manage an average of seven and a half miles per hour. I can paddle with a light load, as I always have an escort boat. This not only allows me to paddle faster, it also saves me a lot of work, once I stop for the day. It is hot today, so I put in two Eskimo rolls to cool down. Or do I like to show off for "my boys"? It is more pleasant to wet myself with a sponge, rather than getting water into my ears, nose and cockpit.

After forty miles, I have done my day's work, and they pick me up. The Navy boat was barely noticeable all day, as they were busy controlling the boats around like a traffic patrol on the road. We drive to the small fishing village of San Juan, with enough shelter from wind and crime. Three other Navy vessels keep order in this small stilt village close to the drug plantations along the estuaries. They are armed with machine guns on all four sides and other fear-inducing armaments. I am getting used to one of the gun barrels being directed at my kayak all night.

While I prepare my dinner on the bow, simple boiled potatoes with mayonnaise and salt, I get another delight in the corner of my vision. "My boys" have a shower. I wonder whether they watched me with the same curious interest, when I peeled off my wet clothing? Life as a woman in a Colombian military camp can become quite exciting. For the night, the guys steer the boat into the middle of the river for the added safety that gives. There are also less mosquitos, and I have a good night's sleep.

Wind and currents ensure satisfactory progress, I am already finished by early afternoon. The men take me back in, and steer directly into a river system edged in the mangroves. Mosquera can only be reached by boat. No tourist ends up here, it is the terrain of the coca growers. I slightly regret not being able to camp freely on the many nice sandy beaches we pass at high speed, but at high tide, they might be completely gone with a tidal range, now four yards high. In the village, I am tempted to join a group of playful teenagers performing some splashy summersaults from the jetty. The river water is deep brown and muddy, so I make do with a clean shower at the nearby police station.

I have covered by lunchtime the short twenty-six miles to Isla Gorgola. I paddle slowly into a coral reef near the coast to delight in the beauty of the beaches and the jungle behind. I am looking forward to a night in nature, but the whole island is a wildlife reserve, and it is not allowed to pitch a tent just anywhere.

The only buildings on the island are a hotel bare of tourists and the police station overstaffed by five guys. The hotel manager explains sadly, that it is not as popular with tourists as it deserves to be, with all what is on offer. Is that because of the many snakes? Or because smoking, drinking, camping, preparing food outside or venturing alone into the jungle is prohibited? The manager takes me to the national park ranger, and both have a long discussion as to whether I would be allowed to pitch my tent at all. I should stay at the hotel for a fair price.

After an endless discussion, I can camp on the wooden veranda of the police station. That would be the safest place with respect to snakes, and I would be allowed to cook my own meals. My goodness, where is the problem, other than a hotel short of revenue? I settle into my tent, and am happy for now. In the afternoon, I find the hotel staff, the policemen and my Navy guys in front of the TV in a darkened room, watching champions' league soccer. Men all over the world have the same interest!

I use the time to go for a walk along the beach, but soon retreat into my tent. A skin care session is the order of the day. But even after a shower from one of my water bags, I still feel unclean. I am itching everywhere. After being coated all day in sunscreen and insect repellent, at night in anti-itch cream and a healing salve for the infected mosquito bites, I would need a proper shower and some skin-friendly soap, plus an air-conditioned room for my skin to dry out and not instantly get covered in salty sweat again. The mosquitos are particularly fond of my behind, and even bite through the tight Lycra shorts I wear in camp. Sitting does not help either. But this is all part of the challenge, and I do not want to complain. There is no way I would have paid for a hotel room giving some of those amenities I need.

There have been inhabitants on this island who had less comfort than me. On a walk with the park ranger, I find an old prison with a capacity for 2,000, closed only in 1984. One can still see some of the ruins, now covered in jungle vines. I see stone benches and tables, which served as an open-air dining room, an old bread oven, primitive toilet arrangements and stock bedding platforms in stone. There is a depressing atmosphere. My guide explains, more than one prisoner has occupied the single cells. It must have been a tough life!

One is not allowed to move around alone here. Due to the presence of snakes and giant ants, one is only allowed to wear high gum boots. Did the prisoners have high gum boots then? A bunch of curious monkeys buzzing happily around in the abandoned ruins.

In Buenaventura, Commander Delgado receives me. I am invited to his Sunday afternoon VIP's barbeque. Pork ribs, fresh caught crabs and fish wrapped in banana leaves plus tortilla chips with guacamole tickle my taste for different food than I usually eat on my trip. Suitably refueled, we talk to a crowd of journalists on a press conference. Commander Delgado offers himself as an interpreter, and is quite glad, for the change not to have to talk about questions concerning drug runners. In this harbor, I also find several semi-submarines and other confiscated drug runner boats. Only last year, the Navy captured thirty of them, and towed them to the Navy base at Bahia Malaga. The high time for smuggling activities is between the end of February and October. My timing in this respect is perfect, as I am paddling, before this busy season starts. Otherwise, the Navy would be too occupied chasing smugglers to offer me any intensive service.

It is a deliberate strategy of the smugglers to send a lot of boats out at the same time, as the Navy cannot be in all places simultaneously. Even if some are captured, the ones that make it are fantastically profitable.

With such intensive care, I have difficulties turning down the offer to stay longer. I can only scratch on the surface of places I am passing through, or my circumnavigation would take several more years! After a day in

Buenaventura, my escort boat crew takes me back to where they took me on board two days ago. My guys perform a hair-raising kamikaze trip. Is this a training run to catch smugglers? At a top speed of fifty miles per hour, the water becomes solid concrete if one were to be dropped off the boat. The tears in the metal lay-up of the boat are due to the daredevil style of pursuing smugglers. My guys seem to be busier than the last days, with many boats on the water to check upon. I am glad they keep those away from me!

Each day starts with going back to the GPS point I ended up yesterday. This morning is the first time I am still on board, when my crew checks on a suspicious boat which has hoped to blast past us at top speed. The three dark-skinned guys in their open boat, equipped with four strong engines, do not look happy having to stop. One pulls a face as if he is expecting an all-inclusive stay on Isla Gorgona with conditions of pre-1984. Three of my Navy men climb over into their boat, armed to the teeth with machine guns and pistols, and turn over the boat's content. The occupants must show their ID papers and lift their t-shirts, to show they are unarmed. But all they find is a tool for measuring the water content of petrol. It is illegal, as it is used in the manufacture of drugs. No more finds this morning.

In Bahia Solano, I am escorted by two soldiers with machine guns on my way from the Navy station into town. I feel like a VIP visitor - or is it like a VIP prisoner? I hope the security situation on the Atlantic coast of Colombia, once through the Panama Canal, is improved. I would like to move around there a bit more freely.

What will be happening in Panama? It is close now, and they have only a small coast guard.

As a good-bye gesture, the Colombian Navy has a special treat for me. I nod off at 8pm on my escort boat. I am about aware that a few fishermen come over to our boat with a few pots of rice and fish. My guys used this special "marine home delivery service" already the last few nights. Another mid-size Navy ship joins our boat, Johnathan starts the engine, and both crafts are off into the night. Meanwhile, I am still dozing inside my tiny bow cabin. But where are we going? At about 11pm, I hear voices. I peep out of my sleeping bag, and see an enormous gray wall reaching up to the sky right next to me. Am I already in the lock of the Panama Canal?

No, we are next to a giant Navy supply ship called "Buenaventura". I reckon it must be at least fifteen times the size of ours. Just before midnight, I am asked if I want to go on board and greet the captain. Sure, I want! I am wide awake again. I climb up a wobbly rope ladder, and am worried for a moment to get squished between our boat and the "Buenaventura". But all is well, and on deck, I am greeted by the proud Commander Juan Aldana. Through the heavy metal doors, he takes me to the officers' casino. This ship is of German origin! Between 1968 and 1998, it was named "Nienburg" and was part of the German Navy until sold to the "Armada de Colombia". Have I had seen it in Kiel harbor in the past? Commander Aldana lived in Germany for two years as a child, and out of all places, it was in "Heikendorf", my own small home village near Kiel! The world is so small! And as he is about the same age as me, we have lived for two years quite close to each other.

I turn down the friendly invite to sleep on board of the big ship, as it is past midnight, and I do not like heaving my luggage over to the frigate. Later, I have my doubts whether that was the right decision. Our small boat is tucked in between the "Buenaventura" and the small Navy ship, and collects a few fat waves. It is hot and humid, and at 2am, the small Navy ship takes off noisily. Sleep is not really coming to me. Our boat is now also in motion. The plan is to make a large circle, and to be back by 6am for breakfast with the captain. On the dot, I climb up the rope ladder again. After the morning meal and a tour of the ship in daylight, I am taken back to the spot I interrupted my tour last night. For many hours, an enormous swarm of fish escorts me. All around my kayak, they jump like mad out of the water. Why do they do that?

Today, I want to reach the border with Panama, from where their coast guard will take over. I am sad to have to paddle past so many wonderful beaches, where I can neither step on land nor spend a night. Just over a mile from the border, a ship from the "Aeronaval Panama" comes up with fifteen people on board, including a TV team from Jurado. I am amazed to see where TV crews are stationed. I play the game and wave to the cameras. Welcome to Panama!

When I finish paddling today at 4pm, a dozen hands help to pull me, my kayak and my gear on the Panama ship. I can spend the night in the captain's cabin, with hot shower and air conditioning - after the last few nights on the small boat of the Colombian Navy with none of that, it is pure luxury. If only my seasickness will not come back again! The ship is on the move all night. Its task is to patrol the particularly dangerous coastline on the border of Panama and Colombia. Next day, same procedure: I paddle my daily distance and get welcomed aboard. We need to be in Jaqué on time, as I still need my official entry stamp for Panama. I expect we would be going up the river mouth, like on the way to Jurado where I got my exit stamp for Colombia. But the ship is too large, it anchors one bay further in Puerto Pina, and my luggage gets loaded into the smaller tender. As I see the rollers in the river mouth, I am glad to be able to hitch this lift. Alone in my kayak, it would be not possible, at least not on this time of the tide. Even the motorboat has some difficulty managing the breakers and the surf. The look on the guys' faces says it all, and I am not looking forward to the way out again.

While I wait for the formalities of my entry to get completed, Captain Edgar informs me they are unable to go with me for the next few days. He explains that the mission for him and his men is now done, and they need to return to Panama City. From now on, I would have to paddle alone again.

Wonderful, this is what I have been longing to do again for quite some time! Edgar thinks, the beaches from here on should now be safe. Really? For the tender to transport the luggage, I would unfortunately have to pay a small fee. Sorry, not needed at all, as I am used carry all my luggage myself! Edgar was not aware of that. I check the satellite images for the distance to Garachine, and it is just under forty-five miles. About twenty-seven miles further, I spot a village where a few soldiers are stationed. If I get there, then next day I could reach the spot from which to cross over to Isla Del Rey in the Pearl Island Archipelago, and the entirety of the infamous "Darian Gap" drug smuggling zone would be behind me.

I feel worn out from a lack of decent sleep the last few nights, and would have preferred to spend a few days recuperating in Jaqué, but the weather window is small until it gets bad again. It would be best to set off tomorrow already. As I am not allowed to camp in the military area, or even to use one of the rooms on the base, I pitch my tent near the entrance. Unfortunately, it was on a spot where some stinky petrol has been spilled, as I found out later.

As we leave late next morning, I am worried whether I would manage the forty-five miles to the next safe landing place within daylight. I want to be on my own as fast as possible, and cannot wait to get going - and to land on a beach I can claim for my own, without tourists, soldiers or drug smugglers. It almost feels like I have lost touch with nature, after all these days with an escort, and guarded nights on boats or military bases.

At least, I have not forgotten how to land through heavy surf! As a nature lover, I pick a small uninhabited beach, even though I knew, they wanted me to land in the next village. When the Navy boat turns up to check on me, my kayak is on the beach, my camp almost ready, and I just give them a wave. The men wave back, but gesture frantically to the other inhabited beach. No, thanks guys, tonight is not the night for social contacts, and I really do not want to tackle this surf again for no good reason. I just want to be alone! But they do not give up. They cannot land the motorboat here, and just as I finished pitching my tent on an elevated dry spot, they maneuver the boat daringly close to the heavy breakers, two of them jump off and swim over to me. They really want to persuade me to pack everything up again, and to go to the inhabited beach next door. "Peligroso, Peligroso... dangerous," they keep calling. But they have no chance to change my mind. I seriously do not think that the guerrillas up in the mountains are going to come down to just this beach this night to kidnap me. No footprints on the whole beach, and I do not believe I will get visitors tonight! But then again?

At half past midnight, a bright flashlight shines on my tent. I see the outline of a heavily armed man. Were they right? Is it "Peligroso", and is this a guerrilla down from the mountains? No, they are three border policemen and a local, who looks like a hunter with his machete and dog. They must have climbed past the cliff separating the two beaches, and want to keep watch over me for the night. Great, I think, now I do not have to sleep with one ear open, listening for anyone creeping around outside of my tent, and I can put in my ear plugs, so as not to hear the surf on the beach. They sit down on a log besides my tent, and talk noisily all night. But earplugs do the job. If only the stench of their cigarettes would not have wafted over to me! A nose plug might be a bit too much protection.

On my launch next day, the surf is still big, and being watched by the men makes me a bit nervous. I fight my way through several lines of breakers, and even need to roll once, until I get out to sea with arduous work. I have to paddle only fifteen miles to reach the beach where I like to put in a longer break. At high tide, this beach cannot be entered from the mainland, so it might be safe. But my guardians of "Senafront", the Panama coast guard, do not see it my way. There are not only the FARC rebels there, but there have also been sightings of crocodiles! This does frighten me the least, as on my Australian tour, these long-teethed fellows have been my frequent nighttime companions. They will not leave me alone, until I promise to keep radio contact.

I cannot remember when I last had a lonely beach to myself just for a day! It had to be just after returning from the Christmas break. During long paddle days, the soul revives, but the body does the demanding work. On a beach like this one in Gajuala, where there is not even phone reception, body and soul get a break.

There is not much to do other than sleep, eat, read, and go for a walk. On my first tour, I spot a shady place in the thickets which have previously been used as a camp. Though I shelter the tent on the open beach with a blanket for a bit more shade, the sweat just pours off me. I gather my stuff and move to the shady campsite. Two fishing boats have been at anchor in the bay since yesterday, and they are coming to the beach to fill up their drinking water out of the little pools created by a rivulet. They help to move my kayak, and are polite and respectful. Did they notice that I am under the special protection of the "Aeronaval"? In any case, it is a good feeling that they are around. The only thing bothering me here are the countless crabs digging into the sand. It is hard to believe how much noise they can make in the vestibule at night!

The forecast for tomorrow is up to fifteen knots north wind, and my plan of getting to Isla Telmo needs me to cover about thirty-five miles. I hope, paddling into the wind will be possible. When I start in the morning, all is quiet. With the change of the tide comes a change of conditions: Now, wind and current are against me. I must go at an angle of forty-five degrees to Isla San Telmo. I doubt I will make that, and must change plan and head for Isla Galera. It is seven miles less, and more southern. But in this direction, I have difficulties going faster than one and a half miles per hour. The current is pushing me southwards. I paddle in the northern direction, but make only westbound progress, even fearing to get washed onto the reef I see on the southern side of the island.

An amazing natural phenomenon is easing this torture: For hours on end, hundreds of stingrays lift out of the water, beat their fins like birds, and slap down into the waves again with a loud clap. This wonderful local wildlife show is only topped by a massive whale showing itself briefly. I have not seen one for weeks!

After a night on the deserted Isla Galera, I dive deeper into the Archipelago of the Pearl Islands. I stay to the right of the main island, Isla Rey, and paddle past Isla Cana towards Isla Espirito Santo. Once again, the company of hundreds of jumping stingrays pleases me. This whole group of islands looks like paradise on earth. Countless tropical dream beaches line my path, they even seem to stay dry at high tide. Panama's coastguard has not been seen for two days, but I am not alone: Various fishermen zip across the sea in their motorboats, as well as a large ferry, a catamaran, and a handful of sail boats. Panama City is close!

My intended twenty miles I have covered by lunchtime. I allow myself the time for a chat with an American - Swedish sailor couple who look like they have lived on their boat with modest means for some years. Another sailor couple, Michael and Ursula, serve me German-style fried potatoes - an unexpected gourmet delight in this region. I thankfully decline their offer to spend the night on board. Here, there are so many secluded beaches, and I am spoilt for choice. Only another three miles, and I can take my pick.

On the penultimate island of the Pearl Archipelago, Isla Bartholomé, I stop for the night. From there, it is only another forty miles as the crow flies to

Panama City. This is normally doable in a day, but due to the strong tides, I need to split the distance: Twenty miles to Isla Chepillo, and then, including a ten-mile detour, a further thirty miles to Panama City.

I unpack my diving mask, and snorkel for the first time on this trip. There is not too much to see this close to the beach, but it gives me a taste of what I may discover in the Caribbean underwater world.

It is a wonderful place to hang out for a rest day, and I change my plan. I will not do a split distance to Panama City, detouring to Isla Chepillo, but add a rest day here, and then paddle the distance in one leg. It is forty miles to the Balboa Yacht Club. I will have to start early morning, and will get in by night time. Never mind, my GPS will show me the way in the darkness.

Workmen disturb my rest day. Hearing a boat engine, I stick my nose out of my tent, and see some men dumping a load of tree trunks. Again, and again, they return with further loads, until it would be enough to build a beach hut. And indeed, when I stroll over to the guy who keeps the night watch, he explains, that it is for the Argentinian TV-series "Expedición Robinson", internationally known as "Survivor". I could tell them a few tales...

The direct route from Isla Bartholomé to Panama City is like a veritable highway, and many different fishing boats and motor yachts are out to spend the weekend either here or there. I count at least twenty-five boats, plus three large catamaran ferries. All wave to me; three people on a fishing boat even offer me a lift. Thanks, but no thanks. When I leave the lee of the islands, the wind and tidal currents are less fierce than feared. A few dolphins and two whales keep the spirits high. I will arrive Panama City at about 9pm. The crew of a small motorboat asks if I would need help. I am still far out at sea just before dusk. I reply, "No, thanks". With the aid of my GPS, I will be able to find my way among the countless lights on the water.

Is that a wise decision, to approach Panama City and the Panama Canal at night? I start to have doubts, when a pilot boat shoots directly towards me. The strong beam from my flashlight makes them turn at the last moment, undoubtedly cursing about this not so well visible tiny floating object in their path. I do have correct lights, but they are pale and small, compared to any other around here. There is no time for radio contact, and they cannot detect me on the radar.

I leave the Panama Canal waiting area quickly, with about thirty large ships behind me. The ships are all well illuminated, but I must look for their anchor chains, to realize in time, who would be about to move. The Panama Canal is not sleeping at night! I remember from the satellite images, I must pass some outer islands on the left, as they are connected to the mainland via a causeway without a passage. I float past a small marina. A lot of the sailboats and yachts are poorly lit, and I nearly collide with the first boat in a dark corner. This massive amount of light all over the canal, harbors and city is extremely confusing. With every dark object appearing, even if it has a few corner lights, I first must figure out what is ahead of me - a dangerous game!

The entrance to the actual canal is bright lit, with red and green lights on both sides. I better stay well outside the shipping lane. Twice, two massive tankers move past me like a massive ghost ship in slow motion, but not in my danger zone. At the side, another pilot boat almost runs me over. But I expected him to cross my path. An earlier boat did the same, and I tried to quickly paddle off to the side.

I hurriedly shine my strong flashlight at him, and get as a reply a beam which nearly blinds me. They shout something across which does not sound like a compliment. Sorry boys, but I am allowed to paddle in this area off the main shipping lane, and you should pay better attention. My red and green position lights are according to regulations. But...just in case, being right does not help me much. The stronger boat sets the rules here...

On my way to the Yacht club, I paddle close to the causeway. Disregarding all the different lights around me, the dam itself appears pitch black. Suddenly, two particularly bright search lights like from a UFO (Unknown Floating Object...) irritate me badly. I nearly get stuck in the mud in a shallow water area just in front of the Yacht harbor. They must be from yet another one of the giants of the oceans sailing inside the canal, secretly and slowly appearing from behind the many yachts at anchor. For me, this feels like a ghostly carnival ride, alone in the darkness in a tiny floating device, with a sea of confusing lights of slow and massive or fast water crafts around. The Pacific says, "Good bye" in a unique way. I am happy this ocean is behind me. I have neither been seriously trashed in the surf, run over, kidnapped nor robbed, and I am still alive and in one piece. It could have been a different story on so many occasions!

Chapter 12
PANAMA CANAL TO
THE CARIBBEAN

Panama Canal to Colombia
March 14th - May 6th, 2013

The white beaches of the Caribbean, the muddy deltas of the rivers of the Amazonas region, and the endless Brazilian coast are ahead, until I get back to where I started from...Buenos Aires!

I need a permit to go through the Panama Canal in my kayak. Despite the help of the German Embassy and my contacts in the Navy, I have received no word. So far, no permit for a sea kayak has ever been issued.

In the Yacht club, I meet Peter and Barkley, who may be able to help me with my necessary paperwork. Barkley is one of the pilots who must be on board on each ship sailing the canal. He has passed through countless times, and can give me many helpful hints. Peter promises to make further contacts within the canal authority. I hope to have the document in my hands before the press conference, which is organized by the German embassy and my host, Hennie of "Paddle Panama". I hope I could announce, I am able to continue without a gap!

The press conference is getting closer, and I still have no reply from the authorities. I am getting impatient, even though there are still many chores to do. I buy provisions for the next three weeks, and I am delighted about the varied offerings in the supermarkets, a real difference to the past weeks! I can get pretty fed up with certain foods, if that is all I get to eat day after day. I have occasionally dumped supplies, just because I got sick of it. It is also important for everything I buy not to melt in the heat in these latitudes.

After the press conference, nothing keeps me in town any longer. I set off without a permit, and hope I can at least sneak through the natural waters of the canal. I deeply regret I must leave out the exciting large locks, and the inaccessible narrow man-made concrete canal section. But at least, I save a minimum of $800 of fees I might have to pay to obtain the permit for the passage of the canal in a kayak! Well, that is if they would have issued me that document at all.

I launch at a boat ramp near Gamboa, fifteen miles after the first locks, and pass under a bridge into the canal region. I will have to cross the shipping lane five times to travel the shortest and most sheltered route to Rio Chagres. From there, it is a clean line to the Caribbean!

I fight against a wind of twenty knots. Other paddlers might have turned around...but what was it one blog reader called me? "She's a lean, mean paddling machine..." Tim and Barkley are in their fishing boat nearby. Barkley as a canal pilot has an official license to drive on the canal, and should the canal police catch up with me, we could load the kayak on his boat.

The canal is not beautiful yet. There are many pipelines and ugly storage facilities and factories along either muddy or man-made banks. After seven miles, the channel widens, and leads through a big lake, where the beautiful natural section is starting to reveal itself. We cross back and forth to find the most sheltered path. It is seriously busy, and many enormous ships are on their way. These ocean giants leave only a small gap for me, when they come close to the mangroves on the banks. But if I stay behind the line of the buoys of the main shipping lane, I am all right. The bow waves of the ships and the small surf they create on the banks are not a problem, but the headwind is a pain! Only once we get to the "Banana Channel" to the right side of a maze of smaller islands, I can get a bit of shelter. There is some danger of submerged trees in this natural world, as this lagoon was only created when the canal was flooded.

Tim and Barkley are relaxed, and pull out their fishing rods, but I am getting fed up crisscrossing in this headwind. For the last time, we cross the main shipping lane and reach the overflow of Rio Chagres in a twenty-five knots side wind and cross waves coming from all directions. This really is not fun!

The lower section of the river is separated from the canal by a dam with a lock where we must carry my kayak over. There is hardly any current, but still a lot of wind!

Frightened to death, I listen to a spooky, muffled scream. Is someone being murdered? No, these must be howler monkeys in the jungle I have heard about, but this is the first time I am hearing them. I cannot see any of these primates, they are all well covered. A few small crocodiles slide into the water from the banks as I pass their resting places. Thankfully, they are not aggressive like the saltwater crocodiles I met in Australia. But going for a swim is no clever idea!

Finally, the river flows into the Caribbean Sea. Done! On the right side of the river mouth, near Fort San Lorenzo, is a slipway for boats. The wild beach on the left side looks far more tempting and quiet for the night. The weather does not yet behave: The forecast is for two-yard high waves and headwinds of up to eighteen knots - marginal, but doable. It starts to rain, but that should not stop me. The conditions cannot be so bad, once I get out of the river mouth into the open sea, right? I should have known better...

On my launch, a mean wave fills my cockpit. I empty my kayak with my sponge, adjust my rudder fin and paddle out to the open sea. But the further I get out, the higher and more chaotic the waves become. I hardly make any headway, and get frustrated. The next suitable landing is far beyond the canal exit. I have doubts, if I can cross the canal entrance fast enough to avoid the ships, and to still arrive in daylight.

My personal swell height limit in the Pacific was around four yards. I must realize, the Caribbean is different, the predicted wave height does not come in rolling calm and slowly, with a long amplitude, like an elevator going up and down. Here, the two-meter waves are short, chaotic, and with the wind breaking them on top.

Altogether, the unfamiliar wave length, the strong headwind, me being weakened by yesterday's tough paddle, two nights with little sleep, and the prospect of the dangerous canal exit with its lively shipping traffic, makes me turn around for the first time since Isla Hornos in Chile...after less than a mile! I paddle back to the shelter of the river mouth, and decide to land on the other side. I only need to survive until Portobelo from breaking waves without wind shelter, after that, I can mostly carry on in a much more relaxed style in the protection of many reefs.

For tomorrow, the outlook is for less wind and lower waves, and I will just have to try again. This time more rested, and with better conditions. I will conquer the Caribbean also!

With replenished strength and a quiet night, I manage to cross the canal exit and Bahia Los Minos. At the end of the bay, I hope to reach one of the small picturesque islands. I have only done twenty miles, but I feel I need another rest day to recuperate completely. The tiny secluded beach I land on seems ideal for this purpose. But I am expected by the banes of my beach life - sandflies! I must hustle to pitch my tent, shower, and dump the luggage inside without opening the doors too long. I need to go out once more to put a black blanket on the tent to protect it from the worst of the sun. The sweat pours down in rivers without me even moving. But it is better to sweat in the tent, than to get bitten by the millions of sandflies outside!

My next stop should be in Portobelo. Once out of the lee of the two islands which have offered me some shelter, the waves are high again. Under these conditions, I will not make much progress. I only see three sailing yachts on the horizon, but that changes rapidly as I get closer to Portobelo. At least a hundred international yachts are at anchor in the bay, all poised to explore the beauty of the San Blas Archipelago. Just opposite of the bay of Portobelo is a small white beach, which looks perfect for the night. But as I get closer, I see that "my" beach is populated with many day trippers taken there by excursion boats. Will that change by sundown?

Soon the beach is mine alone. For the first time in the Caribbean, I enjoy a bath in the lukewarm sea and head out for a snorkeling trip. Later, I watch fascinated an endless row of leaf cutter ants transporting sections of foliage larger than their own bodies. I hope, they do not think my tent is suitable construction material, and dismantle it around me!

If I were to be asked later, which section of my trip was the hardest, I would answer, "The Caribbean", despite all the wonderful beaches and islands which look for millions of holidaymakers like the fulfilment of their dreams. Why? The continuous headwind breaks my average travelling speed down to two miles per hour, and I can only manage twenty miles per day instead of my usual thirty-five. To reach my next stop in Cartagena, I must calculate twice the time and divide up my provisions. The bites of millions of sandflies, and the permanent sweating, even at night, in these sauna temperatures, cause painful skin problems. A cooler wind blows by 3am, but I cannot ventilate the tent properly due to the sandflies. If the wind freshens up during the day, it brings a bit of a cool down, but also harder paddling. I am longing to have dry skin again, and contemplate to check into a hotel with air conditioning in El Porvenir. But the forecast is for low winds and low waves. I must take advantage of that to make progress.

Soon my mood gets better again. The Caribbean and its inhabitants show their most beautiful side. A short stopover in Palmira with its friendly folks, and I reach the first islands of the San Blas Archipelago. I leave behind the small cays by El Porvenir, as they are too densely inhabited, and make straight for one of the San Blas Islands. It does not take long, before I meet some of the indigenous inhabitants of the region. A few Kuna people come towards me in their dug-out canoe, not paddling, but propelled by a small outboard. Civilization has struck here also, and is making people lazy and looking for convenience. "Guys, stick to paddling, like I do"!

The islands, reefs, and the shores lined with mangroves and palm trees are fascinating. Among the four-hundred islands of the archipelago, I have free choice. I decide for the next smallest one, but I am blocked by the reef, and must continue to another one. Here, the landing is easy.

There are a few huts at the other end of the island; I need to ask permission to stay here. About 45,000 indigenous inhabitants live on the San Blas islands. The short-statured Kuna live in a matriarchal society, which gives me a good feeling. My first meeting on their islands with an old lady and a young girl is a warm and welcoming one. The girl speaks Spanish, so I ask if I could camp on the beach for a night. Both nod. Shortly after, the man of the family appears, and offers me a half-ruined hut for a few dollars for the night, or I could take some photos of him for a few dollars. But I thankfully decline. When the tender of a yacht starts to come over for snorkeling in the reef, we have a little chat, and the "yachties" invite me over for dinner on their boat. I have already set up camp, and do not like to leave it unattended for a long time, so I also thankfully decline.

Shortly after, the Kuna man, who a moment ago went off happily with my signature card, returns. Now he is asking for ten dollars - for permission to stay the night. Ten dollars? I am here in a small kayak, not a mega yacht. I explain to him, I already have permission from his wife and daughter, and they did not ask for money.

The world around me is becoming increasingly like paradise. The further I enter Kuna territory, the less yachts I see. I pass picturesque islands, embedded in incredible beautiful reefs. Right in front of me rises a tiny coral islet with two palm trees, just like you see them in cartoons about people being stranded on a lonely island. It would be a wonderful place to camp, but at second glance, I think it is way too close to the densely inhabited island next to it. I carry on.

The second isle I am aiming for is just as idyllic as the first, with a white sandy beach and a palm grove promising cool shade. At the last minute, I see a hut and a laundry line with a solitary towel. The owner might turn up in the evening. On to the next paradise island! I do have a choice of many. The third island also looks like a setting for a "Bounty" advertisement, but the palm grove is missing. It is boiling hot, with not even a breeze of a wind. No surprise this one is not inhabited.

It is just before 3pm, and I am contemplating doing another seven miles before I see it: My personal little paradise island! It measures about fifty by fifty yards, with no sign of habitation. The next islands with villages are far away enough. The isle is surrounded by a grandiose coral reef, and the open palm grove offers shade, as well as a cooling breeze which passes through the trees. It still is early in the day, but other islands I can see on the horizon seem to be edged with mangroves and a few yachts at anchor. I stay here, and will treat myself to a real Robinson Crusoe day, with swimming, snorkeling and relaxing.

I have started to empty the kayak when a motorized Cayuco comes toward "my island". Three indigenous men proudly present me their catch of the day. A squid, two lobsters and a few enormous conches. When they hear where I come from and what I am doing, they are quite impressed. We chat and laugh, and I sign a few cards for them. I ask for their names, and pull out a small list with words in Kuna, and I win over their sympathy. As a sign of their appreciation, they present me with one of the pretty conches. As they set off, I hope they will not spread the word about me camping on the island. I really would like to be alone, and to savor the Robinson Crusoe feeling! My campsite is the ideal spot for a good sleep. Shady, cool, yet away enough from the coconut palm trees. A ripe nut drops down like a small bomb, if I get hit, it can be dangerous!

The boys have not been quiet about who they met on this island. Next day, another Cayuco with a sail instead of a motor arrives. The owner of the island, Alfredo, dressed in gum boots in this heat, comes to have a look as to what is happening on his property. These islands do not belong to the whole Kuna tribe, but to individuals. They have added income by collecting a small fee when tourists make a pit stop. He is as polite and friendly as the three young men from yesterday, and lets me stay on his island without payment. An old school paddler, he has great appreciation of my achievement when I tell him about my circumnavigation. We are chatting with hands and feet. Alfredo is fifty-three years old, has five daughters and one son. His children get on well with modern society, there are computers in school, and he proudly says, the Kuna people are not primitive natives any more since quite some time. They have good reception for cell phones, and one of the islands has a small air strip.

Alfredo sails back to the main island where he lives with his family, and I use the rest of the day for a snorkel trip, and I am exploring of my tiny territory. At one end of the island, I notice an old fireplace, and there is too much flooded up trash everywhere. Being a typical German, I tidy up all the rubbish into a neat pile close to the fire pit, and hope Alfredo will be pleased about this little favor. Now the island looks once again like a virgin paradise, just as if no one has ever set foot on it. Alfredo might one day bring a large trash bag, and take care of the rubbish properly, or at least burn it! I hope...

I spend two refreshing nights on my Robinson Island. It is cool enough to sleep well with the wind rustling in the palm trees, as if rain was falling. Even my maltreated skin has recovered a bit. I am on a 110-degree course sidewind, but the annoying wind is pushing me for a change to go with the flow. I will pay later when I get closer to the mainland, but at least, I can make good distance now. I pass many more paradise islands, but mine from yesterday was simply perfect. Two villages around an airport disgorge new loads of tourists on their way to hotel islands. Some are along my path, but with the dense population, I am not tempted to land. I stick to a friendly wave, which gets a reply from the people.

Slowly, the islands disappear, and I orientate myself again along the coast of the mainland. The further I get to the area of Kuna villages, the simpler and more primitive the huts and hamlets become. In between the palm leaf huts, very few modern buildings stick out, schools, churches or military bases. The Cayucos become simpler, only a few use engines or sails. Near one village without satellite dishes or phone masts, I get into the middle of a whole fleet of these hollow tree trunks, each of them manned by two teenagers. It seems to be a class how to handle these traditional craft while fishing, as each boat trawls a line. For me as a "gringa", it is like a kayak symposium on the water, in Cayucos!

On my way through the Gulf of Uraba, two Islands offer me a place for a night. All goes according to plan, but my skin is badly affected. Sweat, saltwater, and the countless bites from sandflies have turned me into an alien. Especially my lower legs are one open wound. I am now walking on the beaches with long pants, tucked in neoprene socks, as many small biters are hidden in the sand. I cannot sleep for hours on end, due to the itching. My calves are raw from having rubbed them, the scratching attacks drive me crazy at night. I found, the rough side of Velcro does the best job...strong cortisone cream is the only ointment soothing it at least for a while.

I long for a climate without sandflies, and even more for my next break with air condition, when I get to the Colombian border in two days' time - if such luxury is available in this region. But first, I must find a village called Puerta Obaldia. This is where I am to collect my exit stamp for Panama. Another country off my list for this circumnavigation!

I am not sure, if Puerto Obaldia is the village at the end of the bay, or the one I have passed three miles ago. I check my GPS chart and my paper map, and decide to trust the GPS. As I come closer, I see two houses, one could be the "Senafront" building of the passport authority. But as I feared, the last village before the border is NOT Puerto Obaldia. Too bad!

I speak to one of the soldiers on watch in the "Senafront office", and explain my problem. But this station of the coast guard does not have any boats. I would have to find one of the regular shuttles for the trip back to the correct village to get my stamp. Not to worry, for ten dollars I hop into one of the water taxis.

The ride does not take long, and I get my exit stamp quite quickly, bar the fact that the driver of my boat likes to stay, and to drink one beer after the other. But I like to go back to my kayak as fast as possible! I want to paddle around the last headland to Colombia today, the local coast guard is waiting for me! I must organize a different lift, preferably on the cheap.

I speak to a friendly guy at the beach who does know someone with a boat willing to take me back to my kayak. But he charges thirty dollars. A few hours ago, that seemed expensive to me, but now, I just want to be gone. Quickly the deal is done, and we take off.

We return just before 5pm. I will need an hour to get around the headland. I like to do that today, were it not for the bureaucracy! The soldier in the coast guard office thinks, I should go to another office a mile away to do a bit more paperwork. "More paperwork? What for?" I ask indignantly. All is done, all the stamps I need are in my passport! The man insists, but I let him know I do not believe him. The guy in the second office who is supposed to do the paperwork gets to feel my wrath. Really, everything he does is superfluous. He has a look at my passport, checks if I really have the correct stamp, and paints senseless doodles on a piece of paper. Finally, he leans back with a broad grin, and says, "Everything is ok, but you can only leave tomorrow morning."

I beg your pardon??? Why?

"It is too late to leave today, you will need at least three hours to paddle around the headland." "I will need ONE hour!" I am getting thoroughly angry; the Colombian Navy is waiting for me, I will leave today, and just right now! "So far, the gentlemen from Senafront have been very helpful", I grumble, fed up.

"No", he says. "You are not allowed to leave until tomorrow. First, you must have a meal in the restaurant, then to stay a night in one of the hotels".

Aha, that is what it is all about! It might be his brother who runs the restaurant and the hotel. I get louder and louder, until he realizes I really mean to leave right now. Irritated about he must "fight" with a strong woman, he slams my passport on the desk and releases me.

I lose no time to pack my gear, and push the kayak into the water. Headwind and waves are demanding work, but I am in just the right mood to conquer this challenging headland with its reflecting breakers to make some distance. All I need is to be gone from Panama!

A ship of the Colombian coast guard signals me, and I enter the new "old" country. A few guys of the crew give me a cheery wave. It almost feels like I am coming home! My well-known, polite men of the Colombian Navy take me to a simple hostel, where they also go to rest. This village does not have a Navy station where one we spend the night. I have learnt to value the hospitality of the many "Hotel Naval" before!

This hostel has a bunch of huts made from tree trunks. Unfortunately, there are gaps between the trunks, through which one can see. But worse, they let the mosquitos and flies slip in when I turn on the light, which I cannot totally avoid. At least I can enjoy a cold shower, but no air condition. The breeze of the ventilator keeps mosquitoes and heat partially at bay during the night, but after 2am, electricity quits working, and I suffer. It is raining all night, but luckily, the roof is waterproof. In comparison to my tent, this accommodation is not really an increase in comfort. My bitten itchy skin is not able to recover in these conditions, but I appreciate the effort of the Colombian Navy to look after me.

Just like in Panama, the office issuing the stamps for my passport is not in the small border village. Next morning, my Navy men drive me to the town of Carpurgana. I prepare for a wet journey, pack my electronics and passport into waterproof bags, and stow them into my rucksack. I wear shorts and t-shirt, not only due to the warm tropical rain, but because the driver of the small Navy boat only knows one way to travel - top speed! My passport business is quickly done, I change the last of my dollars into Colombian pesos and recharge my SIM card. As I expect to make significantly slower progress in the prevailing headwind, I buy some more provisions, just to be on the safe side.

I am happy to drive out to the big supply ship "Cartagena de Indias", where my companions came from. I would like to have a talk with Captain Castagnera about the next steps of my journey and its safety aspects. This part of Colombia also has its dangers. The supply ship is the sister of the "Buenaventura", where I was briefly hosted on the Pacific side of Colombia. This ship too is of German origin, and was once called "Lüneburg".

The driver of our small boat shows his maneuvering skills. Due to the heavy swell, it is not easy to get close to the big ship. But we manage to attach a rope that holds us close enough to the "Cartagena de Indias" to get hold of the wobbly rope ladder, and I can climb up the massive grey steel wall.

Captain Castagnera welcomes me warmly on board. On the bridge, we discuss the options for the next days. The threat from drug smugglers and the FARC rebels is not as high as on the Pacific side, but should still not be underestimated. I would be more than welcome to spend the next nights on board of his ship, while I head to Cartagena, supervised by his men in the small boat during the day.

OK, I had enough taste of "freedom" the past few weeks in tropical Panama, and thoroughly enjoyed it. But the price for freedom on the beaches is the horrible condition of my skin, with dozens of insect bites and being permanently soaked in saltwater and sweat. The outlook of swapping freedom for security, an air-conditioned and dry place to sleep, and a proper shower in the evening, is tempting. Better sleep equals more miles, an easy formula. My heavy luggage would be on the boat that keeps me company, an added relief when fighting the wind and waves.

We drive back to the hostel in Cabo Tiburon to pack my stuff, and I paddle my kayak to the supply ship. Even though it is only three miles, I fight confused waves of up to two yards high, and headwind of eighteen knots. How am I supposed to get on board the "Cartagena de Indias" from my kayak"?

As slow as possible, I approach the tender of the coast guard from behind. The swell is big, everything must happen fast, so that neither I, nor the kayak, get squished. With some effort, good timing, and many helpful hands, I manage to jump on board. Now, only my kayak needs to be pulled up. As it is not loaded, my men manage that job quickly. All what's left is to get my luggage, my kayak and myself up on the decks of the "Cartagena de Indias".

The luggage is easy, each piece is pulled up quickly through the ten yards high wall without any plunging back to sea. I was supposed to climb up the rope ladder next, but I wanted to know my kayak was safe first. We had to move to the lee side of the supply ship. The kayak is tied into two loops, and off my loved baby goes on its journey through the air up to the high deck. What an effort! Up on the deck myself, my legs are still trembling from excitement.

I am offered to share a cabin with the only two female officers, Diana and

Paola. As both speak good English, we can have a good laugh. The rolling ship makes me seasick, the whole afternoon, I need to spend lying down in the cabin. At least, my skin is recovering in the air-conditioned room. Two more days, and it will be much better. I make some pictures of the worst bits, but my boyfriend Peter does not "allow" them on my website, too much naked skin, he says...

For six nights, I live like a VIP guest on this massive supply ship. Eighty men are at my disposal, until the ship gets another, more important task, and I must "make do" with a small one again. Many thanks for the exquisite hospitality! As we say good bye, the crew poses for an impressive picture in a half circle on the helicopter deck, and another picture is taken with the ship's football team, in German shirts! I give a handstand as an encore... and say good bye!

Since the bay of Uraba, the landscape has changed significantly. Small reefs and long strewn beaches dominate the mainland. I have not seen larger animals for quite some time, and am searching in vain for fishing boats and small villages. The last days, I have gladly put up with the exhausting difficult transfers by tender to the big Navy ship, which navigates miles away from the coast. Today, a new larger ship where I can spend the night in comfort, is waiting thirteen miles offshore, near Isla Fuerte. On board of the "Cabo Tiburon", I am supposed to share the cabin with the captain and the first officer. I am wondering what this happy threesome would offer, and I am surprised... both are women! Captain Liliana and her second in command, Paola, greet me. The captain ladies and her twelve crew men will escort me the next three days to Cartagena.

The closer we get to the city, the larger the houses become on the mainland. To shorten my trip, I use the Canal de Dique. It saves me time going around the wide peninsula, and I might get to the city before nightfall. With the company of many waving fishermen in Cayucos, I glide across some shallow water into the channel. I am not sure if I lost my Navy guards unintentionally, or if they did not dare to take on the Canal, as the water may be too shallow for them. After a few miles, I see a different, smaller Navy boat coming towards me from the other end. It still looks oversized in this narrow side arm. Cartagena has simply sent another boat to escort me into town.

Oh, talking about canals: A few days ago, I finally got a reply to my request to paddle through the Panama Canal with my kayak. The German Embassy has been waiting for weeks for the reply of the canal administration. My request was refused, as it would be "too dangerous" to use my kind of craft due to the lively traffic and the active dredgers that are widening the canal. But like the tale of the hare and the hedgehog, "I am already here".

I realize again that the friendly support of the Colombian Navy is not to be taken for granted, neither my nights on board their ships, nor the official reception in Cartagena with a rendition of their national anthem. Ok, I admit, my honors do not stretch as far as the latter, but I just arrive by chance as it is played for the daily take down of the Columbian flag, including a saluting line of officers dressed in white uniforms.

On the Navy base, I am given the apartment of Commander Hernando Mattos, who does not need it much as he lives with his family in town. The hospitality and help on the Atlantic side of Colombia mirrors my good experiences on the Pacific. Commander Mattos is the Caribbean counterpart of Commander Delgado on the Pacific side. I will meet him tomorrow to discuss the continuation of my tour.

I am looking forward to meeting an online friend from Kiel in Germany in person. Uli Diekmann emigrated to Cartagena four years ago, to supervise the repair of submarines for the Colombian Navy built by the HDW shipyards of Kiel. In care of his address, I have been sent some parcels and mail from Germany.

Uli meets me next morning at 10am, and it is nice to have a conversation in my own language once again. He is super helpful, takes me everywhere, and acts as interpreter when I meet with Commander Mattos. The coast guard has prepared an amazing presentation, with which they explain the topography of the upcoming section, and warn me of the tricky areas.

Unfortunately, they can no longer offer comfortable accommodation on their frigates, they now have other tasks, likely to intercept drug boats? I must sleep again in my tent on land, or on one of the smaller boats they would send up to meet me from the various stations along the way.

It turns out, that Commander Mattos and his men are not so worried about me getting robbed or kidnapped. The region I am entering now is quite safe, although some German tourist have recently been kidnapped near the Venezuelan border. They are far more worried about what could happen to me while I paddle; I might drown or capsize, but THAT, to be honest, is the least of my worries. I have respect, but not fear for the upcoming large river outflows. And if the sea is too rough, I simply have a break and wait it out in a boat, on land, or in one of their Navy stations along the way to Venezuela. How is that a problem?

But first, I would like to enjoy Cartagena's delights. Uli takes me around all the sights and the old town, I could not ask for a better guide. He has done this guiding already to many of his visiting friends, and knows all the special places, including a fifteen-yard high mud volcano north of town. On the way there, I get a sneak peek at the beaches I will be passing in the coming days.

But far more important are shopping and food. Uli is helping to transport the many provisions. I have an incredible appetite for things I have been missing the last few weeks. I gulp a large baguette with a whole Camembert, blueberries, physalis, passion fruit and a pineapple. Once again, I find my favorite sweet, a heat resistant type of "white chocolate", made from coconut, milk powder and sugar, which I first discovered in Ecuador.

I allow myself to buy a few long beach dresses in the old town center. My sporty figure can glam up a bit at times. Uli is so kind to take them with him to Germany on his next trip home, that I do not have to lug them about in my kayak. Next morning, I am off again!

At 5am, Uli and a chap from the Navy pick me up. We just need to carry my kayak across the road, and I am ready to be off. A coast guard boat takes my luggage. The sea is calm, there is barely a breeze, and I make satisfactory progress. Soon the wind is freshening up to first ten, then fifteen and in the end twenty knots. Of course, it is a headwind. It is only 11am, but I do not like to carry on. I signal the boat to pick me up.

I have selected Punta Piedra, just over a mile away, as my next stop, but either the men or I misunderstood something, or my GPS data is faulty. We are heading straight out to sea! The little boat jumps harder and harder on the increasing waves, and two guys need to hold onto my kayak which only rests lightly on two barrels of petrol. Will the driver go as far as Ensenada Amanzaguapo? That would be seventeen miles away, as far as I have paddled today. One might as well go back to Cartagena for the night! A few times, I am tempted to stop the boys and try to head for land by myself. But that is impossible, as the sea is too rough. The only possibility is to carry on. If only one of the engines had not conked out an hour ago...

The driver does his best to steer the boat parallel to the waves. That reduces the jumping and slam downs, but we regularly get a cold shower from the side. The water pump runs continuously to empty all the water out. Everything on board is wet. One of the guys holding onto my boat urgently needs a pair of sunglasses, to protect his eyes from the saltwater. The driver throws some over to him, but they end in a high arc in the water. I carefully give him mine, and he barely has put them on when he falls asleep, whilst holding the kayak in his arms.

If the second engine was to fail, we would be helpless in these waves and without being able to steer the boat, drift towards land. We can only hope to get out, before it smashes on the cliffs. For over an hour now, we battle wind and waves, where do the guys plan to go to for the night? I really need to get off this tub, not only because I cannot bear the slam downs any longer, but also because I start to worry about the state of my kayak. And to imagine I need to sleep here at night?

I am not keen on this kind of Navy help anymore, I like to be back to myself! I will paddle close to the coast, so I can make landfall anytime. There is no shortage of suitable beaches. If only the weather was not so contrary and unpredictable. With some difficulties, we reach a beach where the waves seem a bit less powerful. I quickly pack my kit and let my kayak into the water. As I get in, I bang so hard against the side of the tender I nearly capsize. I have not noticed we turned to the wind side on during the maneuver. A fat wave fills my cockpit with water, but I have neither time nor inclination to pump it out. Maniacally, I work myself through the last 500 yards with a flooded cockpit to the beach. At last, I have done it... I have landed! And I am by myself again.

Next day, I tell my companions that I would like to land and camp on my own each evening, as the situation on land seems to be much safer than on the Pacific coast of Colombia. I get the feeling they are glad to hear this, it gives both sides some independence.

The boss of the coast guard in Cartagena suggests, I might paddle at night, when wind and waves are less strong. I try to start as early as possible the next two days on my way to Barranquillo. Throughout the night, I check, if the wind has calmed down, and if it is light enough to paddle. No moon is to be seen, and only a few stars fight through the morning mist. Or is that even smog? I have noticed the people try to burn their rubbish in the early morning hours; I assume, the industrial center of Barranquillo is not far now. Or is air pollution the reason for the poor visibility? Today, I need to start at Punta de la Garita in a northerly direction, as the swell of up to two yards can quickly build up. I start at 5.30 am, but must stop for the day already after four and a half hours, the wind has breezed up that strong. My kayak is heavy, as it is stowed with all the fresh provisions. I just need to eat and drink more to make it lighter!

I feel safe on the Caribbean coast of Colombia with camping on the beaches. The continuous wind is the only problem, as it covers me and my tent with sand. My encounters with people are nice and relaxed, be they beach wardens, policemen, or a gang of teenagers having a party at the beach. Their curiosity turns to respect and admiration when they read the signature cards about my mission. The Navy keeps their distance, and usually anchors out at sea and does not watch me day and night.

During this last short night, I dreamt the next big challenge, crossing the mouth of Rio Magdalena, was already behind me. But this was only a dream. As opposed to the last three days, the wind has not calmed in the early morning hours, so there is little sense in leaving before daybreak. At half past seven, it blows fifteen knots into my face, and it is likely to strengthen during the day. That is just right for a bull-headed Taurus like me. Defiantly, I fight forwards, and manage at least a ridiculous twelve miles in five and a half hours. By 11am, I am already heading for the next landing spot, which is only four miles to the river mouth. The current of the Rio Magdalena is supposed to be strong, the best time to go around it is early in the morning when the wind is lowest. The alternative would be to use the canals inland, as another paddler from Venezuela on his way to Panama did. But the prospect of the broiling heat and dubious characters living along the canals make me forget that idea. I will simply wait another day, and then crossover this obstacle. The Navy recommends giving the river mouth a wide berth, as the waves created when river current and sea meet are gigantic. Would that be the correct decision? I did not know any better at that time...

Just like yesterday morning, the escort boat is waiting for me. With a headwind of fifteen knots, I paddle out to sea, far away from the outflow. After two and a half miles in the ever increasing and confusing cross waves, I reckon to be far away enough off the current of the river, and try to get closer to land again. All around me are towering breakers from brown walls of river water. I can hardly hear the motor of the escort boat in the crashing of the breakers. From the distance, I notice the boat keeps crashing with a bang on the surface of the water, and the men let the engine howl to go over a wave with better timing. I fear, they must feel dreadful. They suffer more than me in my kayak. I wrap myself around the waves and dance with them, and find it quite exiting to be challenged by these conditions! The boys are a toy of the elements in the boat with too slow a speed for its size and weight. As they want to stay close to me, they cannot take the waves with high speed in a gentle manner.

I am still full of energy to carry on, but the boys signal to me to turn around. I beg your pardon? Why, am I not paddling towards the correct destination? Are we not making progress? Slowly but surely... Later I find out that my guesses were correct: Three of the four young guys were horrendously seasick, and all but the driver had to throw up. More than once, they were afraid they would capsize. As opposed to me, they would not be able to just roll up again in such a boat, and would have gone for a swim. Well, once again, this proves that the threshold of an experienced sea kayaker is higher than those of a small motorboat. So, what is the use of an escort boat against the "danger from the waves"? I can do better paddling just by myself. If I were to get into trouble, my "rescuers" would already be well there!

I am a bit annoyed, but play nice, and release the poor boys of their fate…tomorrow is another day. I signal I am willing to come aboard to them. We must have the kayak and escort boat parallel, with both their nose into the wind and the breakers coming from the front, to do the jump over and loading as kayak as fast as possible. If we had the wind and waves from the side, we would end up with one boat on top of the other, not really a desirable arrangement.

Several times, the escort boat is turned by the heavy waves and drifts off. This is not going to work, boys! Do you even know how to do this takeover? I try to direct them with yells and gestures, and keep my nose into the wind at the same time. I dread to think how they would act if I really were to get into trouble at some point. They abort the first attempt, and I paddle on the spot, bow straight into the wind. After five minutes, the boat comes closer again, this time they manage to stay parallel. Three men line up at the side where they want to pull my kayak up. I throw my paddle over and give one of them my bowline to secure the kayak, while I pull myself up and over to the boat. Now to the kayak, two of the guys are too far at the stern, and the kayak slowly fills with water. It is becoming too heavy to lift! Only two guys and I are fighting with the kayak, the third man is vomiting once more over the railing. At the last minute, I grab the bowline he just let go. If I had lost my kayak here…

This technique is not going to get the kayak on board. I move the boys over to the bow, and three of us are pulling it over the edge on board, the worst way to do this. The hull can sustain severe damage this way. I do not notice any cracking noise as the waves must have swallowed the sounds.

But we have done the job, the boys are knackered. They head for the river mouth with the Navy station, and shoo a crocodile out of the thicket.

The guys resist the idea of playing the same game again tomorrow, and insist on a start beyond the river outflow. I must let the escort boat take me to a place from where my journey can continue - with a new crew and a new boat. My regular crew was responding to a sudden emergency. The new team does not seem to be totally enchanted by their task. I see two of the men making the sign of a cross as we leave. I can understand that, I feel similar as we race at forty miles per hour down the river to its mouth again. Out at sea, we keep an average speed of twenty mph, this short tour is an absolute horror trip for me.

Without glasses to protect my eyes from the salt water, I quickly go blind. All of us are clutching the sides, and try to bend in the knees to counter the impact of the boat as it speeds on the water, engulfed in a cloud of petrol and exhaust fumes. The nightmare continues, even after we have gone around the river mouth with six miles separating us. The driver speeds up to forty miles per hour, as we can see the mainland again. Why do they always have to go as fast as possible? Each time the boat crashes down behind a wave onto the water, my kayak is badly affected. We have tied it securely to some padding tires, but will this be enough to prevent damage? I scream, as if I am getting the injuries myself. Petrified, I let the horror happen. Dear God, I think, get me out of here, straight to Buenos Aires, and better still, straight home!

I wake out of my petrified state as I check the data on my GPS, and see it is high time to carry on again alone in my kayak. I escape the disgusting fuel cloud, and my seasickness calms down again. Almost happy, I paddle in the now much more quiet sea and can make some distance by myself again. After a few hours, I spot a suitable landing place with a solitary tree for shade. Unloading my stern hatch, at least two liters of water glug towards me. I empty the bow compartment, and water has also entered there. I turn the kayak over, and examine the hull. There is quite some damage! The outer coating at the stern has delaminated three hands wide down to the basic structure, and has soaked up water like a sponge. A bit more, and the kayak's tail would be softly hanging down. To make matters worse, I notice a long tear in the hull, bad enough to let a fair bit of water in. I stop looking, take some pictures, and wade over to the escort boat waiting for me. I show the pictures, and explain I cannot do the repairs here on the beach properly, we would better off going to Santa Marta. Said and done, we load kayak and luggage back on board.

In Santa Marta, two men start at once with the repair work on my kayak. As I check their progress the next day, I see that they have cleaned, dried and sanded down the affected areas, and filled them with mastic. Today, everything is covered with fiber glass matting, and sealed with epoxy resin from out of my supplies. When dry, we fill the kayak with water, to see if everything was successfully sealed.

I spend my time with computer work and small chores. Santa Marta is nowhere near as stylish and full of tourists as Cartagena, but even in the poorest quarters, cell phones and SIM cards are for sale at all corners.

Without my notice, the coastguard of Santa Marta has arranged an incredible welcome ceremony. The Navy guys parade to a press conference with a German translator, TV teams and photographers, while some girls of the local school perform a routine with flags and display a welcome banner with my name. A band plays traditional Colombian music, while a young man and a pretty girl in a wide skirt twirl around. I am meant to join them, but I feel uncomfortable dancing, I would like to wear one of the dresses I bought in Cartagena! But the coast guard asked me to paddle to the event, so I am only dressed in shorts and t-shirt. At least I dare to play some drums in the band!

Next morning, before sunrise, I am taken back fifteen miles to the spot I last stopped. This Navy boat is more comfortable, I can even take a nap before I am put back into the water. I paddle twenty miles, before I go back once more to the Navy station of Santa Marta. The forecast promises, the waves and winds will get lower. Will I be able to pass Cabo de la Vela in these conditions? The region between the Cape and the border of Venezuela is infamous for its high winds. Would I be able to cross the gulf of Venezuela like that?

My day starts at half past six in the morning. No wind yet, but I know that will change very quickly. With some effort, I fight my way through the narrow passage near Isla de la Aguja, and turn around the corner into the bay of Ensenada de Concho. I can take a breather in the lee, and have breakfast. But even in the large bays, there is no real shelter from the headwinds whipping up to twenty knots. Punta El Vigua, Punta de Changue, Punta de Gayraca - headland after headland, and bay by bay, I work myself along to make progress.

By 3pm, I have covered thirty-seven miles. There are no beaches to anchor, and we go back fifteen miles to find a little natural harbor. It is possible to take the boat all the way to the beach, and I have an easy job to unloading my luggage. I am looking forward to a night in my own four walls, and feel sorry my escorts must spend the night in the petrol stench on the boat.

To avoid the strong headwinds of the last few exhausting days, I want to use the calm night and start paddling from 1am until 10am, provided I get enough sleep during the day to have the energy for some night paddles.

However, before I continue, I must collect my exit stamp for Colombia in

Rio Hacha, and buy more provisions, which hopefully will last until the next large town in Venezuela.

At this point of my trip, I take a serious decision. The plan was to arrive on May 10th, 2014 in Buenos Aires, my 50th birthday. But I need to take the wind and water conditions as they are, and physically, I can do no more than I have done. I have planned to be in Georgetown, Guyana by now, but the contrary winds of this trip section are the reason I need another two months before I would be there in July. Then, I would only have four weeks to regenerate in Germany. And regeneration I really would need now!

I will split the rest of my journey into three more legs. This current section I will complete in two to three weeks at the border to Venezuela. Like last year, I will be back in Germany between May and August, and then carry on until Christmas 2013 as far as I will get. Next year's summer will be the last three-month wind and weather break which the climate requires.

When I have taken this decision to change my plans, I feel great relief. What is another year on this journey? I will simply arrive for my 51st birthday. The pressure of the schedule has lifted off my brain and body, while I have the prospect of an early recovery period. I am a bit worn by now. My mood is getting bad too quickly, when something does not work as planned, or when a bit of kit breaks. I am also getting sick of my provisions, and do not eat sensibly any longer. I am fed up with the heat and humidity, the skin problems coming along with it, and I am no longer in the mood to take many pictures.

I am still keen to paddle and like to be on the journey, but I need a longer break to recover from the strains, and to find new energy.

My flight home is booked: on May 8th, I am heading back to Germany. Just like last year, I will arrive home May 9th. Hopefully it is a good omen, though it was not planned this way.

Chapter 13
DETOUR TO TRINIDAD

Venezuela to Trinidad to Guyana
August 16th - November 8th, 2013

Back to job No.3... The last three and a half months, I have remodeled Job No.1, my two Janny's ice cream cafés, and Job No.2, the Christmas shop. It is middle of August, and the sea is calling. Venezuela, Trinidad, Guyana, Surinam, French-Guiana, Brazil, Uruguay - these are the next steps on the way back to Buenos Aires. In May, I finished the last section at the border between Colombia and Venezuela, and this is where I restart my trip.

When I leave the plane at the regional airport of Riohacha, the tropical heat and humidity hits me like a fist. A reception committee of the Colombian Navy is waiting for me, friendly and helpful as they were three months ago. Many thanks!

At top speed, we drive on the potholed roads back to Puerto Bolivar. I am back to the coalmine village, where I have spent the last days of May, and I live in the same house on the mining area. The next morning, we leave at 5am to go by boat to the place where I stopped. For five hours, I need to suffer a rough boat trip with the Colombian Navy once more, bending my knees to cushion the impact as we jump high waves. My kayak is well lashed down on good padding, and I stand next to the driver, with my eyes closed for protection against the saltwater spray. I experience this drive like an uncontrolled free fall. I hope, this last motorboat trip, wrapped in petrol fumes, will be over soon. After turning to a southern direction into the Gulf of Venezuela, we reach smoother waters. I can open my eyes again, relax my legs, and start to prepare mentally for paddling. Packing the kayak in twenty knots wind is a balancing act, but soon, I will sit again in my heavily laden boat, and look forward to taking off in the salty fresh air – alone!

After three months break, my muscles feel like chewing gum as I take the first paddle strokes. I also feel the fifteen pounds I added to my weight at home, somehow my rear does not yet fit the seat. I keep the kayak on course, and let myself drift with the wind in a southwesterly direction into the Gulf of Venezuela. I do not like to do more than twelve miles, due to the jet lag, the late start, and the exhausting boat ride. I spot an empty beach with some trees offering a bit of shade. A few bony sheep and goats graze near an abandoned fishing boat. I scare up two wild pigs, I am not sure who got the greater fright - the pigs or me! By afternoon, a pleasant cooling breeze comes up. I want to arrive in Maracaibo latest in four days' time. Until then, a few hours of demanding work on the water are waiting.

I was hoping to cross the Gulf of Venezuela at its narrowest spot with about sixty miles, but the prevailing easterly strong wind tells me, this is not a clever idea. From the other direction, I would have done it. The Gulf of Carpentaria in Australia was more than six times as wide! That one I have crossed without big buzz, eight days and seven nights alone on the water, sleeping in my kayak.

Next day, I manage thirty miles into the Gulf, but notice that I am far away from top form. Paddling in these bath tub conditions is not demanding, but the jet lag and heat reduces my performance. In the western corner of the Gulf, millions of mushroom-shaped, cauliflower-sized jellyfish have gathered. I have some difficulties working my way through this huge biomass - I would not want to be a fisherman here!

The surf has increased. I must go through a minefield of strong breaking waves, and some catch me sideways. I land with some issues after ten hours on the calmer corner of a lively beach. The breakers create a fear-inducing noise. It seems to be a popular Sunday afternoon beach; many young people drive up and down on their motor bikes. A car seems to wait for me as I arrive. Only at the second glance, I notice it is not the police or the coastguard. The driver sits in the vehicle, with its door open, and waves me over. As I march towards the dunes with my gear for the second time, he gets out, walks up to me and asks: "Do you need a driver?" I point at my kayak and tell him, this would be my preferred mode of transport. I put my bow line in his hand, and with a joint effort, we drag the kayak up the beach. The man later tries again to offer me his services, as the beach would be not safe, there would be too many doubtful characters. I only see the young men on their bikes, and I do not care about them.

The same boys annoy me during the night. I have hoped, the beach would be empty by dusk, but until 11pm, three of them are thundering about, shine their headlights directly at my tent, and start asking: "What are you doing here?" I like to carry on sleeping, and do not answer. Now, they start to pull out my tent pegs. No, not with me, boys! I become loud. They are surprised to hear a female voice, but do not give up. I take three signature cards and ask: "Who are you, what are your names and what are you doing here?" Either they did not expect this display of self-confidence, or they were satisfied with the cards. Fortunately, they head off.

Peace and silence is only for a short duration. About 1am, I hear more bikes coming towards my camp. This time, it is a group of four women and two men on two bikes, who must have been told by the earlier three who is camping on the beach. They demand loudly, "Photo, photo!" But all I want to do is sleep. One of the women tries to sneak a peek through the half open zipper of my tent. I shine my bright flashlight directly into her eyes, the girl squeals and runs, and the biker boys follow suit. You are to blame, you should not disturb my good night's sleep at 1am!

In two days, Gabriel in Maracaibo expects me. Our meeting spot is on the southern end of the Gulf of Venezuela, at Balneario Lago Mar. As I turn into the bay, the coast guard greets me with two bottles of ice cold mineral water. They want to escort me to Lago Mar…. "Because of the pirates…" Is the danger really that great that they must encircle me with six boats to shield me from harm? I feel honored, such an escort is normally reserved for the Prime Minister!

We celebrate my arrival with Gabriel, his family and friends with many enormous pizzas. But by 11pm, I am done in and must go to bed. There is a lot to do in the next days.

The Navy thinks it is not necessary to escort me day and night. Thank God… I get a list of coast guard stations where I could stay at night, and I have a widespread network of online kayaking friends who will care for me.

I see an enormous number of old US-American cruisers on the roads of Venezuela, which would not be allowed driving around in these dilapidated conditions anywhere else in the world. Here, they are a normal part of the chaotic traffic, where the strongest sets the rules. A liter of petrol costs less than a liter of clean drinking water!

Resupplying my provisions becomes a problem. There is not much available. Venezuela is a socialist country, and supplying the peoples' needs suffers from bottlenecks, just like in the old German Democratic Republic. On the other hand, some stuff is plentiful. But Gabriel knows secret sources, who can supply what is not in the shops, and I can carry on well stocked with all what I need. He also explains to me the difference between the official and unofficial money exchange rates...

An escort of fifteen paddlers takes me to the end of the Gulf. Once the Navy tender turns off, I am alone again. I go past flat beaches with low dunes with at least fifteen knots headwind. I can only manage eighteen to twenty-five miles per day, it would be much more pleasant to do these coastlines from east to west!

Other than a few pelicans, flamingos and a small school of dolphins, the sea surface of the sea is empty. I should reach Punta Fijo in two days' time. Gabriel found me a hotel in Punta Cardon free of charge. The hotelier lady would be happy to organize a health check on my rash, which developed from heat, humidity, and countless number of insect and mosquito bites. But no thanks, a cold shower, and staying in air conditioned, salt-free and dry air will serve to heal. Should I treat myself to a two-days stay?

The forecast promises low winds, and I stay only one day as I must make the most of that. Lonely beaches and orphaned coast roads besides me, I paddle bit by bit around this usually quite stormy peninsula without incidents. In the distance bray a few hungry donkeys. At the tip of the peninsula, I can spot Aruba on the horizon, one of the Caribbean islands so longed for by German tourists. For me, it is only a sign that I am making progress, despite the ongoing headwind, to finally reach the natural harbor of Puerto Escondido on the eastern side of the peninsula.

I hope to stay the night at the local coast guard station. I can see an aerial tower; the station must be near. As I scramble up the hill, I can see the aerial, but there is no house! A woman confirms there really is no coast guard station in this village. Shame, I will have to do without the shower I have been looking forward to! But the lady has a different idea. She invites me to pitch my tent in her back yard, and my shower is a water butt and a ladle - a delightful refreshment! The place she plans for my tent is almost perfect, too. Dry, shady and level...if it would be not for an ant runway!

The man of the house suggests pouring petrol on their paths, and I have the choice between a tent full of biting ants, or the stench of petrol. I find another place, away from the ant traffic and wind, and spend the night among the large family plus their many goats and chicken. I thankfully decline their offer to share their evening meal, telling my need for a special diet. I am not certain my guts could cope with their dishes. I hope I have not offended the hospitality of this family! I accept gratefully the offer to refill my water bags from their tank.

The family is so kind to help me carry my kayak and luggage down to the water, even though it is only shortly before 6am. By the growling of the morning thunderstorm, I slide through a reef gap to the open sea. The thick dark clouds deliver only little rain. The strong headwind drops a bit during the day, but I do not become faster. An unexpected current allows only a snail's pace of one to two miles per hour. The many ship wrecks tell their own tales of unpredictable currents and waves.

I paddle in a relaxed manner with open spray deck in moderate wind and waves, when suddenly a motorboat races past only 500 yards away from me. All other boats usually take notice and give a friendly wave, but this driver seems to be very much in love with the speed of his fast boat. A minute later, he turns around, and races straight towards me. I stop for a moment to estimate his path, then try to speed up to one side to avoid the collision. But he still seems to aim straight at me, sometimes swerving a bit more left, sometimes a bit more to the right. The bow points high up at top speed, and due to the adrenaline rush, probably also another part of the anatomy of the driver. When the blood leaves the brain...

I wave with my paddle vertical high up in the air, still no sign of turning off his path. I am close to jumping into the water, or at least roll over head down to protect my upper body. I reach for my loud whistle which I wear around my neck in case of emergencies such as this one, and in panic blow as hard as I can. The whistle is swallowed up by the howling engine sounds, and the boat comes closer at high speed. With a last desperate paddle stroke, I can just about escape the danger zone. Still, the speedboat scrapes fully over my stern! With a final effort, I manage to keep the kayak upright, as the wake catches me from the rear. FUCK YOU! All the testosterone and adrenaline seem to have shifted the already small brain into the trousers! The driver turns around, sees my raised middle finger and shouts something Spanish that really does not sound apologetic. I curse him further and shoo him with gestures off to the horizon.

Later, I discover red paint traces from the speedboat on my stern that reminds of the near-catastrophe I left behind. I have a very attentive guardian angel - or I am just plain lucky. On the way to Puerto Cumarebo, I calm down again, and enjoy the scenery. Long broad beaches with low lands behind are the past. Now, small green mountains rise on the horizon, and rocky reefs lie in front of the beaches. Suitable places to land during the day are becoming rarer. Tonight's landing is a bit tricky, I paddle carefully on a small wave over a flooded reef into a tiny rocky pool, where I can climb over more rocks to a grassy spot.

Next day, my endurance is rewarded: Like a mirage, the white club house of the Kayak Club of Cumarebo rises at the beach. About fifty people welcome me, even a TV crew films each moment of unloading the kayak. I can sleep at the house of Noelita, in a room with air-conditioning and fan, wellness for my tortured skin. Richard Colina, himself an experienced and successful race kayaker, has arranged a meeting with a group of youths who stand for their country in international kayak races. It is nice to talk with them, and to feel how my visit motivates them.

Letitia from Surinam, the only one who speaks English in the village, cares for me as an interpreter. Together with Noelita, we visit the local supermarket. I only buy fruit and water, as I still have enough food from what I brought from Colombia, and the offering here is very limited. I do not eat much in this heat anyway, which helps to slowly lose my surplus weight and to get back into shape.

With much less headwind than usual, I can pass the bays until Punta Zauro relaxed. But Venezuela has, next to Colombia, one of the highest rates of criminality of the southern continent, and I must stay on guard. In the last few days there were a few encounters with gentlemen whose intent was not clear.

At noon, I sit on my kayak on the beach and eat my snack. Not long after, a truck stops, and fifteen guys jump down and surround me. Hmmm, what do these dubious chaps want from me? They are not fishermen, despite a few nets and various utensils on the truck. I tell myself to stay calm. Thankfully, nothing tempting of my equipment lies about.

I take one of my Spanish signature cards I always keep handy, and approach the leader in the drivers' seat, smile nicely, and start a conversation in broken Spanish. What my name is, where I am from, what I do, then I ask who he is, if they would be fishermen, and whether he would like a signature card? The driver is perplexed by my chutzpah, gives me his name, and in a millisecond, he takes the signed card, whistles his men back on the truck, and they speed off. I think these "gentlemen" were a local gang collecting protection money in the fishing villages, and they reckoned, I might be an easy and interesting target. My heart is still racing, even when back on the water.

During another stay on a lonely beach which I selected for the night, a man suddenly jumps out of the shrubbery, begs for money to buy milk for his baby, and tells me that this is a place where the drug couriers transfer wares for the ABC-islands, Aruba, Bonaire and Curaçao. His whole demeanor makes me nervous, and I pack my stuff, move to a village and camp near the church.

Another time, after I have just congratulated myself for finding an idyllic beach on an outlying coral island, three young men unexpectedly turn up in a speed boat. They are obviously not fishermen! To stay in control of the situation, I take the offensive, and walk up to them. I talk friendly without being charming, congratulate them about their "stylish" haircuts, and tell them about my son of the same age as them. The motherly approach seems to work. Once I have pitched my tent and want to take my usual shower, I tell them with gestures, that now I would like my privacy. I seem to have gathered some respect, as the boys leave. Nonetheless, I stay alert the whole night, and listen for each engine sound that comes close to the beach. I sleep next to my still loaded kayak, just in case I get further visitors.

With light winds under ten knots, I manage a daily distance of over thirty miles to reach Chichirivice. Rio Tocuyo disgorges masses of brown river water into the sea. The sweet chocolate broth does not mix anytime soon near the coastline with the clear saltwater, and shows a clear border line.

The whole area is a nature reserve, but beaches are packed with holiday makers. I am fascinated by the shops with swim ware. The window dummies have enormous breasts of at least DD cups. I feel underdeveloped compared to all the XXL sizes everywhere. Even more irritating are the advertising placards on the roof tops of the beach shops. Women are depicted showing their rear ends in the tiniest bikini pants in an almost pornographic manner. Showing these in Germany would cause a traffic chaos, if not a notice of public indecency. Different countries, different customs. Venezuela is the country with the greatest number of international beauty queens, but also with the greatest number of cosmetic surgeons.

The network of kayak enthusiasts' functions fantastically well. I know in advance who will look after me at the next several stops: After Nelson and Annya in Chichirivice, and Christian and Cesar in Puerto Cabello, Antonio and Lucy will look after me in Caracas. I should receive my new boat: The second kayak of this trip is starting to hold more repair than original material. I will split the fifty miles to my next stop in Puerto Cabello into two legs, and will treat myself to a few breaks to snorkel on the coral reefs.

On the way to Caraballeda, the harbor of the capital Caracas, the beaches are becoming more rustic, and powerful mountains in the background dominate the landscape. Tourists are barely seen, and taxi boats and yachts are fewer. I meet more fishermen giving me friendly waves. On the last night, I land on a steep pebble beach - not one for beginners or motorboats to stop in. I lug my bags up the steep incline to the first level and settle in.

I love camping on pebble beaches, as they usually are dry, clean and without beasties. This spot is particularly good. From the water, motorboats cannot land, and the coastal road is high on top of the cliffs - no one can climb down to surprise me. After a long time, I am finally able to savor this lonely, hard to get to, and deserted beach for the night. I feel free and for a time, can enjoy my well-deserved break even naked, as there are no spectators, mosquitos or other bugs.

I have just got comfortable in the tent with my e-book, when I hear a few stones roll about outside. Are there stones coming down the cliff? No, but a short, strong wave manages to get over the ledge and find its way into my tent. Hmmm... I laugh about my optimism about the perfect situation for my tent. Most times I get the location right! I wipe out the water, and pull up to higher ground. As if to mock me, an even bigger surprise wave comes into the tent. Now, everything is really soaking wet! I dry-packed the important stuff, but the floor of the tent is underwater. I must move everything out. And for the second time this night, a naked woman in the moonshine must move all her gear to a yet higher location. I hope this spectacle is not repeated!

The first ugly industrial buildings and factories with high chimneys show on the horizon. The rows upon rows of plain, high blocks of socialist architecture are cut off from the sea by a wide highway. Airplanes from the nearby international airport of Caracas regularly thunder over these concrete castles. On many of the simpler houses and favelas, I see blue water tanks on the roof - they are not connected to public water supply. I dread to think what the sewage situation may be like. The penetrating smell of many little streams offends my nostrils.

Antonio and his wife Lucy, my local hosts, live in one of the fanciest tower blocks stretching into the sky high above the favelas. Their apartment is well equipped to European standards. I am even more surprised to hear it is only their holiday apartment, as they live in Caracas. There is a wide gap between rich and poor in socialist Venezuela, just like in all South America.

At the customs office next day, we have no problems receiving my kayak. Thanks to the practical and financial help from Wilhelm, a paddling customs agent. By evening, my new baby is delivered directly to Antonio's apartment, imprisoned in a solid metal transport frame. Antonio plays safecracker, and frees it from its cage. I do the nitty gritty and apply my personal and sponsor stickers and flags of "conquered" countries. They are seven by now, half time, at least according to these numbers.

The stay in the loud metropolis of Caracas is not good for me. My skin has recovered a bit, but the draught of the air conditioning gives me a nasty cold. I must put in another break near Fronton del Fraile after only one successful paddling day to ease the cold symptoms. Mosquitos and ants are a real pain. All my activities take place in the closed-up tent: Washing, cooking, showering, eating, drinking, and the bathroom breaks.

I usually use a sock or such to plug the two small holes where the three inner tent zippers meet. But sometimes, I forget…This night, unnoticed, I am camping on an ant run, and the nasty tiny beasts are marching through the holes across my tent, straight over my pee pot. At night, half asleep, I like to use it to do the necessary, but have never jumped up quite as fast as when they start to inject their acid into my delicate parts. Truly a case of "ants in the pants"!

My path continues along endless beaches. By 10am, the usual headwind blows into my face at twenty knots. A tropical thunderstorm interrupts my strenuous program. I manage to get on land in time, but not to erect the tent. I am crouching next to my kayak, get soaking wet through the massive tropical rainfall, and watch with growing concern a few fishing boats tossed about by the waves like nutshells. The rain is a gift, I can refill a few of my water stores. It has gotten noticeably cooler after the downpour, and I am able to have a good restorative sleep.

The paddling itself is best described as tropical endurance training without much beautiful scenery. The conditions of air temperature of over hundred, and water temperature of lower nineties in shallow areas, garnished with saturated humidity, are less than ideal. It is not surprising the coastline shows no tourists. Who wants to bathe in water which does not offer any kind of a cool down? My skin is looking forward to the next city stop in Barcelona, where friendly locals organize me an air-conditioned dry room. The receptionist of the hotel wants to be extra nice, and asks if I would like a room with sea view? Never laughed out so loud!

After Barcelona, the landscape becomes a bit more varied. Lots of little islands fringe the mainland, the famous holiday place Isla Margarita is not far away. Dolphins give me a bit of entertainment. At Isla Cachimo a few years ago, a group of ten paddlers were robbed at gunpoint, I stay away from that place. Two more days to the last city stop in Venezuela, Rio Caribe, before I head to Trinidad…that should take another five or six days.

I cross the bay of Carupano with the usual fifteen knots headwinds, two miles before Rio Caribe. A boat carrying the local press comes towards me. They want to see how far I have gone, and when I might arrive in town. 500 yards before I finish, they come back again, this time with a TV crew on board. I would have preferred to stay incognito, and to later paddle without attention to Trinidad. I keep getting told that this last bit of coast is the most dangerous of Venezuela.

My host Francisco in Rio Caribe gives me a room in his wonderful decorated guest house. At the immigration office, I get another stern warning: "Peninsula Paria, our easternmost region, is the most dangerous of all Venezuela. Pirates operate there, kidnappings are common, and drug runners use this area for their business with Trinidad," he lists the dangers I face. "Add to that, escaped prisoners like to hide here, as there are neither roads nor cell phone reception. International sailing yachts completely avoid Venezuela for these reasons."

Aramis, one of my paddling contacts, has travelled this route before me, and has information on which villages I should avoid, and which ones might be safe. He gives me a list of good and bad landing places, of course without any kind of guarantee that things have stayed the same. Nothing happened to him, but that could change any time. Some other guys have also paddled this way, but they were a team of three local friends. As a foreign, solo sportswoman in a famous-looking kayak, I do not think I would be in greater danger than the locals. I bet on my experience with people, the prominence bonus, and my self-confidence. Normally, a South American man is a "caballero", a gentleman towards a woman, and the stronger she appears to be, the more he is challenged to be a Caballero. I hope this will hold true even for pirates, drug runners and escaped prisoners, should I meet any. The coast guard cannot and will not support me, and I am glad to be able to stay self-sufficient.

I have developed my own plan: For the next days, I will not bring my website up to date with my current location, and will pass much faster than planned through this danger zone. Only my close friends and family will know where I am. Unfortunately, the TV team from Rio Caribe has already broadcast that I am in the region. I have announced I would need six days to get to Trinidad. With some paddling at night, I hope to cut this down to half. I do not want to stay one day longer in this extremely dangerous, yet so beautiful region of the Caribbean.

With mixed feelings, I pack in a dark corner at the town beach of Rio Caribe, unfortunately with some spectators. The city is already awake, and the market at the promenade quickly fills with people. I do not want the locals to see all my equipment, so as not to raise any desires. Most stuff I have pre-packed in the house. As fast as possible, and with a friendly wave to my friends, I glide into the water in the darkness. I hope it is not obvious which direction I am precisely taking.

I select a route way off shore, as I do not like to be seen from land, and like to stay out of the common way of speedboats. Out here, I feel safer, even if I must fight more with headwind and currents, and there is nothing interesting to see. If someone is intent to follow and rob me, they would find me here too. When I see the first motorboat, I already have an unpleasant feeling. But the men only signal me that it would be easier to paddle closer to shore. I wave back and try to communicate as little as possible.

After lunch, I head for a lonely beach near San Juan de las Galdonas, one of the "good" locations on my list. The beach is not as deserted as I have hoped, but to find completely deserted beaches is impossible in Venezuela. Even the remotest corner has at least a hut, or a group of fishermen. I will wait by pitching my tent, and watch if the three guys close to me may disappear. I stretch out on top of my kayak, and have a little snooze.

Later, I dare to build my camp, but only unpack the absolute necessary. I might set off again a bit later. I do not have a good feeling, as the men just vanished at dusk, and I do not know where they are, and if they may return. I could now use the opportunity to pass the "bad" villages in darkness! Clever idea! At 10pm, I am back on the water, and paddle into the misty night. This night and all next morning, I can make good distance, and hope to find an empty beach by nightfall. The day after, I would reach Trinidad, even if in darkness. That is the plan so far.

I am mostly concerned about not falling asleep. Wind and waves are low, but some current drifts me back if I stop paddling. Suddenly, two boats at top speed race through the darkness along the coast. What are they doing here, in the middle of the night? Haven't I just left the two "bad" villages behind me, or that is where they are coming from? Just as I have gone around the headland of Juan de Unare, the spook starts again. It is 3.30am, and one boat after another race at top speed eastwards like in a parade. I watch them until half past five, by that time, at least twenty-five boats fly past me, thankfully in safe distance. Each new engine sound makes me freeze with fright, and hope the darkness gives me enough shelter not to get discovered and intercepted. These are not fishermen heading out to work! I am quite certain that I have been watching the infamous drug runners on their way to Trinidad. The smugglers like to start in big groups, as the Navy chasing them cannot be in all places at the same time. With hindsight, these were two of the most sinister hours of my whole circumnavigation.

By morning, the traffic calms down, but my stomach does not. I have barely eaten my breakfast of Muesli, milk powder and water, when I feel queasy. I try to remove the bad taste out of my mouth by brushing my teeth, but the saltwater I use for the purpose increases the nausea. It does not take long, I throw up quite violently, and feel a bit better. I would like a real break, but the fear to land at a "bad" place drives me onwards. By late afternoon I relax a little, as I might have passed the most dangerous corners. I can look out for a landing spot.

A bit later, my patience is rewarded, and I spot a bay with two beautiful beaches. There is also lonely hut, but it is too late to carry on further. I do not have a choice, or I must stay another night out. Suddenly, an ear-splitting scream interrupts the silence. Is this a signal from one of the escaped convicts hiding in the bushes? Or are my nerves just stretched to breaking point? I have come across howler monkeys in Columbia and Panama, but this sound is different.

My nervousness is not without reason. As I land, I see a motorboat towing a little skiff passing my bay. And just after having pitched my tent, another boat enters "my" cove. Damn, is there no little strip of sand around here where you do not meet other people? For over an hour, the boat patrols along the beach, while I hide behind my tent and watch what they are up to. Once they shout something like "Hey", but I do not move. I do not even dare to get rid of my wet and salty clothing. Even after they have gone, I shudder a bit when I hear a motorboat…even when none is there. My nerves are tight, I urgently need sleep. Even my food tastes horrible.

I do manage to get some rest until I am woken by a scratch against the tent at 1am. At first, it sounds like a small animal searching for food. Crabs digging themselves into the sand make such noises. To scare them off, I beat against the wall of the tent from the inside, but the scratching does not stop. Is it a bigger animal? Or a rodent trying to gnaw a way in? I take my flashlight and shine it through the fly net outside. There it is again… Now, I hear a nasty sound like that of a material that is being torn, and I am wide awake! Is someone trying to slit open the walls of my tent? My hair stands up on end. A dinosaur claw reaches through a hole in my vestibule! I feel like I have entered "Jurassic Park". In the brightness of my flashlight, I finally see what is trying to enter my tent: A ginormous turtle!

I jump out naked as I am, a welcome target for countless mosquitos. I must get the beast away from my tent before it shreds it! My attempt to push off the one by one yard in a square, 300-pounds heavy creature, is hopeless. The poor animal has gotten wedged in the narrow gap between my tent and kayak. Is it in mating mood, and approaches my dome tent mistaking it for a nice big conspecific?

I pull my kayak out of the way, and the turtle has enough space to turn. She looks for another place to dig a hole for her eggs, and shovels enormous quantities of dry fine sand all over me and my left open inner tent. I am starting to look like a bread crumbed schnitzel, and the beach does not stop any more at the doorstep of my usually clean inner tent. I take a few pictures, and watch her slowly shuffle off. Later, during the night, I hear sand raining down onto my tent a few more times, which shows the turtle is still active. Or is it revenging for the flash I used when taking a picture? She certainly follows me into my dreams.

After the last restless nights, I really want to get to Trinidad as fast as possible, even if I must paddle into the darkness once more. The strange drug runner boat traffic is not good for my nerves. During the day, I also stay away from land as far as possible and avoid any encounters with other boats. I do not even dare to go into the many picturesque bays I am passing. My nerves are done, I just want to get out of Venezuela!

Near the last "bad" village, a large boat suddenly appears behind me. Is this the long-prepared attempt to kidnap me? My imagination shifts into panic mode, even when eight guys in that boat cheerfully wave to me. After they enter a bay, they come back towing a tender, another piece of evidence to me that my kidnapping is imminent. They go past me without paying further attention, only fishing is not what they are out to do. The sooner I am gone, the better!

The narrows between Venezuela and the Paria peninsula is also known as "Dragons' Mouth", a particularly inviting name for this nine-mile passage. I will soon find out why. Most of the distance I can cover in daylight, but the current and tides slow me down to only two miles per hour. Three tankers cross my path, I hope the strong current does not push me into their ways. I can start to relax a bit, as no further watercrafts are in sight. I seem to have the most dangerous part of this section behind me. Did I see real pirates and drug runners? Were there any out there? Am I now safe?

The water temperature of the "Dragons' Mouth" increases, which is fitting for the fiery breath of such an imaginative prehistoric creature. I concentrate on my GPS, and paddle like a well-oiled machine. My backside is rubbed raw by now, and I can only stand the pain with a wet sponge as kind of a cushion between my lower back and the backrest.

Before the sun sets, it hides behind a massive dark thunder cloud above Venezuela. In the distance, I see two bright lighthouses on the Venezuelan mainland, but Trinidad continues to stay in darkness. There should be four lighthouses as per my chart, have they been switched off to make a drug runner's life difficult? Suddenly, a glowing eye looks at me from the water. Is that the dragon? Do they really exist? No, it is only a school of dolphins swimming around me! They playfully jump out of the water, and keep me company for over an hour. They leave bright sparkling bioluminescence in their wake, dive like shooting stars below the surface, and appear and disappear again. It is a fascinating and beautiful, but at the same time spooky sight. One of the marine mammals comes so close to me I smack him with my paddle by accident. Sorry! This bad navigation rarely happens to dolphins. I hope he is not planning revenge, and tips me over. At least the dolphins keep me awake during the strenuous night paddle.

At 10pm, sudden strong vibrations shake the sea. I think it might be some surprising surf or current between the islands, but later I find out it was a veritable force six earthquake. It looks like even nature is trying its hardest to scare me silly in the "Dragon's Mouth", just like the two boats quietly and slowly coming towards me in the darkness. In the meantime, I have put my position lights around my head, as the greater danger now is to get run over by ships, not to get kidnapped. Again, and again, I shine my strong torch in their direction to attract their attention. When they shine a search light strong enough to light up the rocks 500 yards behind me, I know it must be the coast guard. If they do not mistake me for a drug runner who is trying to tiptoe over from Venezuela with a kayak full of merchandise, it is fine with me. Obviously, they estimate me being harmless, and they turn off. Even if usually I prefer the coast guard far away from me, tonight, I would not have minded a little chat on the water. It would have motivated me for these last yards.

I enjoy these anyway. My nose fills with tropical flowery scents wafting over from the land. Underwater, big swarms of fish leave their glowing bioluminescent traces, and on land, glow worms switch their lights on and off. In my fantasy, they could also be people hiding among the dark rock walls, signaling each other to get the timing right for my kidnap...but I am over this fear now, I am too close to my goal, and in safe waters. What is left now is to enter the yacht harbor and find the GPS spot where my kayak friend Glenn is waiting for me. Soon, I see a veritable forest of masts. Countless yachts worth millions of dollars are bobbing in the harbor waters. Even if they are not mine, it is nice to see a bit of luxury after the widespread poverty everywhere in Venezuela. The jetty I land on is made of teak.

But with money comes arrogance and attitude, even from simple employees. The reception I get at 1am on a public jetty near a snazzy hotel is everything but welcoming. I am treated like a hobo. Glenn cannot be reached at this hour; two night-watchmen tell me I must ask at the reception whether I would be allowed to wait here. I have a feeling they only want me to book a room. I thankfully decline, and explain that I would rather wait for Glenn at the jetty, as I do not want to leave my kayak and luggage. They will not accept that. One of the watchmen threatens me with the police. That would be nice, I thought, so I can discuss my problem with someone in real authority. In a dark corner, I change my clothing and take a quick shower. An older hotel employee comes by, and is way more relaxed than his two colleagues when he realizes I am not a vagrant without means wanting to cause trouble. He says I could wait here, and he would come and check on me every hour or so.

I settle on the jetty on my camp mat and try to sleep a little. Without a tent, I feel vulnerable, and ask myself how a homeless person may feel when they must sleep without shelter in the open air. By morning, I can reach Glenn, and I am picked up by his French colleague Michel, who offers me a stay at his house for the next few days. His wife Nevine prepares a wonderful breakfast with toast and eggs, a delicacy I have not eaten in weeks. After a reviving shower, I do not feel quite so tired anymore, and I am ready for the tasks of the day. I need to collect and store my kayak, pop in to immigration for my entry stamp for Trinidad, and to deal with customs.

Just like on the jetty close to the hotel, the reception in the immigration office is not very friendly. A brawny officer wipes the crumbs off his mouth and sends us straight out again. We are not properly dressed. Outside is a big sign on which dress codes for visiting the office are explained in thirteen precise points. I find out, the problem with my attire is that my t-shirt is knotted above the navel with a strip of bare skin shown. Naked feet in flip flops are also not allowed. Have I arrived in a Muslim country? The knot in the t-shirt is easily undone, but I do not carry other shoes nor socks. I put the nicest smile on my face and explain I have arrived the night via kayak, hence my informal clothing. Grudgingly, he lets me enter.

I think the officials might have adopted such unfriendliness to counter the arrogance of wealthy yacht owners. When he realizes I am not one of the elite, dripping in dollars and diamonds, but an internationally renowned sportswoman, he becomes a bit friendlier and is impressed when he studies my signature card. While filling in the forms, I make a few jokes about the, for me, useless questions about crew, tonnage, stowaways, engine size, as these are "one size fits all" forms. The paperwork is quickly dealt with, but as it is not a weekday, but Saturday, I must pay a surcharge of hundred Trinidad dollars. This is unusual, but should I start a discussion about this now? I am glad to have everything done. In the customs office, all goes smoothly. My kayak is well looked after in Meryl's kayak shop. And finally, Glenn arrives himself.

We are invited to an unusual Sunday BBQ: Graham and Russell Henry from Vancouver Island are on the way from Belem in Brazil to Florida. The two young brothers have done just the same section as what lies ahead for me, but in the opposite direction: Guyana, Surinam, and French-Guyana via the Amazon delta to northern Brazil. In contrast to me, they could paddle with, and not against wind and currents. While Russell is busy entertaining some attractive young ladies, I ask Graham if he has any advice for this next section of my trip. "It's going to be rough", was his only comment.

After the tough and tense nervous time of the last weeks, five relaxing days in Trinidad have been good for me. The open sores on my back have improved. I am glad to be back on the water! In my luggage is a hammock, I feel prepared for the muddy coastline ahead.

The south coast of Trinidad hosts a bunch of offshore oil platforms on the horizon, and pumps and refineries on shore. Before I realize the whole Columbus Bay is contaminated with a massive oil slick, I am already right in the middle of it. The sticky mess covers the whole kayak, my paddle, and even my clothing. Absolutely disgusting! I have nothing that will get rid of the black film, rubbing with a sponge or sand does not help. I try my luck with my small bottle of white spirits, but for this quantity of oil, it is nowhere near enough.

As a fishing boat is passing, I take the opportunity and ask the men for help. I must look as desperate as a bird with sticky feathers unable to fly. They carry enough petrol, and are willing to help in cleaning the kayak and even me. One of the men is so kind to rub down my legs before I carry on. "If my wife was watching, I would have a problem", he said with a grin. I will have to stop at the next village for more petrol, to get rid of the rest of this disgusting mess. It is vile. If this had happened in the bush without enough petrol to wash everything off, it would have ruined all my equipment.

I can see from far away the juicy green of the jungle of Venezuela, before I can finally cross back over to the mainland after dusk. It is late before I notice how shallow the water has become. And it is not even lowest tide! This water is lukewarm, and the ground is firm sand one can walk on. From time to time, I must get out of the kayak and drag it along. With headwind, countercurrent, and only a hand's width of water under me, I get about faster in this style. When the water comes back, I can paddle closer to the mainland, but keep a good two miles distance. I find a suitable place to camp, but dozens of greedy horseflies are after my blood.

The coast from here on to the Amazonas is for miles-wide extremely shallow, and in parts very muddy due to the sediment the mighty river deposits. No wonder that after a few days of tricky navigation through the shoals, it happens: I get stuck. Thankfully, it happens on a firm broad sand bank, and not in the endless soft "death" mud. I must now wait five hours until I would float up again to continue paddling. I settle in for the night on the kayak, and roll out my sleeping mat. A water bag serves as a pillow. I need to stay warm, and wrap myself up in several layers of rescue foil. It works out, until it starts to rain heavily. I can solve this problem with the tarp of my hammock. After five hours, I notice how the flood is starting to lift me off the sand bank. I have had worse night's sleep!

The widespread Orinoco delta is nearing. The current from each individual outflow is not very strong, and occasionally, I must paddle far out not to get stuck in the muddy shallows. Inside the delta, I move from island to island, passing the native stilt villages on purpose with just a friendly wave. As a European, I feel a bit out of place here, and my anthropological ambitions are limited on this trip.

I extend my time to three days in the delta, and only paddle twenty miles per day until Boca Grande, the main outflow of the Orinoco. Its natural world is so beautiful, with so much to discover and watch. Directly from the river, there is plenty of freshwater available. Night and day, it is as hot and humid as in a steam sauna, and my heat rash plus a multitude of itching insect bites comes back painfully. Two nights at the pilot station of Rio Barima in an air-conditioned room brings a bit of relief after seven days of continuous headwind. I plan to paddle the 185 miles to Georgetown, the capital of Guyana, in ten days.

The next two days demand all my reserves, paddling is not much fun in the muddy shallow water, with few halfway inviting places to land. I battle through the endless muddy brown shallows. When the headwind breezes up, it stirs up the water to liquid mud. I can only take a break when I find the odd old net pole to tie up my kayak, so as not to drift back again.

Talking about mud, as I suffer from diarrhea during the last few days, my plan to end this section already in Georgetown, and to fly back home to Germany, becomes real. Mid-January, I would continue from Guyana, this time with my partner Peter for company, marking the second time we will be together on this trip. If he knew what he is going to take up now! This section, due to the headwinds and countercurrent, would not be as pleasant as our mutual tour up Chile and Peru. The mud, the heat and the mosquitos do not make the business any more pleasurable.

In the river mouth of Georgetown, I get into serious difficulties. I take the approach to land in a gap between two large boats way too tight, and the current pushes me sideways under the bow of one of the tied up large boats. I can barely keep my head above the water, and I am close to bail out. Only the quick throw of a life ring from above enables me to get me and my kayak out of this dangerous squeeze. Slightly shocked, I greet my friendly reception committee of the Guyana Navy, representative of the town council and the tourism office. Is this mishap a bad omen for the next section?

Chapter 14
MANGROVES, MUD
AND MONSTER WAVES

Guyana to Sao Luis/ Brazil
January 10th - April 27th, 2014

It is the beginning of January, two months at home pass quickly with so much to do. I had to take care of my Christmas shop and prepare for the reopening of my two Janny's Ice cream cafés. Without my fantastic and reliable managers and employees, I would not be able to stay away for such extended periods. Helge's father Werner has looked well after my house, which got a bit of damage in a storm. Not Cape Horn's wind speeds though!

Unfortunately, my partner Peter is not able to free himself of work for his IT business, and despite extensive preplanning, he will not be able to join me. Too bad! He escorts me via long distance, keeps all electronics and website setups under control, and supports me once more with advice and motivation on this next section. This is also a good feeling!

I will be paddling the next leg past Surinam and French-Guyana across the mouth of the Amazonas to Sao Luis. This section is defined by strong headwinds and currents, dreadful heat and a muddy shore, probably until I have reached the easternmost point of the Atlantic coast. With hindsight, it will be confirmed that this section was the hardest of my whole circumnavigation - and the most dangerous.

I quickly finish the preparations for the trip with the support of the nice workers in the tourism office. With the help of Ben ter Welle, the Dutch honorary consul to Germany, I get the exit stamp for Guyana and my visa for Surinam. My shopping for fresh food is done this time in the colorful market halls, not in a local supermarket.

I am starting with a bad cold, not good timing! Once I am on the water, I know I will feel better, even with headwinds of fifteen knots and tides against me. Briskly, I leave Georgetown behind me, and hope to cross this muddy lagoon as fast as possible to reach the Mahacai river mouth.

My first camp for two months! On the beach of a small village, I get the undivided attention of the whole community. What is fun and cheerful to begin with, becomes unpleasant after a short while. Everyone wants to look and give their commentary about me and my tent. Even after I disappear inside, and want my peace and quiet, my tent continues to be besieged. For hours on end, camera flashes light up, and their laughter and shouting does not abate. A few particularly intrusive jokers try to open my tent again to peek inside. I might react a bit unfriendly, but what is too much is too much.

For the next several weeks there is only one subject: Mud, mud, and more inglorious mud. On my second landing, I thoroughly mess up boat and equipment with the mire, which covers the solid sandy ground to a depth of about a foot. It is easy to get the sandals stuck. I can only leave around high tide, or I would be stuck in the quagmire. Given the bad high tide time at 1.30am, I have the choice between shallow water on sticky bog or the rough surf zone, which somewhere out slams down on the start of the shallows. I do not dare to go out too far, I prefer to get stuck in the mud at times, like it happens again after the mouth of the New Amsterdam River. It is exhausting to get up early, to stir up the mud with the paddle, pay attention to the breakers, and to fight the headwind. I ask myself why I chose to go clockwise. Sure, it was a necessary advantage on the pacific, but here since the Panama Canal, it is absolute hell.

Besides some solitary bushes and grass, there is not much to see on this part of the coast. Encounters with other water crafts are rare, there are too many unpredictable shallows. This would have suited me well in Venezuela, but here, it is only boring. Once I run into a bunch of active fishing nets at night, as I do not see them properly in the darkness. The first net throws me back like a vertical trampoline, in the second, I piece a fat hole with my kayak. I am so sorry, dear fishermen, I am mentally already in Nickerie, where I urgently need to replenish my water supplies to last out the week I will need to get to Paramaribo.

I continue another four days through mud, thunderstorms, and headwinds of twenty knots garnished with rain. It is getting cooler, at times I need to put a thin windbreaker over my constantly wet fleece shirt. Before the start of the final sprint to Paramaribo, I allow myself a two days break on the last decent beach for a long time. But it is not a total joy to sit in a tent in the howling wind, while outside millions of mosquitos are waiting to suck the last drop of blood out of me. Thank God, I have stocked up on my electronic library. But only reading and sleeping is boring, I find some more useful things to do: I will shave my legs, paint my toe nails and polish my secret luxury item - my old silver children's cutlery, which fits perfectly into my one and only pot.

No improvement on the continuous mud bath the next day, and a suitable landing place is out of question. For the first time, I must stay in my hammock in a mangrove forest. I need to paddle into the forest at high water, to be able to hang it high enough to stay dry. I am at least halfway protected from the rain and the greedy mosquitos with the integrated bug net and tarp. I use ear plugs, or I can hear more of their buzzing than I like. I am a hammock newbie, and have some difficulties hanging it at the right height and tension. I use my sleeping mat inside, but it slips at the slightest movement and barely keeps the cold and bugs at bay. I can neither stretch out lengthways fully, nor stick my legs up to stretch and relax.

For a comfortable night, I can only take the barest of utensils inside - at least compared to my tent space. I must cook outside in a swarm of mosquitos before I get in. I can only do my regular night pee via Freshette and zip-lock bag with serious contortions inside this wobbly swing. I need to open the Velcro closure on the bottom of the hammock for letting out the collected liquid, in return for letting some mosquitos in. The strong wind is driving the rain sideways at night, and does not keep the inside fully dry. Comfort is feeling different than this camping style. I love my tent! But one hammock is better than no hammock. Next night, I must spend lying down on my kayak, as once more I get stuck in the mud, and cannot find a spot neither for tent nor for my hammock. This style is also not offering an ideal night rest, exposed to mosquitoes and rain in damp clothing.

Only once do I meet a solitary fishing boat. I bet they are wondering what I am doing here, and where I am heading for. That, quite honestly, is what I am starting to ask myself. I get the idea to just paddle through the forty miles to Paramaribo, if I cannot find a dry place to spend the night. But it is a tough job in this headwind! Once, I have a vision of a bright white sandy beach, but as I get closer, it turns out to be a row of white-pink flamingos standing lined up in the mud by the shore. And I cannot just drop where I happen to be, who knows if the next flood is high enough to get me afloat again? No one can walk on the mud, only a helicopter would be able to rescue me here.

What a contrast after my arrival in Paramaribo: I can sleep in the pink princess room of the daughters of my hosts Pieter and Nancy. There could hardly be a greater difference! Cees, the Honorary Consul of Germany, greets me just before dusk at the river mouth from a small boat loaded with kayaking friends. Other than like in Georgetown, landing goes off without a hitch. Many helpful hands pull my heavy kayak up the jetty. After two nights in a hammock and one on top of my kayak in the mud, I am exhausted physically and mentally. Sorry, I am not very chatty and cheerful in the darkness of the late evening. I will catch up with that later during my stay, but now, I am just glad to be able to snuggle into the soft bedding with a "Royal Princess" slogan.

After a single night, I feel noticeably better, even if my bones still hurt and I am covered all over in itchy mosquito bites. I am ready for what needs to be done next: online updates, minor boat repairs, a bit of shopping and my preparations for the next leg to Cayenne in French-Guyana. It looks like there may be a few beaches to stay on overnight, and I may only have to spend one night in my hammock in the mangroves.

I should be able to cover that distance in two weeks. After Cayenne, it is likely to be the hardest stage of the whole circumnavigation. In those 650 miles, I may only find three or four sensible spots to land and recuperate. The rest is mud, mangroves and mosquitoes. I cannot say I am looking forwards to that!

I am savoring the stay in Paramaribo, and the delights of civilization. The former colony of Dutch-Guyana, now Surinam, is noticeably much more prosperous, compared to its neighbor, the former British-Guyana. Shopping is fun and offers more choices. The side by side location of churches, mosques and synagogues is pleasing and harmonious. All is clean and inviting, friendly people are everywhere. I very much like this country! A fancy party of the Rotary Club by the pool of one of their wealthy members is the icing on the cake of my stay. I can dive into a rich buffet and a well-stocked bar. But I really need to first visit the hairdresser! Thank goodness, since my time in Trinidad, I always carry a decent beach dress in my luggage! A well-mixed international gathering parties late into the night, what a contrast to the earlier nights and those still ahead. However, early next morning, I want to be on my way. But "want" may not be the right word here.

Once I have overcome all the excuses I was able to find to delay my departure, I am back on the water at 3.30am at high tide. It is still pitch black, and my eyes must get used to these light conditions on the water. I want to make the most out of the outgoing pushing current before the tide will turn against me. Behind, I still see the glow of Paramaribo's lights, while a few pink river dolphins play in first dawn. An already familiar coastline lies ahead of me, mud and mangroves dominate the scenery. I look forward to using my new little mini-anchor, to be able to take a break while on the water.

I feel a bit sick and seem to have caught a cold in town. A good night's sleep in a comfortable camp is important, but for that, I must paddle long and hard. The frequent rain does not help to please me. A few days like this, and I am already looking forward to the next break. I urgently need to fill up my water supply. Slowly, I approach the border to French-Guiana. Only a broad river separates me from the 11th country of my circumnavigation of this continent.

I land on the city beach of Awala-Yalimapo/ Les Hattes, exactly where the local fishermen have pulled up their boats a moment ago. Their welcome is friendly, and pitching my camp is uncomplicated. I should just put up in the grassy green park of the city beach, and take a shower afterwards in the house of Captain William. I hope to refill there also my drinking water.

This small town is well known among tourists for its turtle hatchings, though few strangers detour here to the most western part of French-Guiana. I might even have time to watch the turtles lay their eggs on the beaches. Like broken table tennis balls, empty egg shells are blown by the wind across the sand. I would have loved to have a look out at dusk, but was discouraged by the clouds of hungry mosquitos. My cold is getting worse, and I have a relaxing stay for two days. I plan to arrive in Cayenne after week.

The next nights I spend as expected - or should I say dreaded - mostly on semi acceptable beaches, and once in the hammock at the edge of the mangroves. One beach I must share with bees and a herd of cows, who are noisily hanging around my tent. The lead bull wears an impressive set of horns, and I do not dare to keep them off with shouts or banging sticks. They may attack and trample all over my camp! I try to do hissing sounds like a big cat might make. That sends them off to the other side of the beach!

Next day, I can only find a thick green wall of forest and shrubbery, with muddy water in front. What I thought were white beaches as per the satellite pictures, turn out to be colonies of thousands of white birds. Both, live a few days ago, and now on the satellite images, I step in the same trap of a bird "mirage". Wishful thinking... Another night in the hammock is unavoidable, with pouring rain and clouds of mosquitos. During the day, I see a rare fishing boat on the horizon, and I am for a moment tempted to ask if I could spend the night on board. But I do not really dare to with the thought, there may still be pirates about. I paddle my way through the muddy shallows. My biggest fear is to get stuck in a mud bank around high tide, with no chance to get flooded onto the next high tide which might be a tad lower in the moon cycle.

Next night, I cannot find a dry landing spot by low tide near the muddy coast, and I prefer to head out back to deeper water, knowing I would have to paddle once more through the night.

Unfortunately, I do not have the Sinnamary delta on my radar, and I paddle carefree along through the darkness. Large river mouths have the unpleasant habit of creating horrendously tall, standing breaking waves, and this one is not an exception. Mountainous wave after mountainous wave pile up high, and break with foaming crests. I must listen to their position, as I can barely make them out in the pale moonlight. In a start and stop technique, and with some slalom, I desperately try to escape the threatening and destructive showers. Several times, I must throw myself with all power into a breaker, so not as to capsize in the darkness. Whether or not I would be able to roll back up in these conditions, I do not like to find out. I can hardly see on my GPS if I am covering any ground at all, and can barely define the direction to go. Its background light is set to a very low level, so as not to distract my pupils, which must still be wide open for greatest vision in the darkness. Desperately, I try to get out of this minefield!

Sometime after what feels like an eternity, I survive the foaming inferno, the water calms down, and all what is left to fight is tiredness. I can read my GPS map again, and know, that just before Kourou, I will come across reefs, rocks and solid dry ground on shore. By sunrise, I feel like I am on a different planet! No muddy coast anymore, but smaller and larger rock scattered offshore. Some of these rocks are so big one could camp on them.

A bit further in the morning after this exhausting and scary long paddle through the night, the longed for sandy beach shows up, easy accessible and lonely. A perfect place to rest my tired bones! I still sing during the smooth landing, as I am so happy that I am still alive, and have found my way through these deadly breakers in the darkness. I flop down onto the sand, and thank all gods and goddesses of the seas for listening to my prayers. From trying to navigate the dark hell with breaking waves several yards high, I have landed in paradise. Or not? What I listen to a few hours later sounds more like the gates of hell were opening again!

A deep, endlessly long, unbelievably noisy grumble sounds out, and the ground around me trembles like in an earthquake. Only a few miles away, a rocket takes off from the Guyana Space Center in Kourou! Unfortunately, I cannot see it in the rainy and dull conditions. I only hope the lift-off is a success, and no burning debris falls on my tent! No wonder all these helicopters were shooing the fishing boats out of the danger zone. Seems like they were not able to reach me!

While having a walk on my day off next day, I spot a large shipwreck a hundred yards up inland. How did that get there? Has the beach "grown", or was it an infernal tsunami that carried the poor ship this high up some time ago?

I paddle through endless fields of shallow water over sandy ground, creating short steep waves in the strong headwind. This is quite a wet business! At first, it is fun to brace into the many splashing small waves, but soon, it is only annoying.

My planned "easygoing" last half day along the rocky coast turns out to be a three-hour daylight version of the nighttime minefield near Kourou. With twenty knots headwind, I am so physically and mentally exhausted when I arrive at the Cayenne Kayak Club, that I am only able to enjoy the evening BBQ for a short while. All I want is just to lay on my bed. Wonderful European luxury including air-conditioning and friendly hosts awaits me. Balm for skin and soul.

I use the three days city stop for preparations for the next deserted leg to Belem in Brazil. My food should last the planned four weeks to Belem, and my water, eleven bags of four liters, for the next fortnight.

My kayak is loaded to the brim, and nearly passes for a submarine, as I paddle through the first rough river mouth behind Cayenne. Nowadays, whenever I look for a place for the night, I must pay close attention to the tide times.

It is the first night, and I must already let myself run aground in the muddy reed, and hope to be flooded up again with the incoming tide. No landing places are in sight. The night on the kayak is not restful due to the chilly wetness and the thousands of mosquitos.

The second night, I spend in my hammock in a forest with tall trees. I am nearly smashed by a massive rotten tree, choosing just this night to change position from vertical to horizontal about fifty yards off my hammock spot.

The third night, I hang the both cursed and blessed hammock too early and too low, as with the incoming tide a few cheeky surf waves try to lick my bottom. Surf inside a mangrove forest?? In the rhythm of the rolling small waves, I am lifting my backside, not to get too soaked. But that is preferable, then to get out into the by now hip deep muddy water, with clouds of thousands of mosquitoes, to try and hitch it higher. After half an hour, the spooky forest surf at night is over, and I find some rest.

Another night, I hope to spend on the muddy coast, which at first looks solid enough to walk on, but it turns out, solid ground can only be found under knee deep mud. Well, at least there *is* some solid ground! Transporting kayak, luggage and human to a four-square yard, halfway dry spot turns into an endurance test for mind and body.

Next day, some sandy banks inside a broad river delta are lurking, and promise an easy arrival. Can I manage to land on this firm sand? Yes - but unfortunately, I must hang my hammock again, due to lack of dry banks among the mangroves. At least I can walk!

Once more, I come across another muddy terrain with low shrubbery, and where I am barely able to hang my hammock in not very solid low bushes. This is more akin to "Jungle Camp", again garnished with thousands of mosquitoes.

Some light shines at the end of the tunnel: The first dry sandy beach! Deliriously happy, I already land by midday, and cannot resist to give my body and equipment a bit of a clean. Hopefully, no water buffalos will visit me at night, as I can see their tracks. After the last few days, I start to look and smell a bit like those primeval creatures.

On the last section before the Brazilian border, the tide drifts me forward at more than five miles per hour. A tropical thunderstorm crashes down onto me, and winds of over twenty-five knots and horizontal rain like out of buckets gives me the feeling, I am drowning above water. The waves in the river mouth of Rio Lamute crisscross from all directions. I can hardly see anything. I brace like mad in all directions, capsize twice, roll up twice, but still feel like the rain drowns me more than the capsizes.

Somewhere near the end of the river mouth, I see at last land. Two younger fishermen are standing in the mud flats, minding their nets just where I hope to land. Wearing a few rags and an old bike helmet with visors protecting their faces against the rain, they live out here with the elements. They have a wheel barrow which could be used to bring my kayak and luggage those 800 yards up to the dry beach. The guys do not hesitate to dump their catch, and to help me while using the primitive one-wheeled contraption smelling strongly like fish. Next morning, they come back with an even bigger cart which is normally pulled by a water buffalo. Together, we manage to move all my stuff a whole mile on low tide to the water's edge to get me started. By myself, this strenuous transport would have taken me more than two hours. As a thank you, I leave them my simple, but solid machete, which hitherto has been one of those pieces of kit I did not have a use for. The two helpful chaps would be able to use it well. Me too, later, but then I did not know that...

On the next easy landing through many lines of splashing low breakers in strong offshore-wind, I find another nice sandy shoreline. I am not alone here. In the afternoon, two hunters come past, armed with machetes and rifles. We greet each other in a friendly manner, and I give them my signature card which explains my trip in Portuguese. I wonder what they would be hunting? One guy warns me of the water buffalos grazing in the vicinity, and mentions that there are also other huntsmen in the area. Meanwhile, his friend is chasing down some rabbits and is shooting with his gun. A brief time later, they pass by again, give a friendly wave, and disappear in the bush.

By half past nine, just after darkness, I see several flashlights through the wall of my tent. Three other, well-armed hunters are paying me a visit. They look like a dad and his two teenage sons. They also check out my card, seem to admire my task, and disappear into the darkness of the bush. Is this a large beat hunt here tonight?

An hour later, after I am already asleep, a sound wakes me. "Click… click… click…!" What is that? An animal? I sit up and listen some more, hear steps and a rustling. Are there more hunters out there? And then all hell breaks loose…

Obviously, someone stumbles over my tent lines, as I hear wild curses, and an enormous machete slices open my tent wall close to my feet.

"Hey, hey, hey!", I call aloud to signal that someone sits inside this tent, and they should please take care. I still believe this is an accident, and someone stumbled and did not intend on purpose to damage my cloth castle.

The guy with the machete seems unimpressed. Swing after swing rains down on my tent wall, and I think I better pull my legs up to get them out of reach of the sharp blade. Suddenly, a gleaming bright light of a torch lights up the tent to near daylight, and next moment, I see a thin long pipe aimed at me through the ugly shattered large hole in my tent. Is someone really pointing his rusty gun at me?

Enraged, the man screams in Portuguese, but I unfortunately do not understand a word. Somewhat calm, I hold out my signature card, hoping he may realize who I am, not to impress him, but to make him see he would not have a nameless victim. I still think this must be a misunderstanding, he cannot want to attack ME? To no avail, he pays no attention to the card I hold up beside his gun barrel.

"Señor, por favor … Señor, por favor … no entiendo …" I keep repeating in a voice one would use to calm down an angry dog. But he just screams louder, and pokes his gun's barrel into my private space. I sit in the slit open tent in the beam of his flashlight like an animal in a trap. He shows me his ammunition, and it sounds like he asks if I know what it is? Sure, I know… I believe your gun is loaded. Or do you want ammunition from me? I do not have any. "Disculpe, no entiendo…"

He waves me out of the tent, I must crawl through the ripped double wall, and he keeps screaming at me. I think I should show him the zippers, and tell him how we use them in Europe to enter and exit a tent, not using machetes! Hundreds of mosquitos enter my maltreated home now through the gaping hole. How am I supposed to patch this up?

I stay calm, and know instinctively that one better makes no surprise movements in front of a loaded gun. The man is not alone. He points me to sit on my kayak next to my tent. I can see out of the corner of my eye, that my reserve paddle in its black bag has disappeared off the deck. Click…click…click…that must have been the cutting noise of the deck lines I initially heard! Did they just want to steal the paddle, and have stumbled over my tent lines? Silently, I try to protect my bare legs from the mosquitos with my long beach skirt.

Is this the end of my journey - and my life? The man still screams at me and waves both gun and flashlight in my face. Suddenly, he turns sideways and shoots. I hope he has not pulverized the stern of my kayak with his shotgun load? That would be an irritating repair, in addition to that of my torn tent…well, that is if I survive this!

The man with the gun tells his companion to crawl into the tent and to search it. What will they take? The guy behaves strangely. Instead of inspecting and choosing what to steal, he throws everything just upside down. Is he looking for something in particular? Only my favorite foldable knife disappears into his pocket, not one of my electronic items or any other valuables. Is that all? Is that it now?

He crawls out of the tent, and in my mind, I make already plans on how to tidy up the ruins. I hope he has not left too much of a mess and dirt, or an ugly smell. Will they please leave me in peace now?

The man with the gun has fun with his machete to slice open my Aquapac with my signature cards. I keep hoping he will read it, but he is only interested in the thick waterproof felt marker pen inside. Or does he think it is a bullet? I hurry to hand him the pen. Be happy with it, let me live and bugger off - now!

.....

The man orders me back into the tent. I still do not understand, but interpret his aggressive gush of words as a warning not to contact the police. And then, suddenly, they are gone. Or not? One returns, and throws my spare paddle bag at me. I have missed that already, many thanks, too kind!

Being alone again, my first thought is to fix the tent to protect myself from the mosquitoes. I start to sew up the many long cuts, which in the darkness is a useless exercise. I am somehow still in shock.

Slowly, clear thought returns. I do not feel safe here anymore, and I just want to leave as fast as possible. It is 2am, and there's high tide. I can leave now, the distance to the water's edge is nice and short. I cannot get rest now anyway, and I feel safer on the water, away from those land-bound hunters. I will go! Under the cover of the dark night, I quickly pack, carry, and drag everything to the water's edge hundred yards away, without using any light. As I sit in the kayak and paddle off, I see a few more flashlights on land. Too late, guys, your "game" is gone! Slightly shocked, but intact. In a shallow bay at the end of a river, I set my tiny sea anchor, and I nap until sunrise.

Up till now, I have managed to keep many dubious characters like those at bay, with a self-confident manner, asserted behavior, an unusual success story, a bit of charm and people skills. But one is helpless and powerless at gunpoint, maliciousness and bad luck. No way I would use any self-defense items like a bear spray or whatever I do not carry anyway, it would have not given me any advantage. This little incident could have ended much, much worse if I would have tried to "fight"!

Understandably, my night's rest is a bit less relaxed the next few weeks. My internal alarm system wakes me at the slightest worrying sound. But I neither have any nightmares, nor do I consider giving up. Like at Cape Horn, it is possible to have an "accident" and continue to drive a car, only with a bit more attention. Most people I meet are friendly, and I am convinced, I am still not running out of my quota of luck. I know that any idea of police involvement is useless, and I do not want any headlines that detract from my sporting achievement. That is the reason this incident is only published here, and not on my blog entries.

I only feel anger towards that choleric, unlucky idiot stumbling over my tent lines while stealing my spare paddle in its bag. For a simple onlooker, I am going about on top of my kayak with a full "battle kit" in view: My easy to misunderstand "rifle case" (the spare paddle in the black bag), my "battle helmet" (who needs a helmet while going for just a little paddle?), and my "bullet proof combat vest", (the life vest with its various attachments...). In future, I will clear my deck completely of all "suspicious", i.e. tempting items, and stow them inside the cockpit during nights. The spare paddle was left on deck, obviously mistaken for a gun, and it was easy for those hunters to be tempted to steal it. And I was even asking the men earlier about what they are hunting here! I also feel anger towards myself for my naivety wearing a light, skin-friendly beach skirt going to sleep.

Two more necessary hammock nights solve the problems of my shredded tent. After a hard fight with some countercurrents of the mighty Amazonas, I can finally turn with the tide into the tributary mouth of the Rio Sucuriju. I am looking forward to a few nights in well-ordered civilization of a small stilt village, but equipped with satellite dishes, generators, and drinking water tanks. I aim towards the larger of the jetties, and I am as always greeted in a friendly manner by the locals. I get a good quarter for my three-days rest in the only two-story house among the fifty stilt buildings of the village. It belongs to the military police and wildlife protection service. In the upper floor, I get a small room, unfortunately without air conditioning, but it has electricity and a powerful fan for at least a few hours at night. And it is very "safe" company!

I must fix my shredded tent and deck lines. No one asks why they are in this state... I would not have given them the right answer anyway. My feet are sore with some fungal infection, and the physical exhaustions of the last days on the water give me a dreamless sleep.

I am to stay here at least three days, until the dangerous "Pororoca" tidal bore in the Amazonas delta abates again after new moon. This ominous phenomenon lets the flood roll in with a powerful current and a high wave, instead of the usual slow rise. There are supposed to be daredevil surfers riding this wave deliberately, but I would rather not try that with my heavily laden kayak!

I integrate into village life with visits and sightseeing. One day, the young locals invite me to watch their soccer match on the outgoing tide on a dry sandbank on the other side of the river. More than thirty men (and one woman - me) make their way in a flotilla of small boats to the natural playground. The outlines of the soccer field are marked with drift wood, and a few high posts they bring along serve as goals. From the distance, it looks as if the players were sliding along like ice skaters in the heat of a mirage on the wet surface. One team is wearing a variety of fancy soccer jerseys with "Sao Paulo Football Club" or "Bayern Munich" printed on, while the other goes topless. All players are barefoot for equality sake. Most guys neither own nor probably cannot afford proper shoes, let alone soccer boots. The daily feet dress code is flip flops for men and women alike.

I enjoy watching the guys playing, and the tide gets lower and lower until the Pororoco is supposed to come. The guys know exactly what will happen, but for me, it is an exciting event! A sound like from a waterfall or heavy rain squall gives about twenty to thirty minutes warning, and within seconds, the Sucuriju River rises with a monster wave by a full yard. The boats on the shore are getting well shaken, despite many hands holding on to them. All players are wet from head to toe. A scary natural phenomenon!

I want to start again after three days of rest in Sucuriju, the monster wave should have run its course the day after new moon. However, I have not found much information about the Pororoca on the internet, other than that it comes in twice. I plan to cross the wide Amazon delta in the lee of the inner islands ten days to my next stop in Chavéz. The further I get into the delta, the lower the winds. And as if to prepare me for a rough time ahead, the night before my departure, it is raining sideways. A hefty storm whistles around the house.

The next day, I merrily paddle from Sucuriju into the big delta. All is well, first a zig zag paddle among some tree trunks to escape the counter current and to get out of the Sucuriju River. When I turn right into the Amazon, the tide runs with me, and paddling becomes easier. When the tide turns again, I am worried about crossing over two of the tributaries without getting swept out. I get out, and drag the kayak in the shallow banks upstream, until I can ferry glide across without getting washed out too far. The water gets shallower with the tide running out, until I must be far from land to still be able to paddle. I will not reach any dry river bank anywhere in daylight, so I might as well stay out and wait, while sitting dry until the water is high enough again for paddling!

The point to get stuck comes earlier than expected. For over an hour before lowest tide, I make myself comfortable in the kayak, eat dinner and can even bend forward for a little snooze until the water rises again.

And rise it does - and then some! I am hearing this murmuring sough for half an hour, and think it is just another incoming tropical rain squall. I do not have another Pororoco wave on my mind at all, since I assume it should be over now. Has it not already happened twice after the new moon? I obviously misunderstood what "twice" meant - sure, it meant twice a day in the tidal rhythm, strong around new and full moon, going down to almost nothing in between. This was not clear to me at this point...how could I have been so naive?

And then the realization at the very last second: "Shit, there comes another fucking Pororoca! Grab your paddle, girl!"

I sit high and dry on a sandbank, four miles offshore, and I am helpless with respect to what is coming towards me in the darkness. I throw myself sideways into the rolling wave so as not to get capsized, lie 90 degrees on my side, and brace and brace and brace with my paddle for my life. Where does this devils' ride take me? Into the mouth of the tributary of Rio Araguari? I have heard, the narrower the river, the higher the wave...

On this corner is a lighthouse, and I can see I am being washed south rather than west. Despite my closed spray deck and tight waist tunnel, the kayak is filling up with the heavy water pressure. Sand, rubble and many pieces of wood fly around me and into my mouth, eyes and nostrils. At some time, I will get washed ashore as a matter of course, but how hard of a landing will it be? Is there a cliff to smash against? I still brace and brace and brace, cannot see anything in the darkness, and scream pointlessly for help.

At a shallower section, I am capsized, can roll up again with one hand and continue to brace, brace, brace... How much longer will I have the strength to do that? My muscles are burning, my sense of orientation is diminishing. Again, I capsize. This time, I am stuck under the heavy kayak with the paddle lying diagonally under me. I must kick myself free and open the spray deck to bail out. Instantly, the kayak is washed away from me.

Luckily - my very serious good luck - I am connected by the bow line to my spray deck, or my kayak and all my gear would have disappeared into the darkness and never been seen again. I have nothing on my body besides a thin layer of fleece. With some effort, I can pull the boat on the line closer to me, and finally I am able to reach the bow toggle. But there is no chance to stand up yet in this only knee-deep water, the current is still too powerful. My legs stick out to the left and right of the bow, I hold the kayak with one hand, and with the other I hold my paddle like for dear life, lay back and lift my behind, and continue to get washed over the shallows in a bumpy, but somehow organized ride.

The shore is getting closer... Will I crash into a mud cliff or fallen tree stump somewhere, with full force? Or better, will I be washed up on a sandy bank? Finally, this ride becomes a bit slower, and in a small deep-water basin or tiny tributary mouth, I somehow come to a halt and can slowly get upright. Are there piranhas floating around? I only lose a sandal in the depth of the pool; my warming rescue blanket and drink bottle are long gone. GPS, flash light and everything else is still there, my pants are down to half-mast. I still have all my extremities, but gained something: Sand and mud in all orifices of

180

my body and kayak. I wade over to the shrubby river bank, and check the kayak for damages. All seems in order, but I must clean my boat from the mud inside! I try to scoop it out with my hands, then with my plastic breakfast box. But the water pressure of my fast ride has turned these finest Amazon sediment particles into concrete. I must scrape it out with a metal spoon, about a whole bucket load!

Finally, I try to clean my clothing and myself in one of the deeper pools of the river bank. Well past midnight, I give Peter in Europe a little wake-up call, "You will never believe this, but it is true…" My ride through hell, as my GPS told me, has lasted about twenty minutes, passed four miles, and the top speed was twenty-two and a half miles per hour. And all that at night, without serious losses or damage. The best surfer cannot do better, and never at night. But do not try this at home!

I crawl into my kayak, wrap myself into my last rescue blanket, and wait for the new day. The waves lap gently at my bow. Is the Pororoco now over?

Peter tells me on the satellite phone, that the monster wave reduces in power over three to five days after its peak. If only I had known that earlier! And it is so logical…Today is only the second day after new moon, but the new wave dissipated here in daylight quite quickly over these deeper pools. I must suffer another night in the hammock, my aching body fairly shouts for a break. The kayak is tightly lashed and pulled up high onto two tree forks. From this position, I can await the sinister soughing of the next wave relaxed. I must have fallen into an exhausted sleep, as I do not even notice the next wave coming in.

Next day, I let quite a low wave go past before I start into a still strong current. Across widely flooded grassland and fences, I reach a farm house with seven friendly workers, where I can recover from the tortures of the last days. Horses, water buffalos, pigs and cows are grazing unfazed on their flooded meadows. I put up my tent inside the wide-open house, to have a bit of privacy. On a rest day, I am partaking of the life on the farm.

The next Pororoco wave is hardly noticeable, it is high time to get going again, and to face new challenges: Strong currents, shallow sand banks, messy water where two currents meet, massive trees and tree trunk obstacles above and below the waterline. In this enormous delta, one can hardly stay safe from experience, but must follow instinct.

Crossing the main channel of the Amazonas to an island in the delta becomes an examination in navigation skills. I get washed out seven miles first, but in the eddy of the other shore, I get to ride the current at more than nine miles per hour. Water buffalos graze on soaking wet meadows, they block the few free places to camp. I must stay overnight in the shelter of simple but friendly family homesteads, where I am a pleasant diversion from their hard farming life. The houses usually are built on stilts on the edges of the tributaries, and nothing can be reached without a boat. You even get to school in a yellow "school boat". The jungle passes like an impenetrable green wall, there is so much to discover. How and what do you live on here? This is a special world!

Just before Chavez, I cross over the eastern channel, and pass the equator for the second time. I keep a beady eye on the GPS, and call my family to celebrate when the display shows only zeros. Can they imagine how much arduous work all this is?

My tortured feet cannot heal properly anymore, the soles are just one painful open sore, and I can barely walk. Due to wearing neoprene socks daily, I have bagged up a massive open fungal infection, but without the socks, sandal straps would have rubbed them, and I would have more abrasions and bug bites. The feet under the deck are wet all day, just like the rest of my skin. The sweet water of the river of the last days has worsened the problem. None of my creams help now. The air conditioning in Chavez only brings light relief.

Finally, I paddle with a lot of current, cross waves, countercurrents and rain out of the massive Amazonas delta and into the Rio Para heading for Belém. I stay with indigenous families in their stilt farm houses, and paddle past the most beautiful homesteads in narrow channels. A helpful gaucho I met at the beach is willing to pull my kayak with his stallion up to dry ground.

In a happy mood, I head for Punta Pesqueiro, the first real holiday resort in Brazil. Gelderson and Priscilla, online friends from the Belém paddling community, pick me up, and take me to their new hotel. Delighted, I move into a cool and clean room. My first meal is a water buffalo steak, what a treat after weeks of rice and pasta!

I must spend the entirety of the first day inside the room to heal my damaged feet. I like to use the recovery time to make plans for the next leg of my journey. Unfortunately, I do not have internet, and it looks like I will have to paddle the next weeks without my broken laptop. That is unpleasant, as ahead of me is an area full of islands and channels, and the tidal range is seven yards. There are no paper charts, and I cannot get my satellite pictures without the laptop. The GPS chart is only moderately exact, and the screen of the GPS device alone is small. At least I am carrying three functioning GPS! I must pay great attention to not only where I am going to, but also when I paddle, in order not to get lost or run dry in this labyrinth of islands and mangrove channels.

The nights, I spend in stilt houses as a guest of families or groups of fishermen. The large tidal range influences the simplest routes. I look for channels connecting the fjords, so that I do not have to paddle past unprotected headlands, but get lost several times and stuck in dense mangrove forest due to the inaccuracies of the charts. At low tide, sandbanks block my direct line across an arm of a fjord, at high tide there is so much drift from the strong current I have difficulties arriving where I would like to get to.

On top of all things, I poke a large hole in the side of the hull, when I surf onto a village beach, side broached in cross waves. Out of all places, there was a stump of an old net pole standing upright on the water's edge. The locals help me to get my injured baby into the garden of a house, where I repair the hole with epoxy resin and fiber glass mats, surrounded and checked out by all the village people.

It is a full moon night in the middle of April, when I arrive in Sao Luis after an exciting crossing of the strong current of the Rio Mearim. My host Jadiel and his girlfriend Sandra give me a luxurious air-conditioned room with en-suite facilities, where I can recover for a few days from the odyssey through the canals and headlands.

I spontaneously decide not to celebrate my 50th birthday in Germany, but to continue to at least Fortaleza. This is likely to take three to four weeks, with a pit stop in Jericocuara. I must make use of the favorable wind and weather conditions until June! After June, a headwind speed of twenty knots is normal until September/ October. After my summer break, I would be able to continue with, hopefully, the last leg of my circumnavigation, the final home run! With freshly regenerated strength, I would be able to tackle the eastern landmass of Brazil with its strong easterly winds and currents.

In Sao Luis, I find a doctor who prescribes antibiotics against the massive skin infections. They simply will not heal themselves under the continuous influence of heat, sweat, saltwater and friction. Easter Monday, I still do not feel fully fit, but want to set off again. The doctor says, I should better take a longer break to give my body a chance to get used to the antibiotics. But I need every single day to fulfil my paddling plan, which is so dictated by the timings of the tides. With a fair-sized audience of beach visitors, I set off at the peak of the tide change at 11am. Soon, the beaches become emptier, with fewer colorful umbrellas and beach huts. There is hardly any music anymore, without which a Brazilian holiday beach would not be complete.

Now I only see fishermen and their boats, or an occasional cow or donkey.

Today, I like to go around a large headland, and to cross the following river mouth at mid-tide. There are already a few dry sandbanks sticking out. The odyssey continues - and I am still stuck with inaccurate charts. Fortunately, it is possible to find suitable beaches for landing without great problems.

In Itapera, two days after Sao Luis, I approach a concrete jetty with the steps reaching the water at low tide. A man runs down the jetty, drops his one and only pants, and jumps naked as God made him into the knee-deep water. This is for the sole purpose of moving his boat out of the way, so I would have space to get in. This is very kind of him, but I would not have minded if he kept his pants on! When he realizes it is a woman arriving here, he is full of embarrassment, and hides behind his boat. I smile, and pull up the kayak. As I carry my luggage to a nearby house, he uses the opportunity to sprint out from behind the boat to where he dumped his trousers. Later, he helps me to carry the kayak from the jetty to the beach. Many thanks!

The winds and currents are giving me some headache. As I slalom around the headlands and river mouths, I have an ongoing fifteen knots of headwind into my face, and the currents does not favor me these days either. Even when the tide changes, the situation does not improve: The wind freshens up so much that I am faster with tide against me and lower wind. "Faster" in this case means one to two miles per hour. I feel totally frustrated. The medications also seem to affect my energy levels. One shitty day after the other - and that will not change until Fortaleza. To my general exhaustion now comes a nasty case of diarrhea. One day I must stop six times. I suspect, it was caused by a jar of pesto sauce which had smelled strange. If it were the antibiotic, it would have started earlier.

I have a difficult decision to make: Should I stop already, due to my overall-worn state, and fly home to recover, even though there are still a few weeks of somehow bearable weather ahead? When I reflect on what has happened so far on this leg, my decision is easy: I need a break NOW. I am really knackered. The permanent tropical heat and humidity, my skin infections not healing properly, the nearly raw soles on my feet, the heavily breaking monster waves that rise from nowhere and caused me to roll a few times, the involuntary ride on the Pororoca wave, the strong countercurrents of the Amazonas, the shallow muddy water and the continuous danger of getting stuck and running dry, the lack of suitable landing places and having to sleep in the kayak or hammock, broken electronics and then getting raided by the hunters. I decide to paddle back a few miles to civilization, where

Jadiel can collect me from Humberto de Campos, and take me back to Sao Luis.

I lose no time to arrange my return to Germany. I get an online flight ticket, clean my equipment, repair a few places on the kayak with epoxy resin, and sort out things to throw away or to take back to Germany. The boat and most of my gear stays with Jadiel in Sao Luis. This is where I want to continue my journey in October. The flight back to Brazil is booked, on October 16th I will continue. I wonder how my boyfriend Peter will react to my appearance. I have lost ten kilograms, but gained ten years of age!

Chapter 15
RECIFE: PADDLING NORTH – AND SOUTH

Brazil: Recife to Sao Luis
October 25th - December 2nd, 2014

Brazil: Recife to Rio de Janeiro
December 3rd - February 5th, 2015

The break in Germany has lasted longer than intended due to the premature end of the last leg. I have recovered well, both mentally and physically. My sponsor Hilleberg was once more so generous to give me a new tent, that way I do not always have to look at the patched rips from the machete attack. I am well prepared for my last section, and expect to paddle five to six months before I will return to Buenos Aires. By Christmas, I will have reached Recife. I hope my elderly mother will stay fit until I return, she has caused us a bit of worry during the summer. I arrive in Sao Luis after my five-month summer break, and get a warm welcome from my faithful helpers Jadiel and his friend and translator Lucas. The plan is to take me by car to the beach I exited from at the beginning of May. It is well over thirty degrees centigrade, hot and humid, and the wind is strong.

When we arrive near the dunes at the position I left off after an adventurous journey, I get a knot in my stomach. There is only one thought in my mind: I do not like these conditions! The view of the sea is even scarier than a few months ago. The next 620 miles would be a permanent headwind of twenty knots, garnished with an endless wide breaker zone which I might only be able to break through while the swell and tide is low. Safe take out spots would be rare - all conditions to be avoided when planning a paddling tour. But there is no alternative. I do not like the prospect of only being able to paddle three to four hours per day at a speed of up to two miles per hour or less, and to cross a seriously gruesome surf belt twice a day. On the upcoming distance, that might be hundred or even up to two-hundred dangerous landings, where each time I would be risking life and equipment, and would endure torturous hours on the beach with mosquitos or in the sauna tent.

Not that I was not aware of this beforehand, and not that I want to skip any part of my circumnavigation. But what for? Only so that I can say I am the only person to have paddled this section, plus - into the wind!

I find a different solution: My circumnavigation will not have gaps, but a little blemish. This coming leg, I will simply reverse my direction. I will drive to Recife 930 miles south of Sao Luis, and then paddle north with the wind and currents to Humberto de Campo. This is the hardest, most difficult decision of the whole tour, but the most sensible. I do not want to start to hate the sport! And I might do if I must fight just a few more miles into the wind. I do not think I must prove myself to anyone anymore. And at fifty years old, I am mature enough to take this decision.

On the beach and during the whole drive back, I continue to think if this decision is really the right one. Back in the apartment with Jadiel and Sandra, I feel anything but heroic. I have a chat with Jadiel, and my decision is confirmed: I will drive to Recife, and paddle backwards to Humberto de Campo!

The drive through the night is adventurous: Three friends go with me, and we take turns driving through the darkness over potholed roads without any signs. My kayak is riding on a made-up roof rack, and in these road conditions, I am quite worried about my baby's well-being.

In Recife, I have a quick visit to a dentist, as I have lost a filling. As I stand on the beach next morning, I do not feel really fit. I must find my rhythm again, and accustom my muscles to the demanding work out. Thankfully, today I find beginners conditions, and that is how I feel. I am happy again, once I leave the harbor wall behind me, and have direct sight of the picturesque beaches. Many holiday makers are mobile, I view Brazilian beach life at its best.

I am careful not to hit yet another maniac guy on a jet-ski or powerboat flying over the water, I prefer slow and harmless fishing boats around. For the first night on the beach, I find a little corner away from the holiday traffic and party noises - a promising beginning. But I must get used again to bush camping! Several times that night, I stick my head out of the tent, to check if there is no one around. Each strange or unusual sound sets me off.

On the water, the change in direction does not yet pay off. The wind hits me sideways, not too helpful nor friendly. But when I cross the first bay, I feel

I am pushed along. I leave behind the skyline of Joao Pessoa with its hundreds of sky scrapers as fast as I can. The wind conditions are more difficult than expected. More than twenty knots are always demanding work, even when it is a tailwind. I must be on high alert all the time in case of a surprise breaker from behind, and at times, it feels like a ride on a cannon ball. On a landing, a high breaker capsizes me. My rolling in the foaming water does not work out, so I swim next to the kayak, and let myself drift ashore. Should I have cancelled this whole section? This is not how to manage the planned thirty-five miles per day. Next morning, I need three attempts to get out, including a capsize and roll up, before I can continue my journey towards Natal.

Not all is working smoothly. I cannot rely on meeting helpful people in each village to get free accommodation. In Pipa, where I have intended to end a day, I only find some guest house owners charging rates I do not like to afford. I prefer some quiet beach five miles beyond the popular holiday resort for my planned rest day, adding another hour and a half to my daily work.

The rain pours down on my tent at 4am, what a wonderful feeling, when I can turn around and go back to sleep. After only ten days, everything hurts from the continuous fight with the breakers and the surf. I do not make much ground speed, when I ride up and down the mountainous waves, it feels like the vertical distance I cover is higher. It would be nice if my GPS could record that!

It should get easier, once I have gone around the eastern landmass of this continent, and I can go more westwards. In this section, I feel like a pupil who is kept in detention. I am no longer sweating like I did last May, but still, the first rashes appear. Tomorrow I will arrive in Natal, and will be able to look after the bodies of both myself and my kayak.

The lumpy waters at the harbor entry of the large town make me seasick before I arrive at the local yacht club. Everything looks nice and promising, it is the right place to recover. I smell the tempting flavor of an asado, the Brazilian BBQ, which I am spontaneously invited to by a group of sailors. Before I can indulge in fried steak and sausages, I must finish the regular chores to make myself at home, and quickly give an interview to the local paper. Hustle with your questions, guy, I am hungry!

Tomorrow, I will reach the easternmost city of Brazil, Torous, after which the coastline bends to the westward direction. Turtles of all sizes and a few dolphins keep me company. The countless wind turbines and dozens of kite- and windsurfers love the strong wind, I do not. They are attentive enough not to run me over, but the hiss, especially when the windsurfers swoosh past me, is scary. For safety's sake, I lift my paddle if one of them gets a bit too close for my comfort. Who knows if they have as much control over their toys as I have over mine?

That wind is really getting on my nerves. One would think a strong pushing wind around and over twenty knots must be fun, but to control a two-hundred-pound kayak in these conditions is not pure enjoyment. Pleasure paddling is something different, pleasure camping, too, for that matter. There is hardly a beach without a big party till late at night.

This coastal region is not particularly exciting, windmills dominate the view and continuously remind me of the fact that this is an area of strong easterly winds. A pit stop on this tough section is near, and I reach the Yacht Club of Fortaleza after twelve days without a break. A relaxing stay with friends, and I continue fresh and with renewed energy to the last part of this long, reversed leg. Unfortunately, I must continue without my laptop, as it stays in town for repairs. Another two or three weeks along this stormy, unfriendly coast, and I have made it!

Along endless beaches and dunes, I am almost glad the waves give me a pounding, or there would have been several times where I would have fallen asleep due to boredom or tiredness. The only entertainment here are swarms of jumping fish. The more I get westwards, the more the sea and surf calms down.

The coastline soon looks familiar: Green lines with a thick mangrove forest broken by many river mouths. Instead of countless surfers, there are rustic fishing boats, which do not look unlike surf boards. The jangada, the craft of the Brazilian fishermen here in the north, has a large triangular sail hitched on its tip. With a simple bench on top, it looks like a mix of a stand-up paddle board, surf board, and a small open boat. Three men crew these boats as they whip though the waves on their fishing trips. The jangada men also have races with their toys, and obviously enjoy the wet elements.

The water is getting shallower. I leave the popular holiday resort of Jericoacoara with its hundreds of, for me, dangerous wind surfers quickly behind me, and shortly before Pedra do Sal, it gets uncomfortable once more. At over twenty-five knots wind, I ride across a wide bay and around the very rough rocky headland into town, which impresses with a big lighthouse and massive granite rocks. Like the teenagers, I have fun climbing them, and explore the rural holiday location.

And after a final day with monster surf and three capsizes, I once again enter a labyrinth of mangrove fringed islands and channels, which I already got to know on my way south. This time, wind and current pushes me without effort on the calm water. It feels like I am in a different world, where I can listen to the sounds of the jungle. I count my blessings when I arrive in Tutoia, where I finish this reverse leg with a calm day.

I take the bus to get back to Jadiel in Sao Luis. I will rent a car to drive back to Recife, this time just by myself. My kayak and some of the gear I will collect on my return journey. I am welcomed to Sao Luis for the fifth time now!

It is the end of November, and barely four weeks to Christmas, when I would like to be in Salvador. 700 paddle days are behind me. For the next three days, I expect stress, but dry traffic stress. I must drive for three days via Tutoia and Fortaleza, where I collect my kayak and my repaired laptop. Navigating on land proves to be more difficult, despite a hired GPS with road maps. The tool can only be as good as its maps, as many roads are dirt tracks, and neither signs are posted, nor they are marked on my map. A few times, I get stuck in loose sand. I worry about my kayak, since the "roof rack" are only a few foam pads, which was as good as I could get it. The traffic is, compared to European standards, horrendous. My baby and I will have to survive these roads. it costs me 1,500 Euros on this return trip to get to where I was five weeks ago.

The Yacht Club in Recife is fanciful and well organized. All around me, workers tinker and repair stuff in their shops. I have seen a few Yacht Clubs in this region, but this is one of the better ones. I enjoy qualified help on repairing and refreshing my kayak. The club employs a PR manager, who helps me with my press engagements. I get to meet curious and sympathetic paddlers, and enjoy the attention. They help to motivate me for the final leg with their enthusiasm. Many thanks!

I miss the VIP treatment in the Yacht Club of Recife when I head south the next day. I continue to visualize my final goal of Buenos Aires. The next longer pits stops are in Brazil are Salvador, Rio de Janeiro and Florianopolis. Paddling inside the many reefs will be interesting, and hopefully, I will have moderate winds.

Along the long beach of Boa Viagem, I must once again think about sharks. These toothy beggars were ever present, particularly along Australia's northern coast line, and I had encounters daily. The curious beasties follow closely and unnoticed behind, until they decide to give it a bump to find out what kind of fish I am. Mostly, they bump with the mouth shut, but the last and strongest one in Australia took a bite, and left a hole and a tooth behind. He must have told all other sharks I am not edible, as they are also around anywhere in South America, but I never had any closer encounters.

The sea around Recife is supposed to have the largest number of sharks anywhere on earth. Asking paddlers what they think about that situation, they say: "it should be possible to paddle there…," and when I ask if they have been there, the usual reply is, "No, it's out of limits for small water craft!"

Ok, but you let me start and paddle here? Well, who cares…I remember my Australian experiences and reckon, "this here" cannot be worse. Nonetheless, I am glad to deal with this bit as fast as possible, and best without seeing any triangular fin, unless it is a dolphin!

I am barely 800 yards away from the mainland, when I see two jet skis rushing towards me. Two guys from the coast guard come to pick me off the water. Paddling here is not allowed! One of them has such poor control over his jet ski in the bumpy water, that he heftily crashes a few times into my kayak. Or is that his way to emphasize his commands? I am angry, as the sharks are kind enough to leave me alone, I really do not need these kinds of bumps now. With some difficulties, I fiddle a signature card out of my day hatch, and explain why I really must go along this beach without any gaps. It is only a ridiculous five or six miles of "shark infested" area!

One of them races back to shore with my statement and card, and comes back with his lieutenant, who is speaking good English. He is very impressed by my achievements, and does not want to impede me. He decides that they simply join me with the jets skies on the most dangerous section. I do not mind, I have some nice company, and it creates the possibility of a potential shark choosing a jet ski over me.

It is windy and rainy. I can see my only sparsely dressed companions are starting to get cold, all without helmet, jacket, PFD or wind protection. With no view of any triangle fin, our three crafts are riding through the shark infested area. Once we have passed most of the reefs, the beach is getting lower, and I aim towards a calm river mouth with the skyline of Recife as a back drop. I reckon I do my frozen companions a big favor to stop early. My invite to come back tomorrow at 5am to set off together is rejected with thanks. That would be too early, and anyway, the most dangerous bit is now behind. That is just what I hope to hear! A fun ride with one of the guys on the jet ski ends this short escort. Were there really that many sharks?

Whenever I can find shelter between the mainland and the outer reef, I thoroughly enjoy paddling. The shallow water is calm and clear, and a light northeasterly wind pushes me forward. This region in the state of Pernambuco between Tamandare and Sao Jose do Coroa Grande can only be described as a paddler's paradise: A reef giving shelter on the left, quiet beaches on the right, much to see and to discover, not too hot, easy landing sites, and dream locations to stay overnight. I think I have earned this treat after all the earlier tortures!

In Maragogi, the beauty of the reefs has created a popular snorkeling and diving tourist destination with a variety of water colors the like I have not seen for a long time, all shades of blue and green. The choice of paradise beaches is so big, it is hard to pass some, when my paddling quota for the day is yet to be filled. These beaches are clean and cared for. Every few hundred meter you will find rubbish bins that are well used.

Around Maceio, I experience the full Brazilian joie de vivre: The bass of Samba music just thunders across the bay, families sit under sun umbrellas stuck into the shallow water. The houses along the promenade are only half the height of those in Recife. I see joggers, power walkers and cyclists; fitness seems to be a popular pastime. Beach wardens set up umbrellas and loungers, and even rake the sand. From my wet vantage point, I can watch an exotic Hindu wedding, with the water strewn with flowers. Nice, but unfortunately most of them are wrapped in plastic foil.

On the beach, two groups play football, one team wears shirts, the other does not. That might be the why women's football is not that popular here? The ladies seem to prefer to take their string bikinis for a walk. You show what you have, and sometimes a lot, which is not always aesthetically pleasing. However, going topless on the beach, like it is a common habit in Germany, is not a choice. I prefer to wear shorts and t-shirt, I stir up enough attention as it is. The temperature has now thankfully moved from "unbearable" to "I can handle this", and skin problems are within limits.

It is now middle of December, and I am making good headway. Paddling outside the reefs is a challenge, inside it is usually calm. After Macaio, I am paddling next to red and white cliffs which are so beautiful I would love to peek into every canyon. But I need to carry on, as I am still on a schedule. I will paddle this last leg without my regular Christmas break. I am wondering how a town stay would feel over the holidays, it is packed to the limits everywhere. The only thing reminding me of Christmas these days, is chewing gum with cinnamon flavor. I just carry on, tune out the Christmas time, and try not to think too much of my loved ones at home on the day.

How will I best cross the upcoming multiple large river outflows? Riacho Breiao is still comparably easy. I slip into the entrance just behind a long barrier reef, to paddle along Francis Beach. I feel like I am in the longest bath tub of the world, or on a kiddy's playground, with so many different floating devices in and on the water. The beach is crammed full of tourists, with one sun umbrella seeming to be glued to the next.

Lagoa de Roteiro is also sheltered by a barrier reef, but I cannot find a safe entrance on the north side. Anxiously, I paddle along the unprotected outer side with heavy breaking surf, hoping to find a way to enter the calm lagoon. At the end, I see a few fishing boats leaving, the narrow entry feels dangerous and spooky for a non-local. I squeeze through with good timing, and I find a quiet corner to pitch my tent, with only a few tourists in sight. Unlike them, I must do without a comfortable room with air-conditioning and mains power.

Rio Couripe is a bit more of a challenge. I prefer to avoid the sheltered but crowded bay just after the village, but also cannot face going into its river mouth. It has sandbanks all over with heavily breaking waves. The area after seems better, and I land safely in the shade of a palm grove on a quiet lagoon beach. But the deep bass of the Samba parties in the town still thumps all the way over here.

The coastline between the next large river mouths of the Rio San Fancisco, Rio Mosqueiro and Rio Mangue do not offer safe take out spots. The last protective reef at the headland of Pontal de Peba I must leave behind, as I have not done anywhere near a day's paddle. The only possibility is to fight my way through the breaker zones of the large river mouths, to find a quiet beach.

I am impatient to get to the first wide river to land safely, and dare to go through a wide heavy breaker zone to the open beach before the river, in the hope of finding a strip of calm water in front of the last breaker. With a bit of luck, I manage to stay upright on the way in. Unfortunately, there is not much of a calm strip of water to be found, and I get washed high up the beach a few times. Finally, I am fed up with this useless attempt to paddle in sheltered waters, and I head straight out again. This was a superfluous and risky endeavor I really should not have bothered with!

I now sneak through the challenging breaker zone at the mouth of the Rio San Francisco, my heart is pounding heavily, and I must do several high braces. But I reach quiet water upright, can cross the river, and land safely. But I must get out again in the morning!

Same game again in Pirambu, I land safely without capsize through a nasty surf belt, but a bit too early, and decide to drag my kayak on its bowline through the eight-hundred yards distance into the calm river mouth. Walking the kayak in the surf belt is a dangerous exercise, any higher wave can lift the boat and wash it up the beach. If my legs are in the way, they would be broken. The kayak tips over a few times, and even with the cockpit cover on, it is arduous work to turn a two-hundred-pounds boat.

It is impossible to estimate if the water is calm out at sea where the big rivers empty into the Pacific. It would be a detour of endless miles to try to give the river mouth a wide berth, and who knows, depending on the tide, if it is really calm out there. A fisherman on his bigger boat has an easier job to safely go in and out of a large river mouth, with his lookout from higher up. A few fixed GPS points to find the unbroken line of the main current might also be of some help. But unfortunately, there is no fishing boat to be seen, whose path I could follow. Rio Aracaju, I try to pass with a wide berth, but I end up in a minefield of cross breakers, like at the river mouth I had to cross at night a few weeks ago. Just get out of here!

At Rio Mosqueiro, I go back to my tactic to break through the surf belt at the river mouth. Once more, it is an evil minefield, I must roll twice, and I am washed ashore, but at least sitting upright and not swimming. My camp on the other side of the river is quiet, but the sand here is as powder-fine as flour, and sticks to everything and everywhere.

I am now trying to cross the penultimate river of this kind, Rio Mangue Seco, I keep my nerves, and find a narrow, but unbroken gap between the heavy breaking rollers. I paddle endlessly between tall white wave walls, until I finally get to the safe calm water inside.

Until Sitio, I cannot find any safe landing place: A sharp black rocky reef surrounds the beach. It is hard to see if anywhere might be a safe gap to go in. But there are fishing boats on the beach - is the black stuff not rocks? On a few smaller waves, I carefully come closer for a better look, and the decision to land or not is taken out of my hands. A sudden high wave gets me, and surfs me straight onto the black mass. I expect to hear an ugly crunch and the splintering hull of my boat, but I discover the black stuff is a carpet of soft black baby mussels. Lucky... this time!

When I try to land for the next night near Subauma, I break my nose... I search for the correct path through the outer reef, and think to have found it near some markers. I hesitate one second too long, get grabbed by a fat rolling breaker once more, and I am surfed straight over the dangerous reef. Unfortunately, there was a rock in the path of the reef gap, and I hit it, nose first. I pitch pole, capsize, bend underwater far forward on my deck, and hope to protect my head from further contact with any reef rocks. Thankfully, I am already wearing my helmet! I manage to roll up again all right, drift into calm water, and my view goes straight forward to my bow pointing at the beach.

"Fucking hell!" I curse roundly, the whole nose of my kayak is bent forty-five degrees to the left! I paddle the short distance to the beach as fast as I can, and with a jerk, I bend the nose back to where it should be. Unfortunately, I forgot to take a picture of it first! I quickly unload my soaked gear from the front compartment, which is now showing big cracks. Good dry bags pay off! At least, my own nose and all my bones are without damage. Have the few dolphins who came alongside for a while today brought me luck?

The worst crash in my kayak career is still thankfully not a total write-off. But even the damage at Cape Horn was easier to repair! Doing it at the beach here will be difficult, even though a few fishermen are offering their help. I hope my contact in Salvador can pick me up. They will come in a few hours, and already know a person who can do such a major restoration.

It would be difficult to do such a trip without the support of friends. Paulo, Daniel and his wife Jessica have arrived, they like to take me to the house of their friend Emiliano in Lauro de Freitas, a village just before Salvador. On the way, I am baffled by the number of filigree bridges across the highway, could they carry a person across? These bridges are for monkeys to cross safely from one side of the jungle to the other. I can visualize one of those funny creatures hanging upside down, grinning directly into the face of a passing trucker!

I am staying at the large old family home of my friend. I have it all for myself, it is like a palace, with a pool and big courtyard, air-conditioning and fast internet. Total luxury! Gustavo, my genius "kayak doctor", manages to fix my severely dented vehicle. Many thanks!

I do not like to intrude on any of the families here over Christmas, and carry on. My friends take me back to Subauma where I crash landed three days ago. The prospect for the next few weeks is giving me a good mood: There should be low following winds, low waves, safe take out places, and a beautiful and varied coastline. This section of Brazilian coast is my best Christmas present!

I do not have any plans as to where to stay, I take it as it comes on the many options on this coast. I am doing my best to ignore that today is December 24th. My beach for tonight has not only the usual palm trees, but also a large pine tree, the first one since a long time! I cannot avoid some upcoming Christmas feelings. I imagine burning candles on the pine tree, and treat myself to a few half molten pralines of white chocolate which I saved for this special holiday. I call my family to wish them a "Merry Christmas", a strange feeling while sitting on a tropical beach in the heat. The beauty of the reefs I pass on my way to Morro de Sao Paulo is another Christmas present.

New Year's Eve is no big party for me either, other than making good progress - and a few last white chocolate pralines for a feast. And while I paddle in warm water in the higher seventies, Peter at his New Year party in Denmark takes a heroic swim in the icy Baltic Sea.

On the beaches of the Brazilian state of Bahia, high summer season continues. All places are packed to the last square yard, but on a slightly more secluded beach after Porto Seguro, an obviously overheated couple takes the cocktail "Sex on the Beach" literally. I am nearly tempted to set my small anchor and enjoy the view a bit longer. They are so engrossed they do not notice my silent approach, but the wind and current pushes me on far too quickly. As I turn around, I can see the guy is taking a deep draught of his cocktail...

It is not a promising idea to look for accommodation in these holiday centers at high season without having made contacts ahead of time. Even if my skin demands a bit of air-conditioning, the hotels here look too fine and expensive, not something I would like to pay for. I head to a small beach restaurant, fill up my water bags, and treat myself to grilled cheese and delicious coconut ice cream. I paddle around the cliffs to find a quieter section of the beach, here only a few paragliders swoop above me. I hope that they all know what they are doing, and are not likely to fall on my tent! Vultures are circling with them. As an ex-skydiver, this sport does not look exciting to me. Far more interesting would be the tiny ultra-light plane one can hire for a tour over the beaches, but despite the pilot throwing curious glances over me and my kayak, his paying customers are obviously more important.

I like it better back out on the reefs, where dolphins and turtles have their own party with a sting ray jumping high out of the water. I land close to a village with a plastic kayak rental, and hope none rents mine out for a premium while I pop into the village. I spotted a few shops from the water, and hope to stock up my supplies a bit. I have run out of fresh fruit, and I am delighted to find maracujas, carrots, apples and bananas to replenish my vitamins. Without regular fruit and fresh vegetables, I might be getting sick more often. There are no oats or muesli, only a kind of a baby porridge which I can mix with the last of my oats. Pasta and water makes my shopping trip complete, I can live well again for a few days. Decent food is essential to keep the spirit up on such a journey, and it is easy to get fed up with monotony.

One night, my kayak has an ancient neighbor. Six men are moving an enormous eleven-yard, twenty-five-year-old dug-out canoe. It is powered by six men with single-blades, each two and a half yards long, and five pounds heavy. By comparison, my high-tech carbon double-blade weighs only 630 grams, and is just over two yards long. They load a two-hundred-yard long and a yard-wide net, which is weighed down with stones at the bottom and has swim floats at the top. I am invited to help on some real men's work, but fortunately, it is only to help with the preparations to disentangle and fold the net. I feel honored, and would love to join them tomorrow on their fishing trip, but I better should keep going.

This reef zone looks easier than I have expected for the homerun. I have had many exhausting and dangerous passages on the 15,000 miles I have covered so far, which make this leg seem harmless. It has not been too often as pleasant as it is here: Calm seas, mellow winds, balmy temperatures, beaches with easy take out spots, sleeping places that at are easy to find, few mosquitoes, no rash, no open festering sores, no dangerous animals and nice people everywhere - it could hardly be better. I have solved all sorts of problems and survived all sorts of dangers, nothing can shock me much anymore, but it is also difficult to become enthusiastic. I might be sated after all these impressions and experiences? Sometimes I am paddling like in trance with my eyes shut.

But you should not count your chickens before they hatch: I was just thinking of how perfect everything is, when the conditions change again. Behind Conceicao, I once more must fight on long straight beaches with strong wind and an unpredictable surf, and landing is everything but simple. Nearly all my electronics die at the same time, I must make a pit stop in Regencia. I thread my way through heavy breakers into the river mouth after a stressful paddle through fifty miles of strong following wind, which needs all my concentration.

Felipe, my host in Regencia, convinces me to stay three days with him, and not to take a longer break later in Victoria as planned. He supplies me with everything I need: A room in a friend's guesthouse, internet at a research and rescue station for turtles, and his help to get my electronics sorted. Nothing speaks against a longer break here, the last three weeks, I had only two rest days on the beach.

Turtles go with me the next days. This region is a preferred one to lay their eggs on the beaches. The water is a cool twenty-two degrees centigrade, and the surfers even wear wet suits. I paddle fast to pass the ugly harbor of Vitoria quickly, including all the uninviting skyscrapers of the city. Soon, the landscape becomes natural again. High mountains rise, and the coast is broken up by reefs and cliffs. The strong following wind of up to thirty knots is back, and my two-hundred pounds kayak looks like a submarine when a wave rolls over it from behind, and submerges it for a moment. Was this not what I have asked for? Were the earlier conditions not too simple and boring?

I hardly find beaches without people now. When I think I have found one, it is not long, and fishermen walk or bike up to the beach, and settle with their rods and nets for an evening catch. Some of them stumble over my tent lines, and one guy even tries to peep into my tent as I settle in to sleep. With a hiss I usually reserve for stray dogs, I chase him away. He runs as if he has seen a ghost!

Another day, some extended Brazilian families turn up and park their cars just beside my tent, with a full sound system in tow which serves the whole beach. Great music, but at this volume? More than once I must flee my tent, and distract myself by going for a walk. When I see Ilha do Santana on the horizon on my way to Cabo Frio, the choice between the island and the large town of Macaé is not a hard one. I decide on the island, and paddle the twenty miles happily across, with following wind and favorable currents. The first sandy bay I reach looks good, no people, no houses, only a large colony of sea birds, a few vultures and – unfortunately a large quantity of rubbish. My solitude is soon over. Five trawlers anchor in the bay for the night, one close to my spot, and he turns up the music. The disco hits from the eighties remind me of my teenage years, but here, I really do not need them. Different countries, different customs...

Next day, I have a bit more luck. I paddle back to the mainland, and find on the next four miles some of the most beautiful rocky cliffs and beaches of all Brazil. Near Rio das Ostras, I discover another promising-looking little island. Will I find the quiet and peace I am craving for here, with no music, no people, just enjoying the scenery like Robinson? I treat myself to this island after only twenty miles, as I can still feel yesterday's fifty-five-mile section. The path through the rocks towards the miniature coral beach is not easy, but hopefully it prevents larger boats from landing here.

Happy and content, I pitch my tent in this natural idyll. I have a swim in the sea, wash my hair and, bare of clothing, let them dry in the sun...until this massive sailing ship turns up. It is a beautiful two-master, but it disgorges at least seventy tourists. And of course, their loud samba music thunders across the bay. But I am lucky, they only swim and snorkel around the ship at anchor. They are not allowed to enter land here. Thank God! Entering this coral island barefoot would be quite unsuitable anyway. After an hour, the spook is over, and the ship leaves again. Heavenly peace returns to my "private" holiday island!

The snow white perfect beach of Cabo Frio is my next destination. Already the rocky coast along Cabo Armacao dos Buzios with its little sandy bays is a paradise, and I cannot stop looking into every nook and cranny. The beaches around Cabo Frio top everything. On the satellite maps, the white sand glows through the clear waters on those most perfect beaches of all Brazil. The most popular and whitest beach right at the windy cape I have for myself in the evening, once the many boats have taken the day trippers home - and once I have convinced two soldiers I am harmless, and gone by tomorrow. I turn down their offer to spend the night in safety at their base, as I am already settled comfortably. Later, I regret that, as a strong downdraft is pulling at my tent all night.

After the delightful, reef-protected beach of Saquarema, and the rocky headland of Punta Negra, there is only open coast for a halfway stop on the last sixty miles until Rio de Janeiro. The headwind freshens up after noon as forecasted, and it is high time to get ashore. The last twenty-five miles to Rio de Janeiro I will do tomorrow, I think.... The straight-line steep beach with its small dumper is not a problem to land, even though I mistimed it. I end up being washed up and down the beach for a while, and my cockpit fills with water. At that point, I was not aware about how this coast could change...although I saw the many wrecks along Punta Negra.

Bright light shines in my tent at night, with sheet lightning flashing up every few seconds. After a few hours, a thunderstorm, the likes I have not experienced before, breaks loose. I listen for the increased sound of the breakers, the sea is up, and I stay down, happy to turn around once more for a rest day.

In the morning, I evaluate the new situation: I am feeling trapped! I can forget about launching for Rio de Janeiro today, and for the next four days. Yesterday, there was an easy swell height of two feet. This morning, the swell is two yards high, and by Sunday, it will be two and a half. That means, the last wave will pile up to four yards just offshore, and then slam all its gathered power in a single dumping breaker onto the steep beach. The wash up fifty yards to the third level plateau nearly reaches my tent. Such breakers, I have only seen once in my sea kayaking career, and that was in New Zealand in the corner of Birdling's Flat. It seems they are not an everyday event here either, as a lot of people gather on the beach to watch the display of nature's power. I take pictures until my fingers hurt, even though I know that no picture can show the true dimensions and destructive forces.

To be stuck here for four days just a short distance before the major pit stop in Rio de Janeiro is not to my liking, and I decide on plan B: I will ask my kayaking friends hosting me in Rio to collect me here. Flavia and her friend Carla come this afternoon, and we drive to the Yacht Club where I can store my kayak for the few days I will be in Rio. My accommodation is a tiny apartment in the beautiful old town of Urca, south of the center. It belongs to Rafael and Catharina, who have vacated it especially for me.

I really am ready for a bit of civilization: Freshly showered and wearing the only beach dress I am carrying; Flavia and I visit a typical Churrasceria. I am hungry for everything but rice, pasta or oats. Afterwards, she gives me a tour of Rio by night. The famous Christo's statue rises surreal in the darkness, high above the sugar loaf.

For four days, I enjoy their hospitality, and play a bit "normal tourist". But now, it is time to really paddle into the bay of Rio de Janeiro! The sea has calmed down, and my launch off the ugly dumper beach works fine with good timing. I enter the wide bay of Rio between the tiny Ilha de Menina and the northern shore, and find something what I later sell on my blog as the "Jumping turtles of Rio de Janeiro": I pull a half a yard long, unfortunately very dead, but well-preserved turtle with some difficulties onto my foredeck, and it becomes a great picture of a supposed "stowaway". Even some locals were wondering about this strange unknown new species...

The world-famous Sugar Loaf of Rio lurks near Ilha de Veada. Entering Rio Bay, the right-hand side of the river is a military exclusion zone, why is the water there full of yucky dead fish? On the other side are a few old forts, and a shadow play gives me the impression of guns aiming at me out of the windows and arrow slits.

At last daylight, Flavia and two friends find me with their kayaks, and we paddle among the countless boats and a few catamarans into the harbor bay of Rio de Janeiro. Slowly, the metropolis turns into a sparkling sea of light, and Christo hold his protecting hands over all.

Chapter 16
HOME RUN!

Brazil/ Uruguay/ Argentina: Rio de Janeiro to Buenos Aires
February 6th – May 1st, 2015

As I leave Rio, a small group of seven friends in five kayaks are leaving the harbor with me. The sugar loaf, Christo, and the world famous, but today deserted beaches of Copacabana and Ipanema, are soon behind me. Only a short little distance is left, 1,500 miles to Buenos Aires!

The archipelago between Rio de Janeiro and Sao Paulo is a paradise for sea kayakers. On Ilha Grande, I meet Christian Fuchs, one of the most experienced sea kayakers of Brazil. He has paddled most stretches of the Brazilian coast himself, and given me countless bits of valuable information, hints and contacts. I get a shady place for my tent inside the boat house of the ranger, and have a day off with snorkeling trips, to recover from the windy and bumpy approach on the outer side of the islands.

In the popular area around the capital Sao Paulo, it is difficult to find a place for the night. The best beaches are either built up, "private", or reserved for the military. My next city host is waiting for me on the aptly named Ilha Belha, the Beautiful Island. It seems to be a popular place for wealthy house- and boat owners, and it holds the largest and fanciest yacht harbor of all Brazil. I would like to explore the caves at the outsides of the island with paddling friends, or to watch the samba schools for longer, but my schedule pushes me continuously southwards. I might be back one day!

On the way to Ilha Dos Gatos, I feel as if I am in the middle of a regatta of hundreds of motorboats and jet skis. It is a beautiful Saturday, and who can blame the owners of any floating device for being out here?

It seems that most of them have the same destination in mind as me, the beautiful beaches of Ilha Dos Gatos. I find a halfway secluded spot for my tent, after a group of half-drunken young men luckily vacated it. In the air and sand hangs a scent of grilled meat, beer and digested beer, until a cleaning thunderstorm comes down on my campsite. All yachts across the beach flee to a sheltered anchorage, and I enjoy the fresh air and quiet after the rain.

Around the metropolis of Sao Paulo, deserted beaches are rare, and I have a bad conscience when I hide my tent under trees on a military beach, or I must sort myself out with rangers and beach wardens pointing at "no camping" signs. A landing in a thunderstorm, garnished with two rolls, washes me up the beach at Praia Grande, where my new host Leo can collect me.

I must put in a day off in Guarau, as I suffer from vomiting and diarrhea. The next beach is beautiful and deserted, but barricaded behind fierce surf. After a capsize, I must swim to reach it. The launch off this beach next morning is similar tricky with a double line of dumpers.

I am fighting my way with a pounding heartbeat through the breakers at the mouth of Mar Pequeno, to look forward to 130 miles of relaxed paddling among sheltered islands and canals. The fishermen watching my arrival in their protected bay show respect, they would not go out in their motorboats through those waves created by the ebbing tide!

The five days inland in the Mar Pequeno, the "Small Sea" with its surrounding canals, is like another paddling world. I can recover on the mirror smooth water away from the ongoing threat of dangerous breakers while starting and landing. I am enjoying the vegetation on the banks right next to me, getting lost in mangrove channels and camping in small villages among friendly people. In Maruja, I can hear the powerful roar of the surf right across the promontory over to my quiet camp by the river. But I would also quickly get bored on this relaxed paddle style only. It is all about the changes!

Back at the open coast, I have another challenging landing in the confused waters of a small river mouth, before I find shelter behind Isla Sao Francisco do Sul, and in the house of my kayaking friends Nina and Alan. The attractive and friendly couple feed me the best home cooked meals! Paradise cannot be better!

Gradually, it is time to make some plans for my arrival in Buenos Aires! At the latest on May 1st, I would like to be back at the Puerto Madero Yacht Club, the place where it all began in August 2011. It stays exciting, as I do not have much time to play around. If wind and weather were to delay my arrival in time, I would have to skip a bit of the journey. I must be in Germany on May 9th in Augsburg, where the first "World Paddle Awards" takes place, and I am among the final three contestants!

I still have two months to complete my trip. Sao Francisco do Sul to Florianópolis takes four days. On one of those, I get into trouble with the right rudder line breaking on a bad timing. I can barely control the kayak in a strong side wind with rough waves. With a massive effort and endless sweep strokes on one side only, I manage to stay away from the rocks. With some knots and tricky footwork, I can finally maneuver into a sheltered bay. I stick my head upside down into the bow to replace the broken cord. This steering system is the only one I would use on an expedition, but I should have checked often for wear and tear of the rudder lines, and should have replaced them in time! This is not my first replacement of those...

At Cabo Santa Marta, I surrender for four days to the severe weather and the loving care of Sonia and Jamie, before I face an eighty miles unprotected beach. Two somewhat merciful stops along that way do not change my decision to paddle inland for the next 430 miles. A chain of lagoons and lakes, all connected with canals is lurking as a detour chicken way, as the open coastline is fully unprotected, and launchings and landing would be wild. In Chuy, I would be back on the open sea, this is my last stop in Brazil. I will need another two weeks for Uruguay, and my circumnavigation of South America will be complete!

Leo, my final land contact, gives me a hand with the short portage to Lagoa Itapera. He joins me on the first day in this beautiful peaceful world with low current, low wind, but endless fields of water lilies and reed. In these serene surroundings, it is good to pause where one fancies, at a reed-covered wooden jetty or a place with a particularly pleasant view of the mountains. We take our time!

The canal connecting this lagoon to the next one reminds me of small rural rivers in Germany. There are buzzards on the banks, storks and vultures, and fat milking cows everywhere, just like at home, minus warm water, solitary palms, banana farms and the mountains in the background. In the second lagoon, Laguna dos Quadros, the headwind is becoming stronger.

I do not know whether Leo can scent his house on the opposite lagoon bank, or if he is bored while we are paddling and chatting. Like all men paddling with me, he likes to show me he can paddle faster than my sedate travel pace after six-hundred days in South America. In my 180-pounds kayak, I carry the red lantern for my well rested companion in his fully empty kayak, who enjoys zooming away a few hundred yards ahead. Sometimes, I am allowed to catch him, and then the game starts all over. Male paddlers joining me for a few hours are all the same! Even if I initially ask them to take it easy, as my boat is heavily laden, and I have a few more miles on my clock. I change up to competition mode, catch up, and hook my boat stealthily to his, so he has something to pull! By evening, he points out a wonderful hidden spot to camp, and heads home to the other side of the lagoon after a wonderful paddling day together.

It was a good decision to leave the open coast, and to wiggle my way through these hundreds of miles of interconnected lakes, lagoons and canals. After all these battles with the surf and dumpers, I feel like I am in the chill out lounge after an ecstasy trip. Or like I am going back to my beginnings. This paddling on calm waters reminds me of the time I started to paddle years ago, with my little son Helge in the back hatch. We loved just to explore the nature, without sporting ambitions.

Travel styles, not just in sea kayaking, can vary, depending on whether you are alone, with a partner or in a group, with or without sporting ambitions, for research or perfect documentation, or just for the fun and a relaxing holiday. As a solo paddler, I have the advantage of independent decision making and no partner-stress, but it also has disadvantages in dangerous situations. I like to be a loner, but my brain gets rusty on the long run without the input of a good chat. The impressions are less different than when out with a partner, as the sporting goal is the main factor. Who knows what the style of my next kayak trip will be?

Sometimes, the connecting canals of the lagoons are fairly clogged up with water plants and reed, and the entrance is hard to find. At the exit of the first lagoon chain, Leo is waiting in his manually built Greenland style kayak.

He helps me with the second short portage into the two largest lagoons, Lagoa dos Patos and Lagoa Mirim. Together with his partner Tiane, he escorts me out to the windy open water. On this southeastern corner, it feels like I am at sea again, with shore surf and a strong headwind. At the end, I must have three days off on these beautiful sandy beaches of Lagoa de Patos, enjoying some exotic and familiar flora and fauna. Thousands of ducks are at home here, as well as turtles, beavers and capybara, a water pig. Spanish moss hangs in long bunches, and a pine forest is used commercially for collecting the resin of scored trees. In one lagoon bay, I paddle through a floating thick carpet of green algae platelets like in a vegetable soup. Luckily, there are only few people, farms or boats, and I savor the solitude!

In L'Aranjal, I am hosted by the local surf and kayak shop, and two paddle friends join me in a double kayak through the connecting canal between the two large lagoons. The current is straight against us, and this shortcut is starting to feel like work. Antonio and Guillherme as locals enjoy camp life a bit different than me. They are not bothered by the millions of mosquitos, spread their gear everywhere on the meadow like a yard sale, and cook right next to a fresh cow pat, but in the lee of their tent. I prefer to withdraw straightaway into my tidy tent free of wind, mosquitoes and fecal matter. A few colorful, "authentic" gauchos with a herd of cattle ride past, with manly rough shouts to keep the cows at bay. I climb out of my protective cloth hut, and pull out my camera like an "authentic" tourist!

The crossing of Lagoa Mirim is once more a windy business, I am crossing from the northwestern to the southeastern side, but real wind protection is nowhere to be found on the shores. I really do not want to know what the coast is like offshore in these conditions!

Guilherme and his friend Kenneth like to help me on the short portage to Chuy. They plan to meet me in their kayaks some distance out. Guilherme paddles with beginner Kenneth too far away from the end in strong downwind. Now, we must paddle back together for eight miles against a twenty knots headwind. No problem for me, I bend over and almost lie on my foredeck, and keep shoveling with good technique, training and experience. Kenneth soon reaches his limit, with no experience and bad equipment. Luckily, I see a tow belt around Guilherme's waist. I do not carry any as a solo paddler, and only have my bow line. Now, diplomacy is needed, as no one likes to be towed. I suggest a merry threesome, with me in the middle. We would stay together, and can still make satisfactory progress combining our efforts.

I have overstayed in Brazil longer than my six-month visa allows, I would have to pay a hefty penalty. As I am not certain when I would ever be coming back to Brazil again, I choose the possibility to pay this, when I next arrive in this beautiful country. Proudly, I stick the final flag on my kayak hull: Uruguay! Just barely three weeks, and my epic journey will be finished. The entry stamp for Uruguay is not a problem, we can go back and forth; no one bothers us when I like to start still in Brazil.

The open sea greets me with the gruesome familiar surf belt. I cannot get to sleep properly with the prospect of fighting breakers again, but I want to keep going! Three thumping jumps down the crest of a wave, a zig zag stop start technique, and I am out of the breaker zone. That should be the last one, the landing spots in Uruguay all have some form of shelter...or so I thought.

On Isla Rasa near Cabo Polonia, I close the fauna loop on my trip with the northernmost seal colony on the eastern Atlantic coast. Wonderful, I am nearly "home"! I savor the noises from the grunting and glistening seals in the morning sun. Unfortunately, my left rudder pedal is slowly disintegrating into its laminated components. A "bandage" of duct tape and cable ties heals the wound. Why should the equipment fare better than its user?

Just before Punta Del Este, I meet a group of six Argentinian sea kayakers. They are on a trip to La Paloma, and excited to meet me here. They have been following my blog entries, but have not been online for a few days. After a short nice chat, we head off in different directions. I have just completed my daily quota of thirty miles, and my desire for like-minded company arises. I quickly turn around, and decide to catch them up. They think it is a wonderful idea to camp together, and head for a lively city beach. I would never have headed there on my own, but the guys have a different travelling style. The group experience is more important, than to cover distance or to reach a destination, and any curious locals are just carried along.

I make myself useful by preparing the mutual dinner, chop vegetables and knead a dough to bake bread over the fire. We all eat from the big pot. A few bottles of wine make the rounds, and so close to home and in like-minded company, I am in best party mood and will not let the wine pass me by. My body is not used to that, and as one of the guys plays a few tunes from "Brave Heart" on his violin, I am feeling decidedly soused. On a trip, and particularly when paddling the next day, I rarely drink, but this nice evening was worth a hangover. I manage to stay upright on my drunken stumbling way to my tent, where are the guy lines? I must lie down, and secretly throw up into the sand of my vestibule. Next morning, I start first, and have considerable difficulties, please, I do not need any capsizing now!

Behind Punta Del Este, my loop around the continent comes near to closure. I turn into the big mouth of the Rio Plata - this time from the north! As a confirmation of my loop, I spot my first penguins, and I feel excited, just like when I saw the first northern seals on Isla Rasa. The water is still in the higher seventies, these two are the northernmost representatives of their kind on the Atlantic coast.

The beaches of Uruguay seem clean and tidy, a pleasure for me and the last holiday makers. With Casa Del Pueblo near Punta Bullene, I see the most impressive artistic buildings I have ever seen! All in white, and it seems to not have any straight wall. Uruguay is one of the richest countries is South America. I paddle from headland to headland, but not in the best condition after a short night with a solid hangover!

The strong current of the mouth of the tributary Arroyo Pando is hopefully the final occasion where I must use my last reserves. Just as I am trying to give the breakers of the river mouth a wide berth, the wind freshens up to twenty knots from southwest, and steepens the waves to an ugly size. I should have ended my day before crossing this river mouth. Or I should have tried to break through the surf into the calm river water sideways, as I usually do. After the worst is rounded, there still is no quiet water. High time to land in this wind! Unpredictable cross waves let my heart beat faster, but I manage to stay upright and surf ashore near some houses.

The next three days' forecast is stormy, and my partner Peter from Denmark is waiting for me in Montevideo. I have two weeks left until my planned big arrival celebrations in Buenos Aires on May 1st. Kayaking friends promise to pick me up here this evening, but have difficulties to find me in a maze of tiny dirt roads in the darkness of an evening sandstorm. I do not have phone reception in my sheltered corner, and must climb up a couple of times a steep windswept dune, to check for messages.

The reunion with Peter is the first highlight at the end of my trip. He has come over from Europe to Buenos Aires already a couple of weeks ago, to work in his IT business, and to be finally part of the celebrations. As to join me on these three weather days off, he has taken the fast ferry over to Uruguay.

The kayaking group in Montevideo is looking after us splendidly with sightseeing, meals out, and celebrate my success by presenting me a little trophy. Many thanks! But first, I must "paddle" to Montevideo!

Two kayaking friends are joining me on my final leg to the capital of Uruguay. While we are having an animated chat with not much paying attention to the sea, an embarrassing "accident" happens: A small wave surfs me over the stern of my neighbor, and I throw him over. For a moment, I sit crossways with my kayak on his turned over hull, and prevent the poor chap from rolling back up, so he must bail out. That could have ended up being nasty! Never take your eyes off the sea, even when chatting!

Meanwhile, Peter has taken the ferry back to Buenos Aires, and prepares my official arrival on May 1st, in cooperation with the Argentine Navy and local kayakers. My options are, either to paddle up the Uruguay shore of the Rio de la Plata to its final group of islands, and to safely hop from one island to the other, or to cross over thirty miles at the narrowest point near Colonia de Sacramento. The former will take me four to five days, the latter only one, but it is not open for kayakers due to the number of fast ferries, and general high ship traffic.

It is nearing autumn in this part of the world. I am wearing all my warm clothes, and at night, my thin sleeping bag with a fleece liner is no longer warm enough. In the morning, cold and wet fog swirls about and makes me freeze for hours. It takes me four days to get to Colonia, and the landscape reminds me of home again, like in the lagoons in southern Brazil.

But I am too early! I neither want to hang around in Uruguay for a whole week, nor I like to make a week-long detour through the islands. I prefer an "unofficial" and incognito arrival on Friday, April 24th, while crossing the massive Rio de la Plata, illegally. Thirty miles in rough winds and strong currents is a full stressful paddling day. I am simply not in the mood the same evening to attend a big party with dozens of representatives from the press, and like to savor my arrival for a while (nearly) on my own. I do not announce my arrival on my website, but simply publish my daily report a few days later.

The official reception is planned for May 1st by the Argentine Navy on their historical sailing ship "Fregata Sarmiento", a counterfoil to our German "Gorch Fock". Many VIP's, ambassadors, press, and lots of local kayakers are invited to join the party in the city harbor of Buenos Aires. By then, I am fit again, have slept well, recovered, and visited the hairdresser to better smile into the many cameras.

I am meant to collect an exit stamp in the Uruguay harbor of Colonia, but strangely there is neither a slipway to land on, nor an office in which this could happen. Or did I not look properly? Steep harbor walls and fat ferries block my way. Ah well, that solves the issue of inconvenient questions with regards to my further direction of travel. Who needs an exit stamp? Are the Argentinians going to send me back to get one? Not likely.

The last night in Uruguay, I feel like a hobo, camping under the shelter of a steep cliff in some reeds, right underneath a busy noisy street. My final night on a South American beach, and I am still alive! The fast ferries whoosh past my beach with thunderous noise.

I plan to paddle as far northwest as possible, to stay out of the way of the fast catamaran ferries, but I am not sure, how the strong current and side wind will influence my path. In the end, I will have to somehow share the harbor entry with those jet monsters. I can make out the city skyline twenty-five miles before I get to the shore, now I am only navigating by sight with an occasionally GPS check for drift from wind and current. Buenos Aires, I am back again!

The last night before I set off for the very first time on this trip, I went to see the musical "Evita" with Peter in Hamburg, close to my hometown Husum. Now, after nearly four years, I am closing the circle. "Don't cry for me, Argentina..." - Argentina (and the rest of the world) does not need to cry for me, I am back!

The song is in my brain and on my lips, while I am paddling the last miles into a colorful red sunset over Buenos Aires. I sing it wholeheartedly, with tears in my eyes, also in memorial of my friend Alejandro, who sadly cannot greet me anymore in his hometown. I have a melodramatic arrival, straight out of a picture album. Down south, while I was in life-threatening danger in an unexpected storm, he drowned, being surprised by just the same storm along Staten Islands. I had a few hairy situations on my long way up the coast, but thankfully, I am alive and in one piece. Tears are blinding my eyes as the song carries me into the safe entrance of the yacht harbor.

My partner Peter, my sister Edda, my faithful friend Ricardo Kruszewski of SDK-Kayaks, and after Alejandro, my main organizer in Argentina, plus two other friends, stretch their necks out to spot me coming around the corner. Their quiet applause is enough recognition for today. I am exhausted in body and mind, and all I want is Peter's shoulder in my bed.

A week later, dozens of boats and jet skis of the Argentine Navy, and a whole flotilla of local paddlers escort me on my "official" arrival. Well rested, beaming from ear to ear and waving happily to the crowd like a queen, I pass the last mile towards the Fregata Sarmiento to the boisterous sounds of the Navy marching band on the "Ladies Bridge". I am deeply touched by the honorable official reception on this wonderful veteran sailing ship. The ambassador of the European Union, the German ambassador, representatives of the city of Buenos Aires, as well as countless VIP's and local paddlers, press, and camera teams of half a dozen TV stations, have come to my honor. Later, I find out that the last German given a military reception on this ship was the President of the German Reich, Friedrich Ebert – in 1925!

After 16,800 miles, 850 travelling days of which I paddled 605, I have achieved the impossible - I am the first person ever to circumnavigating South America in a kayak. And I might stay the only one for quite a while.

Back home, a week later with perfect timing, I am honored to receive the first "World Paddle Award" out of the hands of the president of the German Canoe Federation. Maybe, I deserve it a bit!

EPILOGUE

"Well behaved Women rarely make History!" This quote is historically attributed to either Laurel Thatcher Ulrich, Eleanor Roosevelt or Marilyn Monroe, and sticks as a decal on my kayak.

That is me - I love to live only to a degree within the norms society demands, I love to swim against the stream, polarize people, and do not have role models or gods in the traditional sense. My parents have named me "Freya", the Norse Goddess of Love. My kayak is named accordingly "Goddess of Love to the Seas".

Were these four years of effort worth it? YES! Was I ever going to give up? NEVER! How did I do it?

In the first few weeks, I could already visualize my arrival celebrations in vivid mental images - and that is how it came to happen. I stay focused, I visualize my success. in fact, I am a typical Taurus. Well organized, stubborn, versatile, flexible, dexterous, enduring, persistent, and pertinacious. Add a tiny quota of luck, whatever that might mean. Self-confidence, strength and emotional control grow with the achievements. Many qualities must work together to make it a successful circumnavigation. Success starts in the head, and a Taurus has a very solid one.

Life goes on after a success. The question most often asked is, now what, quo vadis? I do not think I will yet become a sporting "pensioner" - maybe, a "North Island" follows the "South Island"? Who knows...

Thank You to:

Peter Unold, my partner – for continuous mental, practical and IT-support, for the graphics in this book, to have been a wonderful paddling partner for four months, and a life partner for the time being and to come

Helge Hoffmeister, my beloved son – to let me go, to be proud of his mom and to understand why she is doing what she is doing

Werner Würger, Helge's caring dad – to look after our wonderful son, and after my house while I am away

Andrea Höhn and Ilona Sierks, my shop managers – for their brilliant self-sufficient managing of my two Janny's Ice cream shops and my Christmas shop

All my other about forty employees – to keep my shops with great engagement in working order

Alejandro Carranza and Ricardo Kruszewski – for support in Buenos Aires before and after the trip

All my local hosts and helpers – to give me a home on the way and any support I can think of

The local Navy's and Coast Guards – for their support and protection on and off the water

The German embassy's – for their support and contacts to the local Navy's

My blog readers – for their supportive comments

My audience on my public speaking engagements – for their support to visit my talks

Udo Beier – for his regular write-ups in German publications

All the many press people – for their help to give me a high-level public profile

Karel Vissel, my reliable weather-man, – to send me the forecast twice a day

Point 65 – to develop and provide my "Freya" kayaks, and for financial support

THULE – for financial support and roof racks

Epic kayaks – for 18-x sport kayaks and wing paddles

Hilleberg – for the many tents I needed

Kokatat – for dry suits, PFD's, jackets and pants

Haglöfs – for outdoor-clothing

Global Marine Networks – for the satellite phone and x-gate program

ICOM – for the VHF radio

ACR – for the Personal Locator Beacon (PLB)

Hennessy Hammock – for the hammock

Snapdragon – for spray decks, cockpit covers and backrests

North Water – for cockpit- and underdeck bags

Seal Line – for the dry bags

Therm-A-Rest – for the sleeping pad

MSR – for water bags, cooking gear and miscellaneous

PackTowl – for outdoor towels

Aquapac – for all the many electronics' dry bags

Cocoon – for their silk pareos and sarongs

Skwoosh – for their gel-seat pads

Native – for their sunglasses

BlüBandoo – for their cooling visors

Klaus Vogt – for co-writing this book in German

Stefan Lutterbüse, Bastei Lübbe – for publishing and editing this book in German

Edda Stentiford, my sister – for translating to the English version, editing my blog entries and broad support

Julie Ortiz – for editing the English version

To YOU – as the reader, buying and enjoying my book!

22551279R00123

Printed in Poland
by Amazon Fulfillment
Poland Sp. z o.o., Wrocław